Foreign Bodies

Foreign Bodies

A GUIDE TO
EUROPEAN MANNERISMS

Peter Collett

SIMON & SCHUSTER

LONDON·SYDNEY·NEW YORK·TOKYO·SINGAPORE·TORONTO

First published in Great Britain by
Simon & Schuster Ltd in 1993
A Paramount Communications Company

Copyright © Peter Collett, 1993

Simon & Schuster Ltd
West Garden Place
Kendal Street
London W2 2AQ

Simon & Schuster of Australia Pty Ltd
Sydney

A CIP catalogue record for this book is
available from the British Library
ISBN 0-671-71063-X

Typeset in 11/13 Garamond by
Hewer Text Composition Services, Edinburgh
Printed and bound in Great Britain by
Butler & Tanner Ltd, London and Frome

Contents

To My Parents

Introduction

In all the circle of knowledge, there is not perhaps a more pleasing
employment than that of comparing countries with each other.

Oliver Goldsmith, 1760

There are many ways of comparing countries, but the most
fascinating comparisons are those that focus on the inhabitants
of other countries and the ways that they behave. And yet, if you
pick up a guide book on, say, France or Germany, you will find
almost nothing on the subject. There will be a lot of information
about the history and architecture of the country, and probably
descriptions of the local customs and cuisine. But you won't find
anything about the local mannerisms. You won't discover how
people in those countries insult each other, what amuses them, or
how they employ their bodies to communicate with each other. In
fact, you are likely to get the impression that their mannerisms are
unimportant, or that they are no different from your own – neither
of which is true.

This book sets out to show that mannerisms are extremely
important, and that if we take the trouble to study other cultures
we are likely to be rewarded by the discovery that they differ
from us in the most unexpected ways. Mannerisms are important
because they form the basis of the social exchanges that take place
between people, and because they can very easily give rise to
misunderstandings between people from different cultures. We
are often tempted to assume that mannerisms are somehow less
important than values or attitudes, or what people actually say to
each other. This simply is not the case. The way that people behave
is crucial, not only to the sort of impression that they make on each
other, but to how they feel about themselves.

A great deal of our behaviour is over-learned and automatic, so
that we no longer notice what we are doing, or how other people
behave. If you make a point of watching how people gesticulate

1

with their hands, you will notice that they often use the same hand postures, and that these postures differ from one country to another. This does not arise from people deliberately setting out to copy each other, but from a process of unconscious mimicry, which forms the basis of learning in childhood and the development of social conventions. The fact that certain actions operate outside conscious awareness makes them all the more interesting, because in some cases it means that they still await discovery and careful investigation.

In spite of their importance, psychologists have only recently begun to show an interest in the cross-cultural study of mannerisms. There are several reasons for this. Firstly, psychologists have traditionally been more interested in what goes on in people's heads, rather than how they behave. Those with an interest in behaviour have usually tried to investigate people's actions in the laboratory – hardly the kind of place to put someone at ease, or to encourage them to behave spontaneously.

The other major reason behind psychologists' reluctance to study mannerisms cross-culturally is historical. During the eighteenth century there was an enormous upsurge of interest in other countries, which was accompanied by a desire to apply scientific methods to the study of different races. Unfortunately there weren't any scientific methods to speak of, so scholars had to make do with phrenology. Phrenology was based on the idea that someone's character could be inferred by inspecting the shape of their head and face. It provided a convenient model and easy methods. Armed only with a pair of callipers, a tape measure and some drawing instruments, scholars went off to the remotest parts of the world to take cranial measurements of the natives and to collect skulls. The problem with phrenology was not its lack of precision, but the fact that it didn't know what it was measuring. Conclusions about the significance of cranial bumps and facial angles were simply plucked out of fresh air, with no attempt being made to measure or understand character independently of the shape of the head and face. In the end phrenology went the way of most pseudo-sciences, but not before it had cast a long shadow over the study of cultural differences.

The other development that helped to discredit cross-cultural comparisons was 'race psychology', another pseudo-science that generated an enormous amount of interest in Britain, France and Germany. Race psychology wasn't particularly interested in observation, or for that matter in quantification. Phrenology had at least had the decency to measure people's heads, but race psychology preferred to rely on unbridled speculations and whimsical conjecture about the character and 'soul' of different races. This would have been of little consequence, had the new discipline not been taken seriously and used in support of racist theories. At the very centre of race psychology was the idea that different races have different mentalities, and that these are inborn and genetically determined. Race psychology could not accommodate the suggestion that cultural or national differences in behaviour might be due to non-biological factors, and there was therefore no place for the notion of change. Race psychology remained respectable up until the Second World War, but by the nineteen-fifties it had been thoroughly discredited. In its wake, however, it managed to leave behind the impression that all cross-cultural comparisons are somehow linked to biological notions or to theories of racial superiority – which couldn't be further from the truth. It also managed to encourage a counter-movement, in which people tried to play down the differences between cultures, and in some cases even to deny that they exist.

During the eighteenth century some of the most respected philosophers of the day – people like Diderot, Montesquieu and David Hume – became involved in discussions about the nature of national differences and their causes. For example, the English philosopher, David Hume, produced a thoughtful analysis of national differences, where he insisted that 'Men of sense allow that each nation has a peculiar set of manners, and that some particular qualities are more frequently to be met with among one people than among their neighbours.' Numerous explanations were put forward to try and explain national differences in intelligence, courage, indolence and melancholy. The soil was one explanation, religion another. The form of government was also considered to be an important influence on behaviour, as was the climate.

Climatic theories of behaviour go back a long way, at least to the time of Hippocrates. Aristotle, for example, compared those who lived in cold climates, like the northern Europeans who were reputed to be brave but intellectually deficient, with the Asians who lived in a hot climate and who were known to be clever but cowardly. The Greeks, he noticed, lived in between, and this made them both clever and brave – ideal qualities with which to conquer the world, provided they could somehow be united.

Theories of climatic determinism re-emerged in the sixteenth and seventeenth centuries, when they were dusted off and reinvigorated, usually to account for the superiority of one's own nation, but sometimes to try and explain its complexity. For example, Sir William Temple, writing in 1690, suggested that the variegated character of the English people 'arises from our Clymat, and the Dispositions it Naturally produces. We are not only more unlike one another, than any other Nation I know, but we are more unlike our selves too, at several times, and owe to our very Air, some ill Qualities as well as many good.' Temple recognised, however, that the changeable English weather was responsible for the spleen of the English, and their tendency to melancholy. 'This makes us unequal in our Humours, inconstant in our Passions, uncertain in our Ends, and even in our Desires.' Half a century later, Horace Walpole echoed these sentiments with the observation that 'In England, tempers vary so excessively, that almost everyone's faults are peculiar to himself. I take this diversity to proceed partly from our climate, partly from our government; the first is changeable and makes us queer, the latter permits our queernesses to operate as they please.'

The problem with the climate theory was that it failed to explain how countries at the same latitude, and with very similar climates, could be so different. There were additional problems for those who accepted the theory, but who disliked some of its conclusions. For example, English adherents to the theory objected to the fact that they were supposed to be like the Dutch and the Germans, whom they regarded as dull and cloddish, and very different from themselves. But the big problem with the climate theory was its inability to explain how nations like the ancient Greeks and Romans, which had once held sway over the known world, had gone into decline. Like phrenology and race psychology, the climate theory had no place for change. It was wedded to a static view of the world, one in which nations neither advance nor collapse, and where the habits of people never change.

We are all susceptible to the myth of historical constancy, the idea that nations never change their ways. Certainly, there is evidence to support this view, and one doesn't have to look too far to find cases where communities have behaved in the same way for centuries, and sometimes for millennia. But there are also numerous examples of social habits that have changed dramatically, and which make a nonsense of static theories. For example, there is a great deal of evidence to show that Scandinavians are extremely conscientious about personal cleanliness and hygiene. This, however, was not always the case, and the Arab historian Ahmed ibn Fadlān, who met Scandinavians on the Volga in 992, described them as anything but clean. 'They are the filthiest race that God ever created. They do not wipe themselves after going to stool, nor wash themselves after a nocturnal pollution, any more than if they were wild asses.'

Studies of national stereotypes repeatedly show that the Germans are considered to be bellicose and authoritarian by other Europeans. This image of the Germans emerged round about the middle of the last century. Before that they were regarded as peace loving and rather timid. Machiavelli, for example, described them as enjoying their rough life and not wanting to go to war, while Madame de Staël, who observed the Germans while she was exiled from France by Napoleon I, remarked on their 'independence of spirit', which she sharply contrasted with the French, and the fact that they showed every sign of 'lacking in military spirit'. In fact the characteristics that are now said to be displayed by the French and Germans were totally reversed then. France was a tightly organised military machine, with everything that implied, while Germany was weak and indecisive. 'Nothing is odder than the German soldiers,' wrote Madame de Staël. 'They fear fatigue or bad weather, as if they were all shopkeepers or literati . . . woodburning stoves, beer and tobacco smoke create a heavy and warm atmosphere around them which it is difficult for them to leave . . . Among them a general who loses a battle is more assured of obtaining forgiveness than one who wins of being applauded.'

Ralph Waldo Emerson provides us with a British example of the way in which people can change. Emerson arrived in England in 1833, and returned to America fourteen years later. In that time he was able to observe the English at close quarters, and to compare them with his compatriots. Many of the things that we now regard as typical of Americans he noted as specifically English, like their obsession with money and success, or their overfed appearance, which he contrasted with that of the bony Americans. Of the English he wrote, 'There is no country in which so absolute a homage is paid to wealth. In America there is a touch of shame when a man exhibits the evidences of large property, as if, after all, it needed apology. But the Englishman has pure pride in his wealth, and esteems it a final certificate.' It is difficult to reconcile this description of the English with what one finds in England today. This all goes to show that there is nothing immutable about people's social habits. What is characteristic of a community today probably wasn't a few centuries ago, and won't be in years to come.

The study of European mannerisms presents a special challenge, not only because they are so diverse, but because Europe is in the throes of momentous upheavals. On the one hand there are centripetal forces bringing nations together in an attempt to exorcise the past, and create a unitary structure with a common identity, while on the other hand centrifugal forces are at work, with local identities being asserted, people being flung in every direction, and states being torn apart. The clash between these two opposing forces raises a host of questions about the political future of Europe, and the shape that the European community is likely to take. It also raises some extremely interesting questions about the styles of behaviour and the mannerisms that people are likely to adopt in the future. Will the French, for example, become more similar to other Europeans in their comportment and demeanour, or will they reassert their national identity by retaining and possibly exaggerating those mannerisms that make them so typically French? At this stage, the only sensible answer to this question is the one that the Chinese communist leader, Chou En-lai, gave when he was asked whether he considered the French revolution to have been a success – 'It's still too early to say.'

Address

When people address each other they sometimes have a problem deciding what to call each other. In England there are three choices as far as names are concerned. One can either call someone by their first name, by their last name, or by their title-plus-last-name – for example, one can address John Smith as 'John', 'Smith' or 'Mr Smith'. It is very rare for people to be addressed by both of their names (e.g. 'John Smith') or by their title and both names (e.g. 'Mr John Smith'), although there are places where people are addressed by just their last name (e.g. 'Smith'). In English public schools, for example, it is not unusual for pupils to address each other by their last name, and for the teachers to do likewise. This convention of last-naming people can also be found in gentlemen's clubs, which are in many ways an extension of the public schools.

The choice between first name and title-plus-last-name depends on factors like familiarity, formality and social status. For example, people who are unacquainted are much more likely to address each other with title-plus-last-name in a formal situation than in an informal setting, where they are more likely to opt for first names. People also tend to use title-plus-last-name when there is a difference in social status, and first name when they are of similar status. In the final analysis, however, the choice boils down to a question of social distance: when people want to demonstrate their closeness they tend to opt for the more familiar form of the first name, and when they feel the need to keep the other person at arm's length they usually resort to title-plus-last-name.

In societies that possess these two forms of address there is usually sufficient consensus about when to use first names and when to use title-plus-last-names. However, different societies can have very different norms about the use of these forms of address, both in terms of when it is considered appropriate to use each form, and when it is right for people to start using each other's first name.

In Germany a great deal of emphasis is placed on titles, and people expect to be addressed as *Herr* or *Frau*, or by the title of their occupation. Elsewhere professors and doctors are referred to by their titles, but in Germany it is a case of *Frau Professor* or *Herr Doktor*. The man with two doctorates is sometimes referred to as *Herr Doktor Doktor*, and someone like Albert Schweitzer, who had doctorates in medicine, music and theology, might reasonably expect to be addressed as *Herr Doktor Doktor Doktor*. In practice, of course, things are not that rigid, and someone who has two doctorates is usually addressed as if he only had one. There is a story about two German academics, which although it is probably apocryphal, is nevertheless very revealing about the German attachment to titles:

> Two academics, Schmidt and Müller, are in the university canteen. Schmidt has a doctorate, and Müller has two. They have known each other for many years, and have always addressed each other as *Herr Doktor*. Schmidt says to Müller: 'Herr Doktor Müller, we have been acquainted for a very long time. Don't you think it's time for us to dispense with titles and address each other by first names? 'I have a better idea,' says Müller, 'I have two doctorates, while you have only one. I suggest that we cancel one doctorate each. I will call you *Herr*, and you can continue to call me *Herr Doktor*.'

Because Germans set great store by titles, they are quick to take offense when they are not addressed properly. Everyone, or almost everyone, has a title, and is therefore a properly constituted individual. As Carl Jung said of Germany, 'There are no ordinary human beings, you are "Herr Professor," or "Herr Geheimrat," "Herr Oberrechnungsrat" and even longer things than that.' The attraction of titles is that they pigeon-hole people, and therefore add to the orderliness of society. But in doing so, titles also define people in terms of their occupations, so that what someone does by way of occupation becomes more important than who they are. Then, of course, titles confer status. They are like verbal insignia, informing everyone about how much respect and deference the person with the title deserves.

It is no wonder that so much effort is expended in the pursuit of titles. In his book on Germany, John Ardagh describes how German businessmen vie with each other to acquire honorary consulships of third-world countries so that they can be addressed as *Herr Konsul*. 'Of the forty-one consuls in Stuttgart, only five are foreign career diplomats; the rest are local Germans with "honorary" status. Some of these have a serious and worthwhile job to do. Others work for countries as tiny and remote as Haiti and Chad, which have virtually no contact with Baden-Württemberg, and I would guess that a third or more have bought their titles. A businessman never admits to having done this, yet he will probably feel that the large sum has been well spent. He gets no diplomatic immunity, but has perks of other kinds ... He gets invited *ex officio* to the *Land* President's annual party; he can throw a posh party himself on his country's national day. The 'CC' plaque on his car helps him with the police – needless to say. And his wife too enjoys her kudos as "*Frau Konsul*". There is a touch of the absurd about two minor Swabian tycoons solemnly calling each other, "*Ja, Herr Konsul*", "*Nein, Herr Konsul*" – but that's Germany.'

The Swedes are also obsessed with titles. For example, if you want to look someone up in a Swedish telephone directory you need to know their title as well as their name, because everyone is listed under their surname, their occupation and their first name or initials. Titles are also an essential part of conversation. When one is addressing people formally it is not sufficient to call them by their last name; one also has to refer to their professional title, *and* address them in the third person. In his book on the Swedes, Paul Austin tells us that 'the only polite way of addressing a Swede, in Swedish, is by his title. *God dag, Ingeniör Johansson, och hur mår Ingeniör Johansson idag* (literally "Good day, Engineer Johansson, and how is Engineer Johansson feeling today?").' To foreigners like the British and the French, this obligatory reference to someone's title seems very strange, but the habit of addressing someone in the third person singular seems even more peculiar because it gives the impression that they are actually two people – one who is being addressed, and another who is replying on their behalf. According to Paul Austin, the reason for this is 'the lack of any generally viable word for "you". There is *du*, which is intimate. And *ni* which, except in the plural, tends to have such overtones of disdain or, at all events, standoffishness that one hesitates long and debates with oneself before using it.' This sounds like a convincing explanation for the Swedish preoccupation with titles, except that, as Austin himself recognises, there are other peoples, like the Germans and the Danes, who are adequately equipped with second-person pronouns, but who are equally devoted to the use of titles.

For the Swedes, as well as the Germans and the Danes, titles are a means of enlisting language to record people's occupations and to keep everyone in their proper place. The habit of referring to titles has the effect of creating an obstacle between people, one that presupposes that occupation is more important than anything else. The use of titles ensures that conversations remain formal, because it is extremely difficult to be casual and intimate while one is constantly making reference to the other person's occupation. Addressing someone in the third person also increases the distance between the participants, giving the impression that they are not in a position to speak for themselves.

The conventions surrounding forms of address in Britain are very different from those in Sweden. When the Swedish academic, Eric Geijer, visited England in 1809, he noticed that the English addressed each other without using titles.

> The general tokens of politeness are just the same in England among the upper and the lower classes and between the two. One addresses every man as Sir! which I should translate as Herre (which it actually means) were it not that one uses the English word also for one's horse and one's dog. One calls every woman Madam (pronounced Mam) and this is free from all the Swedish trouble of addressing everyone by his title. When two coal-carters meet, they ask: 'How do you do, Sir?' and two lords begin their conversation in no other way.

Although the basic egalitarianism of English greetings is still in evidence, terms like 'Sir' and 'Madam' have given way to less obvious signs of mutual respect. 'Sir' is still used in shops and restaurants, and so is 'Madam', although with noticeably less enthusiasm. When it is used, 'Madam' is pronounced 'Madam', while the earlier pronunciation of 'Mam' is now reserved for the Queen. 'Mr' and 'Mrs' continue to be widely used, often for very different reasons. In an Oxford college, for example, the college porter might address a Fellow as 'Mr Smith', and the Fellow may reciprocate by calling the porter 'Mr Brown'. The superficial symmetry of this exchange hides the fact that in the first instance

'Mr' is being used as a form of respect, while in the second it is designed to remind the porter of his subordinate position. In both instances the use of 'Mr' serves to increase the distance between addressor and addressee.

The way that people address each other in Britain has definitely changed since the last war. Up until then Sir and Madam were employed as mutual signs of respect. Over the past few decades, however, Sir and Madam have changed their tone, becoming more one-sided and deferential, which is why they have fallen into disfavour. But there is also another important factor at work, and that is a generalised reluctance to address people by anything other than their name, and in many cases a reluctance to use any name at all. A professor in Britain is no longer addressed by his title as a matter of course, and he is frequently not even addressed by his name. This avoidance of titles and names represents the ultimate in linguistic cop-outs, because it means that one doesn't have to acknowledge any kind of relationship between oneself and the other person. It is certainly a very English solution to the problem of deciding what to call people.

English speakers are different because they only have one word for 'you' singular, whereas other European languages have two. This was not always the case. Up until the seventeenth century English also had two pronouns – 'you' was the respectful form of address, and 'thou' was used to inferiors. 'Thou' was regarded as a demeaning form of address, hence the expression 'to thee or thou' someone, meaning to treat them impolitely, to look down on them. In *Twelfth Night*, for example, Sir Toby Belch tries to lure Sir Andrew Aguecheek into a duel, saying 'Taunt him . . . If thou thouest him thrice, it shall not be amiss.' In a similar vein, Sir Edward Coke is reputed to have set upon Sir Walter Raleigh after his trial, saying 'Thou viper . . . I thou thee thou traitor!' 'Thou' disappeared from the English language during the seventeenth century, probably because it had become insulting, but not sufficiently damning to be retained as an insult. The fact that it was adopted by the Quakers, as their only form of address, may also have hastened its demise.

French, German, Italian, Spanish, Russian – in fact all the European languages, except English – possess two singular second-person pronouns. The origins of these pairs of pronouns are Latin, where the familiar form of 'you' was *tu*, and the more formal version was *vos*. Historical linguists tell us that Latin provided the impetus for the distinction in French between *tu* and *vous*, and that many of the other European languages borrowed their pronouns from French. German, for example, began with the distinction between *du* and *Ihr*. In time *Ihr* gave way to *er*, and later on to *Sie*. Spanish and Italian began with *tu* and *vos*. In the case of Spanish *vos* gave way to *usted*, and in Italian it was replaced by *lei*. But what was the reason behind the evolution of this dual system of address? According to Roger Brown and Albert Gilman, the Latin of antiquity had only one word for 'you' singular, namely *tu*. It also had *vos* for addressing people in the plural. Originally the Roman Empire was centred on Rome, but as it expanded it became necessary to establish a seat and a second Emperor in Constantinople. Round about the fourth century B.C. people began to address the Emperor in Rome with *vos*, implying thereby that he was a plurality, which in a sense he was because there were two of them. Later on people recognised that *vos* could be used to address other important individuals, and this led to the dual system of address that we know today. It is generally accepted that the French, whose manners were aped by most of Europe from the twelfth century onward, were largely responsible for introducing the dual system of address to other countries. In England the distinction first appeared as 'thou' and 'ye', with 'ye' giving way to 'you', and 'thou' eventually disappearing altogether.

Because English has only one word for 'you' singular, there isn't ever a decision to be made about which pronoun to use when addressing someone in the second person. The only problem is whether to use 'you', or to avoid it altogether. In fact, not long ago it was thought to be rude to 'you' people of importance – one would not, for example, address one's aunt or uncle as 'you' because this was regarded as too familiar. Societies that have two forms of address are very different because people have to decide whether to use the familiar 'T' form (like *tu* or *du*) or the more formal 'V' form (like *vous* or *Sie*).

Decisions about whether to address someone with the T form or the V form depend on social conventions. According to Brown and Gilman, variations in the use of T and V can be explained in terms of two dimensions – one being the power dimension, the other being the dimension of solidarity. Differences in power are expressed asymmetrically, by superiors giving T to their inferiors, and receiving V in exchange. Solidarity, on the other hand, is expressed symmetrically, by superiors exchanging V and by inferiors exchanging T. That, anyway, is the basic theory about how T and V are used, although there are disagreements about certain details of the model. One of the things that has been noticed is that the situation can influence decisions, so that people who normally exchange T may decide to switch to V in order to appear more formal, or to disguise the nature of their relationship. This habit of switching back and forth between T and V was apparently very pronounced in pre-revolutionary Russia, where, according to Paul Friedrich, 'two officers might exchange *vy* while discussing military tactics, but revert to *ty* when chatting about women back in their quarters'.

Societies that possess the T/V distinction can differ in terms of how they decide which form of address to use, the frequency with which they use T and V, and the ease with which people move from exchanging V to exchanging T. The Italians, for example, use T more often than the French and the Germans – or at least the former inhabitants of West Germany. In Italy most pronominal address is reciprocal – people either exchange *tu* to show their equality or intimacy, or else they exchange *lei* to demonstrate their mutual respect and distance. Most instances of asymmetry occur where youngsters and older people are involved, and this is most noticeable in working-class circles.

The French are much more attached to V, and this is probably a legacy from the days when husband and wife would address each other as *vous* rather than *tu*. Sartre and Simone de Beauvoir also addressed each other as *vous*, presumably to distinguish themselves from all those Parisian couples who were busy swapping *tu*. In fact the French use of T and V is rather different from that of other European countries, because they use V extensively, but not with family and friends. Children grow up exchanging T with their parents, and with their friends in school, and this, it has been suggested, is why there is such a strong association in the French mind between friendship and family membership. French politicians tend to use *tu* when they are being chummy, and *vous* when they are being serious. President Mitterand is reputed to use *vous* whenever he addresses his colleagues, and they of course give him *vous* in return, thereby establishing a relationship based on mutual respect rather than camaraderie.

The situation in what was West Germany is very different from the former German Democratic Republic. In the west *Sie* is used extensively. Strangers exchange *Sie*, and so do work colleagues who need to show their respect and keep their distance. As people get to know each other better they start to reach the point where an exchange of T would be more appropriate. The process of switching from mutual *Sie* to mutual *du* is fraught with all kinds of social dangers that need to be carefully negotiated to ensure that nobody is offended. Typically the switch is initiated by the superior. Both parties then retire to a bar, there to celebrate their new relationship with a *Bruderschaft* ceremony. The two individuals raise their glasses, entwine their arms, drink each other's health, and may even conclude the ritual with a kiss. A few minutes ago they were *Sie* to each other; now they are *du*, and unless they have a serious disagreement, they are likely to stay that way.

Like other communist states, the German Democratic Republic was dedicated to the eradication of social distinctions, and this extended to certain forms of address. The party made strenuous efforts to discourage the use of *Sie*, with the result that *du* became widely used, especially in political circles and in the armed services and the police. Recent research by Sigrid Jakob at Oxford reveals that *du* continues to be used much more by East Berliners, but that its use is confined to people whom they know rather than to strangers. As one might expect, the reunification of Germany has started to affect the way that people relate to each other. Comrades in the east, who formerly addressed each other as *Genosse* and exchanged *du*, are now beginning to use *Sie* – just as they did before the Berlin Wall was built.

Linguistic habits have also been forced to change in other communist countries. In nineteenth century Russia there was an enormous gap between the nobility who exchanged *vy*, and the peasants who exchanged *ty*. In remote parts of the country there were peasants who had never even heard of *vy* being used in the singular. In most of the country, and certainly in the cities and towns, T and V were employed asymmetrically within the family; parents gave T to their children and received V in return, and husbands gave T to their wives and were addressed as V. The use of *vy* was also heavily institutionalised. It was decreed, for example, that witnesses in court should be addressed as *vy*, whereas prisoners should be addressed as *ty*. There were also army regulations, stipulating which ranks were to be addressed as *vy* and which as *ty*. After the revolution of 1917 these decrees were countermanded, firstly by the Provisional Government, and then by the Bolsheviks, who insisted that all military personnel should address each other as *vy*, both on and off duty, and regardless of their rank.

The Russian system of pronominal address was extremely complicated before the revolution and, in spite of all the changes that have occurred, it still continues to confuse outsiders. The Russian author Gogol regarded the complexity of the system as its great virtue: 'It should be said that if we in Russia have not yet caught up with the foreigners in some things, we have long overtaken them in the means of address. It is impossible to count all the shades and niceties of our means of address. The Frenchman or the German will never grasp or understand all the particularities and differences.' Russian modes of address have changed a great deal since the revolution. Within the family asymmetric exchange has given way to reciprocal use of T; non-reciprocal uses of T have definitely become taboo. In several cases the unions have succeeded in persuading management to address the workers as V, in order to show them the respect that they are due. In spite of the shift away from non-reciprocal forms of address, Russians can still convey all kinds of subtle messages. This is partly because every Russian has three names – a first name, a patronymic and a surname. The way that these names can be selected, shortened, made into diminutives and then combined with *vy* and *ty*, provides Russians with an enormous vocabulary for defining their relationships.

As societies become more democratic one would expect to find non-reciprocal forms of address disappearing, and a greater use of reciprocal T rather than reciprocal V. Over time V should start to become redundant and might even disappear altogether. In fact the evidence suggests that this is not happening. True, there has been a shift away from non-reciprocal forms of address – the changes that have taken place in French and Russian families are a good example – but in some cases reciprocal V has actually increased

at the expense of reciprocal T. This is happening in eastern
Germany, where people are abandoning the imposed conventions
of the communist era, and shifting from an exchange of *du* to an
exchange of *Sie*. There is therefore no reason to expect that V will
eventually be replaced by T. After all, the English abandoned T
altogether in the seventeenth century, and they have managed
with V ever since. There is nothing inevitable about the changes
that take place to pronominal forms of address. They can shift in
various directions, and they are likely to do so as they respond to
the demands of governments, fashion, and the changing nature of
people's relationships.

Beckoning

One of the great advantages of hand signals is that they can be seen from far away. When people are separated by a large distance, or in a noisy situation, they tend to use their hands to communicate with each other. Using gestures, they can ask people to come to them or to go away. They can also greet people at a distance or bid them farewell. Because people all round the world convey these messages, one might reasonably expect there to be a universal hand gesture for each message. We find, in fact, that this is not the case, and that even within the narrow confines of Europe there are dramatic differences in the ways that people beckon, dismiss and wave to each other.

In northern, central and eastern Europe there are two gestures for beckoning. One is the 'index-gesture', and the other is the 'fan-gesture'. In the case of the index-gesture the index finger is used to summon the other person. Here the hand is positioned so that the palm faces up, and the other fingers are usually curled on to the palm. In the case of the fan-gesture the palm of the hand also faces up, but now all four fingers, the whole hand, or even the entire arm is used to call the other person. (The fan-gesture is so called because it looks like the hand is being used to fan the face.) These two gestures tend to be employed in different situations. Because the index-gesture is more imperative in its tone, it is more likely to be found where one person is entitled to summon another – the case of the parent calling the child being the typical example. As a rule, adults do not beckon other adults with the index-gesture, unless, like the customer calling the waiter, they have the right to do so, but even under these circumstances there is a strong preference for the fan-gesture, simply because it is more respectful.

In Mediterranean countries like Spain, Italy, Greece and Turkey, beckoning is performed differently. In these countries there are also two gestures, one being the same index-gesture that is used elsewhere in Europe, and the other being the 'paddle-gesture', where the hand is held palm-down, and all four fingers, the whole hand or the entire arm is used to call the other person. (The paddle-gesture is so called because it looks as though the hand is being used to paddle a canoe.) The difference between the fan-gesture and the paddle-gesture is in the position of the palm and this can easily give rise to cross-cultural misunderstandings.

When an Englishman, for example, visits Italy, he can easily mistake the paddle-gesture for a signal meaning 'go away', especially when the person performing the gesture raises the hand high in the air and brings it down rapidly. To the Italians this simply looks like an exaggerated beckon, one that is either designed to be more visible at a distance, or to convey a greater sense of urgency. For the Englishman, however, this gesture means 'Go away' or 'Go further away'; it certainly does not mean 'Come here'. This confusion can give rise to all kinds of misunderstandings. For example, when a visitor from northern Europe is summoned by an Italian policeman, he is likely to misconstrue the gesture of the raised hand sweeping downward as a suggestion that he go further away. This could of course have extremely embarrassing consequences.

The potential for cross-cultural misunderstanding is increased by the fact that in Italy the fan-gesture is used as a wave. Elsewhere in Europe people wave by moving their hand from side to side, with the palm facing forward. This gesture is used at a distance, both to greet people and to bid them farewell. In Italy, however, the wave is performed by moving the hand back and forth, with the palm up – in other words, with the fan-gesture! Whether it is performed with the hand held close to the body or with the arm extended, to a northern European the gesture looks like it is saying 'Come here'. To the Italian, of course, it means 'Hello' or 'Goodbye'.

The Italian fan-gesture can be performed with various degrees of emphasis, ranging from a gesture where both arms are held up high and rocked to and fro, with the palms facing back, all the way down to an almost imperceptible movement, where the fingers are quickly closed on the palm. To complicate matters, the Italians sometimes turn this abbreviated gesture over, so that the palm faces down rather than up, which makes it look exactly like a miniature paddle-gesture, meaning 'Come here'. To an outsider it can all be very confusing, but fortunately for the Italians it is not, because they know from the context that the gesture is intended as a wave, and not a beckon.

Most beckoning gestures in Europe are performed with the hand but the head is also used, usually by jerking it to the side, and people sometimes snap their fingers to beckon someone. This gesture is very old, and it was widely used in ancient Rome to summon servants. Petronius informs us, for example, that 'when a gentleman wanted his chamber-pot, it was a common way of speaking to make a noise with the finger and thumb by snapping them together, this was called *concrepare digitos*.' The fact that this gesture was associated with servants, and more specifically with the toilet, may explain why it is regarded as rude today.

Cleanliness

The history of Europe shows that concepts of cleanliness have changed dramatically over the centuries. In ancient Rome, for example, bathing was an integral part of most people's lives. For the upper classes it was a daily occurrence, and for some of the more hydromaniacal Emperors a pastime enjoyed seven or eight times a day. There were public baths and fountains in every part of Rome, and enormous feats of engineering were undertaken to bring fresh water into the city. According to *Clean and Decent*, Lawrence Wright's fascinating history of the bath, Rome at its peak provided no less than 300 gallons of water per person per day – most of it for the purposes of bathing. This figure is all the more striking when one considers that the corresponding figure for a city like London today is about fifty-one gallons, with about thirty-four gallons being used for domestic purposes, and the rest for commerce and industry.

Things were very different in medieval times. By the twelfth century plumbing had virtually disappeared, hot water was in short supply, and baths were few. People bathed infrequently, but when they did immerse themselves in water it was usually in pursuit of pleasure, or as a form of sexual foreplay. It was common, for example, for lovers to bath together before retiring to bed – not through any desire to be clean, but simply because the luxury of bathing together heightened the enjoyment of what was to follow.

Medieval books of etiquette did not insist on the need to bath, but they did stress the virtues of washing the hands, face and mouth each morning. In fact, the habit of washing the hands was widespread, largely because the fork had not yet been invented, and because people ate with their hands. Hand-washing therefore became a necessity, and very soon an intricate ritual emerged, full of expectations and hidden meanings. Lawrence Wright describes a typical scene at the table: 'At the top of the table an important person might wash separately, but it was polite to share the bowl with one's neighbour, and pleasant to play *manus manum lavat* (one's hand washing another) with one of the opposite sex. Neglect or refusal could be a calculated insult. Water was poured over the hands from a jug while they were held over the bowl. The water might be scented or strewn with rose-petals, but soap . . . was not brought to the table.'

Apart from the ritual of hand-washing, water played a very subordinate role in everyday life, and bathing had very little to do with cleanliness – Queen Elizabeth I, for example, is reported to have only bathed once a month, 'whether she need it or no'. At the same time, the streets were full of rotting debris, and the state of people's homes left a lot to be desired. In a letter to Cardinal Wolsey's physician, written about 1530, Erasmus offers the following description of a typical upper-class English home: 'As to the floors, they are usually made of clay covered with rushes, that grew in fens, which are so slightly removed now and then, that the lower part remains, sometimes for twenty years together, and in it a collection of spittle, vomit, urine of dogs and men, beer, scraps of fish, and other filthiness not to be named. Hence upon a change of weather a vapour is exhaled very pernicious in my opinion to the human body.'

The situation on the other side of the channel was no better. By the sixteenth century the French had become a nation of hydrophobics, due largely to the development of theories about the harmful effects of water. It was believed that the surface of the skin was permeable, and that hot water especially was capable of opening the pores and exposing the body to attack from unwholesome air. Water, it was said, exposed the body to plagues and pestilential vapours; it weakened the organs and ligaments, and could even cause death. Bath-houses and steam-baths, which had previously enjoyed enormous popularity, were now regarded as dangerous denizens of illness and disease. To immerse the body in water, especially water that had been in contact with other people's bodies, was to invite all kinds of dangers.

There were occasions that demanded bathing, but these were strictly medical. They were conducted under the supervision of a doctor, who took care to ensure that after the bath the patient was properly wrapped in protective clothing, and then sent off to bed to recover from the ordeal. Children required special protection from the penetrating effects of water because they were particularly vulnerable. They were therefore anointed with fragrant oils to seal the pores, and then swaddled to shield them from diseases that might penetrate their skin. In the case of children, baths were kept to a minimum. For example, the legs of the Dauphin, the future Louis XIII, were never washed until he reached the age of seven. When Louis XIV's doctor decided to bath him, it was purely for medical reasons. The doctor reported that the king did not enjoy the experience. When the king was immersed in the water he developed a terrible headache, so the treatment had to be called off. A year later the doctor repeated the experiment, but it ended in failure because by this time the king had developed a total aversion to bathing.

To keep themselves clean – or rather to create an illusion of cleanliness – the French aristocracy resorted to flannels, powders and perfume. Books on hygiene recommended that dirt and body odours should be removed by wiping the body with scented linen or compounds of herbs or rose petals. For example, a book of manners, published in 1671, advised that 'Children should clean their face and their eyes with a white cloth, which cleanses and leaves the complexion and colour in their natural state. Washing with water is bad for the sight, causes toothache and catarrh, makes the face pale, and renders it more susceptible to cold in winter and sun in summer.' It was essential, however, to remove or mask offensive odours. This could be achieved by judicious use of perfumes, by regular changes of clothing, and if it was absolutely necessary by washing only certain parts of the body. Regular replacement of clothing, particularly linen garments, was the main way that people avoided appearing dirty. It made people look clean, even if they didn't smell particularly sweet. Louis XIV, for example, did not wash very much, but he made up for it by changing his shirt three, four, sometimes five times a day. Henry IV was also renowned for his extremely fine linen, which he changed with enthusiastic regularity. This did not help him very much because, according to Mme Verneuil, he went around 'smelling like carrion'. In fact it is said that his personal odour was so overpowering that his future fiancée, Marie de Médecis, almost fainted on their first meeting.

The condition of Paris during the eighteenth century presented a real danger to health. The smell of cess-pits and decomposing carcasses was everywhere, and when the streets were not being used as a public toilet, they were being filled with the contents of chamber pots from the windows above. The stench of excrement and urine greeted people at every turn – so much so that the young Rousseau was moved to comment 'In the Palais de Justice, in the Louvre, even in the Opera, one is pursued by the unpleasant odour and infection from the latrines.' In a vain attempt to protect themselves from disease and discomfort people resorted to all kinds of fumigants, aromatics and perfumes. They armed themselves with camphor amulets, boxes of herbs, and bottles of vinegar – the contents of which were exposed to the nose as soon as the stench became too over-powering.

The idea that water represented a danger to health was also widespread in England during the eighteenth century, and it was commonly believed that sweat was the body's way of keeping itself clean. Society was much more tolerant of body odour than it is today, and cleanliness, such as it was, had more to do with appearances than personal hygiene or comfort. Consequently, although people washed their hands and face fairly regularly, they seldom applied water to their armpits, their feet or their genitals, and they showed even less enthusiasm for bathing. As late as 1801, a doctor observed that 'Most men resident in London and many ladies though accustomed to wash their hands and faces daily, neglect washing their bodies from year to year.' Soap did not come into general use until about 1824, when the Leblanc soda process allowed soap to be produced on a commercial scale. It was only after this that people, both in England and on the continent, started to recognise the virtues of soap and water and the importance of keeping clean. But as Europeans acquired new habits of cleanliness they adapted them to their own conditions, and in some cases to the old practices that they were intended to replace.

One of the earliest attempts to find out how often people take a bath was conducted in 1850 by Henry Mayhew, the great chronicler of life in Victorian London. Mayhew asked sixty-seven down-and-outs whether they ever took a bath. He reported that fifty-nine said 'no', two said 'sometimes', two said 'yes', another two said 'yes, in the Thames', and one person turned out to be deaf and dumb. A somewhat more representative survey, conducted in 1950, showed that 20% of Londoners 'never' took a bath, partly because only one in three houses at the time actually possessed a bath. Research conducted in 1978 showed that the figure for people who never took a bath was down to 3%, and that 40% of the population bathed or showered every day. Recent research shows that the corresponding figure today is 60%. These figures reflect the steadily increasing numbers of baths and showers in Britain, as well as a growing commitment to personal cleanliness and hygiene. Although similar trends can be detected in other European countries, people's attitudes to cleanliness differ enormously from one country to the next.

The French, for example, have a very different approach to cleanliness from, say, the British or the Germans. A poll conducted by Francoscopie, a French market research company, revealed that the average French adult uses 4.2 bars of soap a year, which is about half the number consumed by the average Briton. Only 19% of men and 32% of women in France take a daily bath – compared to the overall figure of 60% for the UK – and only 5% of the population wash their hair every day. This neglect of personal hygiene is even more pronounced in the case of dental care, where the use of items like toothbrushes and toothpaste remains conspicuously low. According to a recent report by Euromonitor, 'around 2.75 tubes of toothpaste are consumed annually by each inhabitant of France, which on average allows only one spread load on a toothbrush per person every three days, while the average French citizen buys a new toothbrush only once every seventy weeks'. This ties in with the finding that more than half of the population of France goes to bed at night without brushing their teeth.

What are we to conclude from these findings? Is it the case, as numerous observers have claimed, that the French are dirty and smelly, or have they simply found alternative ways of keeping themselves clean and smelling sweet? The answer is that the French are not as clean as, say, the British or the Germans, because they take far fewer baths and showers, but this is offset by the fact that they have other ways of dealing with body odour. Recent research by Taylor Nelson, a British market research company, shows that the use of 'wet' cleaning products like soap, bath additives, shower gels and shampoos is much lower in France than it is in Germany, Italy and the United Kingdom, but that the use of 'dry' cleaning agents like astringents, cleaning lotions, wipes and eye make-up remover is higher among French women than among women in these other countries. This shows that while women in France rely on methods other than soap and water to keep themselves clean, French men do not. As a result, French *men* are not as clean as their counterparts in Germany, Italy and the United Kingdom.

This reliance on 'dry' cleaning products has a very long history in France. When they decided, during the sixteenth century, that water was a danger to health, they resorted to other means of keeping clean. One method was to replace garments that had absorbed sweat and body odours; another was to rub the skin vigorously with a flannel or a piece of material that had been impregnated with perfumed lotions. These 'dry' methods continued to be used up to the end of the eighteenth century, when the cleansing properties of water were rediscovered. But while other Europeans were experimenting with soap and water, the French continued to harbour a suspicion that water is bad for the skin, which explains why they continue to take fewer baths and showers than other Europeans, and why lotions and astringents are so popular. When a French woman uses a lotion to clean her face she is doing much more than removing dirt from her skin; she is also reinforcing a tradition of personal care that goes back hundreds of years.

The other aspect of personal hygiene that has a long history in France is the widespread tolerance of dirt. Central to French thinking about the body is the notion of *terrain*, the idea that the body is capable of resisting germs without external assistance, and therefore that a little dirt, rather than causing any harm, may actually fortify the constitution and protect the body against illness. The French, it seems, have a much more organic attitude to dirt – they see it as part of the natural state of affairs, something to which they should try to adapt, rather than something to be totally eliminated. This partially explains why the French spend 50% more on fresheners than Italians and Britons, and three times as much as the Germans. The French market for toiletries and cosmetics is the largest in Europe. The bulk of this market is made up of skincare products and fragrances, rather than colour cosmetics, like lipstick and eye shadow. This shows that French women attach a great deal of importance to wearing a good perfume and that they are more concerned about the condition of their skin than wearing make-up.

German women also attach high priority to skincare, but less importance to perfume and make-up. For the German woman what counts is a natural, youthful look, which is why they are such heavy users of skin creams. They are also devoted to anti-wrinkle creams, which are used by almost a third of the female population. German men are also heavy users of face creams and lotions, partly, it is said, because the average German male is so vain. Research has also shown that there are differences between east and west Germans. For example, west Germans wash their hair twice as often as east Germans. They also use twice as much styling gel, and twice as much anti-wrinkle cream. It is only in the case of deodorants that the east Germans exceed the west Germans, largely, one suspects, because deodorants serve as a cheap and convenient substitute for perfumes in the east.

The case of the British is very different from that of the French and Germans. In Britain women spend proportionately more on make-up and fragrances, and less on skincare. For the average British woman what matters is looking smart and smelling attractive, even if a large element of artifice is involved. Skincare is not terribly important for British women, partly because the mild climate is so kind to their skin, but also because they are more resigned to the lines and wrinkles that come with age. Another important factor appears to be the long-standing association between skincare and medication. In the United Kingdom skincare products are more likely to be used as a remedy for a skin problem, rather than as a regular means of protection. Moreover, the vast majority of face creams designed for men are medicated, which explains why British men surreptitiously resort to the creams and lotions purchased by their female companions.

In the league table of personal cleanliness the Italians come out at the top, and the Spaniards at the bottom. Italians take more baths and showers than people in France, Germany, Britain and Spain. Where both men and women are concerned Italians are the heaviest users of soap and bath additives, and where just women are concerned they are also the heaviest users of cleaning lotions.

Skincare products are also important, especially make-up products associated with the eyes, but sales of fragrances are low – possibly because Italians bath and shower so often. The composition of the fragrances market is also unusual, because more than 90% of women's fragrances consist of toilet waters, and sales of men's fragrances are actually greater than those to women.

The Spanish case is a mirror image of the Italian one, because the Spaniards pay very little attention to baths and showers, while engaging in copious consumption of fragrances. Fragrances are used in enormous quantities by both men and women, and they are applied with equal enthusiasm to children. It is estimated that 60% of men regularly use a fragrance – typically an eau-de-cologne – while children are virtually weaned on the stuff. Dousing young children with a fragrance may strike some people as rather strange, but one needs to remember that children in Spain are really just small adults. Like their parents they are constantly on display, and that is why they also need to smell good.

Driving

When people get behind the wheel of a car they often change out of all recognition. We have all experienced the sort of thing; a friend offers us a lift home and then proceeds to reveal a side of himself we never even knew existed. One minute he is the kind and considerate person that we know so well; the next minute he's hurtling down the motorway, weaving between the traffic, throwing insults at other drivers, and generally behaving as if he were possessed by some automotive demon.

What is it about cars that brings out this side of people and turns them into highway kamikazes? Is it, as numerous psychologists have suggested, that driving is an anxiety-provoking experience, and that this makes people impatient and bad tempered? Or does it have something to do with the inherent symbolism of the car and the atavistic responses that cars evoke in people? Psychologists have spent a great deal of time investigating things like reaction times, visual acuity and speed estimation, in the hope that a greater understanding of motor skills will help to explain why drivers become involved in motor accidents. Young men, it appears, have these skills in abundance. The fact that they are involved in more accidents than any other sector of the population suggests that a shortage of motor skills is not the main explanation for car accidents. The clue to dangerous driving probably has more to do with the opportunities that the car provides for self-expression and the acting out of fantasy.

The unique thing about cars is that they extend our ability to act on the world, making us stronger and faster, and inviting us to pit ourselves against other drivers. At the same time they foster the illusion that our ability to outstrip other cars is a reflection of our own capabilities rather than those of the car. Speed and risk are also important clues to the understanding of drivers, not only because these sensations are enjoyable, but because they project the whole

28

business of driving into a realm of unreality, where drivers imagine that they are in complete control of their destiny, and where they fail to recognise the real dangers of the road. Being in a car creates a sense of inviolability, the feeling that one is protected from the outside world, and that people can't get at you. That is one of the reasons why people are likely to insult each other from the security of their car, and why they find it so easy to depersonalise other drivers, regarding them merely as the occupants of cars, rather than as individuals in their own right.

The way that someone drives says a great deal about the kind of person they really are. Driving style is therefore a kind of litmus test, showing the side of people's personalities that they don't normally reveal. The same is true of nations, not only because people in other countries drive very differently, but because their driving style often reveals something about them that is not immediately evident in other situations. Take the case of the Greeks, who always come across as courteous and considerate – certainly not the kind of people one would think of as competitive or given to taking unnecessary risks. This image of the Greeks does not get a lot of support from the accident statistics, which show that, relative to the distances that people travel, Greece has more deaths on the road than any other European country. Portugal comes next, and Spain, which has about 9,000 deaths on the roads every year, comes third. France, with slightly fewer, is fourth, while Britain, with about 4,500, is near the bottom of the league table.

For a long time it was assumed that deaths on European roads could be explained in terms of factors like bad roads, confusing sign-posts, and the poor quality of the cars – it has been suggested, for example, that the high death toll in Greece is due to the restrictive import taxes, which encourage people to drive cars that should have been dispatched to the scrap yard. Recently, however, it has become apparent that although environmental factors play a part, they are not the only causes of accidents, and that the way people actually drive their cars is the real culprit.

Travellers to Greece, Italy and Spain are often astounded to discover just how little respect is shown for traffic laws. Drivers in these countries frequently 'crash the lights' by going through an intersection after the traffic lights have changed to red. Everyone knows that there is a delay between the traffic lights in one direction turning red and the lights in the other direction turning green, and that this provides a few seconds during which they can safely get across to the other side – assuming of course that nobody going in the other direction decides to jump the lights before they turn green. The habit of crashing the lights frequently ends in an accident, not between cars going in different directions, but between cars going in the same direction. Because it has become the norm for cars to crash the lights, this sets up an expectation that everyone will do so. That is why, if a car stops suddenly when the lights turn red, it is likely to have several cars collide into it from behind.

British drivers are very different. They are more hesitant about crashing the lights, and they usually wait until the lights have turned green before proceeding. In fact it is not unusual to see drivers in England waiting patiently for the lights to turn green, even at the dead of night, when there isn't another car around for miles. To the Italians and the Spaniards, not to mention the French, this kind of behaviour appears totally bizarre – it is the kind of thing one would expect of Pavlov's dogs, not human beings. An Italian driver behaves very differently in these circumstances. Provided that there are no other cars around, and there is no chance of his being apprehended, he will simply ignore the red lights and drive on. As far as he is concerned, the traffic lights are only there to be obeyed when other cars or the police are around, although there are some Italian cities, like Naples, where the local drivers appear to be totally unaffected even by traffic regulations, the presence of other drivers or the police.

I remember an episode, some years ago, when I was in Italy with a group of English friends, and we were driving round one of these seaside towns on the Adriatic coast, looking for a restaurant. Eventually we found a policeman, so we stopped and asked him for directions. The policeman decided that, instead of giving us directions, he would accompany us to the restaurant, so I climbed into the back seat, he got into the passenger seat, and we set off. At the end of the street we came to a set of traffic lights, which were red. Naturally our driver came to halt, waiting for the lights to turn green. At this point the policeman turned to the driver, removed his Ray-ban sunglasses, and, with obvious bewilderment, asked him what he thought he was doing. By way of explanation, the driver pointed at the red traffic lights. The policeman made a series of dismissive gestures, replaced his glasses and said 'Nonsense! If everybody behaved like this the traffic would come to a complete stand-still. Move on! *Avanti!*'

The attitude of Italians towards traffic regulations is very different from that of the British. This is not to suggest that the British follow the law religiously, because they don't. They will happily park on double yellow lines, and they are not averse to speeding on the motorway, but as a rule they tend to follow traffic regulations in a way that makes the Italians look positively anarchic. Italians view traffic regulations as flexible guidelines, something they can afford to ignore, provided the police don't cause any trouble and nobody gets hurt.

In countries like Spain and Italy, parking has become a problem of epidemic proportions, with cars parked in the bus and taxi lanes, on the pavement, and sometimes two or three deep on the main thoroughfares. These problems are partly the result of inadequate parking facilities, but there is also an element of ostentation in the desire to park one's car where it can be seen and admired, not to mention the sense of satisfaction that comes from leaving it in a prohibited zone. After all, it is another way of thumbing one's nose at authority. The French have had this kind of problem for years, and it is not unusual for parts of Paris to be completely snarled up by parked cars. In order to reduce *stationnement sauvage*, the city authorities have designated several 'red routes' through Paris, where it is prohibited even to stop one's car. There was a great deal of opposition to the *axes rouge* when they were first introduced, but this soon quietened down, and traffic is now moving freely.

The way that people react to traffic jams varies enormously from one country to the next. The British, for example, are accustomed to Bank Holiday traffic jams and bumper-to-bumper driving through the countryside. Unlike, say, the Italians, who produce an cacophony of honking horns whenever the traffic comes to a halt, the British tend to be rather phlegmatic and philosophical about the prospect of being held up for hours. The Germans have a very similar attitude to traffic jams, although recent research by an institute in Hamburg shows that a surprisingly large number of drivers actually enjoy the experience. The researchers discovered that the majority of drivers disliked being trapped in a traffic jam, or *Stau* as it is called. They found that there were several strains of '*Stau* fever', with symptoms like anxiety, aggressiveness and feelings of malaise. However, it also emerged that one in five drivers experienced what they called '*Stau* lust' – they actually got a thrill from being trapped in a traffic jam. Some drivers said that they liked the feeling of camaraderie associated with being in a traffic jam; others reported that it gave them a perverse sense of achievement to know that they had been through the ordeal.

One of the ordeals that all drivers have to face is how to get from a side-road on to a busy main road. In Britain it is not uncommon for cars on the main road to offer a space to those entering from the side road – either by flashing their lights, or by leaving a gap. On the other hand, in countries like Spain, Italy and Greece, a car that is trying to get out of a side road is hardly ever offered a space on the main road – unless, of course, it happens to be driven by an attractive woman, or the driver manages to catch the eye of one of the drivers on the main road. Otherwise, the only way to get into a main road is by edging forward slowly, so that one of the cars on the main road is eventually forced to let one in. Similar patterns can be observed on roundabouts. In countries like Spain, Italy and France, drivers frequently jostle for position, weaving in and out of the traffic, and doing everything to get ahead, regardless of the effect that it has on other drivers.

These cultural differences in driving styles appear to be connected to divergent attitudes about the obligations that the individual has to other people. Latin countries, for example, are renowned for their 'collectivism', which means that while people are totally devoted to their immediate reference group, they are not too concerned about the welfare of those who fall outside its boundaries. Typically the reference group includes the extended family and work colleagues, and possibly the neighbours and people who live in the same locality, but it certainly does not include the faceless mass of people on the road. The average Italian, for example, has obligations to his reference group. When he gets in his car, these obligations no longer apply, because other drivers fall outside the scope of his reference group, and he is therefore not obliged to treat them with courtesy or consideration. The British, on the other hand, have a much weaker sense of reference group, and the obligations of the individual are not dictated to the same extent by group membership. The British are also motivated by a desire to get on with other people and to give them a fair chance – what Ralf Dahrendorf refers to as the 'public virtues'. Consequently they are often just as considerate to strangers as they are to people whom they know well, and this is especially evident when the 'cost' of being courteous is low – which of course it is when one motorist makes a gap in the traffic for another. It has to be said, however, that the courteous behaviour of British drivers appears to be in decline. There are places, like the inner cities, where it is almost non-existent, and where, for all the consideration that is shown, one might as well be driving around in Paris, Madrid or Rome. Whether this decline in motoring manners is simply a feature of modern city life, or something that is about to engulf the whole country, remains to be seen.

The Italians, as we have seen, like the French and Spaniards, appear to have a rather anarchic attitude towards authority, and this has a pronounced effect on the way they drive and the way they relate to other motorists. In Italy and Spain this anarchic attitude is combined with an immediate concern with the here-and-now, rather than with any long-term consequences of one's actions. The Spaniards also have a peculiar fascination with the subject of death, which seems to have inured them to the dangers of driving. This fascination with death is certainly very ancient. It predates the *autos-da-fé* of the Inquisition, when thousands of heretics were burned at the stake, and it is certainly as old as the ritual of bull-fighting, which celebrates death. A few years ago the Spanish police became concerned about the number of cases where youngsters were killed falling out of cars, or being knocked over by cars. It emerged that bored youngsters had invented new ways to die in a car accident. One method involved climbing from the window of one car into the window of another car as the two cars sped down the motorway – a trick that didn't always work. Another deadly stunt, usually done for a wager, involved a youngster standing in the middle of the road, with his eyes bandaged, so that as cars came round the corner they were forced to cross to the other lane to avoid hitting him.

One of the great attractions of cars is the opportunity that they provide for self-expression. Motorists are able to use their cars not only to control and alter their moods, but also to fortify their self-esteem and to project an image of themselves as certain kinds of people. Central to the image that drivers try to project is the impression of competence and control. In some countries this includes the ability to take risks, and a readiness to compete with other motorists. French drivers, for example, do not like to be beaten by other cars, and they sometimes react very negatively to being overtaken. The objective of French drivers, says Richard Bernstein, 'is to get ahead, to be first, but to do so cleverly, stressing speed and manoeuvrability, those necessary attributes of the physically less powerful'. In France, and in countries like Italy, Spain and Greece, driving has become a test of character, and in the case of male drivers, a measure of their manhood. That is why male drivers in these countries are so much more opportunistic and aggressive, and why they are so ready to shout at each other, gesticulate and honk their horns.

A few years ago, Joseph Forgas, an Australian psychologist, conducted a fascinating study of horn-honking in Germany, France, Spain and Italy. Displaying either an Australian or a German sticker on the back of their car, he and his wife pulled up at the traffic lights, and when the lights turned green, they remained stationery and measured how long it took before the drivers behind started to honk their horns. There were striking differences between drivers in the four countries. German drivers proved to be the most patient, waiting about seven and a half seconds on average before they honked their horn. Not surprisingly, Italian drivers were the most impatient. On average, they only waited about four seconds. French and Spanish drivers fell between these two extremes. The interesting thing about these results is that France, Spain and Italy emerged as being very different from Germany. These three countries have a distinctly macho attitude to driving, whereas Germans do not.

The only macho aspect of German drivers is their love of speed and their resistance to any attempts to impose a speed limit on the *Autobahnen*. The car lobby still talks about '*Freie Fahrt für freie Bürger* – free roads for free citizens – and German drivers continue to treat the *Autobahnen* like test tracks, hurtling along at break-neck speeds, flashing their lights to clear a path before them. Since the Berlin wall came down hordes of clattering Trabants from the east have appeared on the *Autobahnen*, obstructing the path of all those speeding Mercedes and BMWs, and increasing the accident rate into the bargain.

Fast driving is a source of great enjoyment to a large number of people, partly because it creates certain physiological sensations, but also because it gives drivers a sense of control over their destiny, and allows them to experience the thrill of taking risks. Motorists who drive fast tend to base their decisions on subjective assessments of their car and their own driving abilities. The problem with this kind of calculation is that it totally ignores the role of other drivers, and it is also notoriously inaccurate because drivers over estimate their own abilities. Drivers know that accidents occur, but they somehow think that they won't become involved. It's a case of the 'not me' syndrome, the belief that one is inviolable, or that one can always extricate oneself from a potentially sticky situation.

This is very evident in the case of seat-belt wearing. In most European countries seat-belts are now compulsory. The law, however, is no guarantee of compliance, and in countries like Spain and Italy large numbers of drivers continue to reject seat-belts. The excuse they give is that seat-belts are dangerous, or that they are uncomfortable. They seldom mention the fact that seat-belts tend to undermine their sense of inviolability, and in the case of men, their macho identity. Not long ago the shops in Italy were selling T-shirts which had a realistic image of a seat-belt printed across the front. You could put one of these T-shirts on and drive for miles without raising the suspicions of the police. What happened to the T-shirt if you had a head-on collision was another matter altogether.

Expletives

Most languages have two sides to them – a public vocabulary consisting of words that are acceptable and inoffensive, and a netherworld of obscenities, oaths and curses. These expletive items of language usually begin as inoffensive words, and once they have exhausted their capacity to shock, they return once again to the lexicon of ordinary, inoffensive words. European languages differ enormously, not only in terms of the sheer size of their expletive vocabularies, but also in terms of the types of swear-words that are available, and how often people use them. In the past most swear-words consisted of oaths, whereas today the emphasis is much more on curses and invective. 'The crude history of swearing,' says Geoffrey Hughes, 'is that people used mainly to swear *by* or *to*, but now swear mostly *at*.'

The ancient Greeks, for example, swore by the gods – men by male gods like Zeus, Jupiter and Mars, and women by goddesses like Minerva, Juno and Venus. But the Greeks did not confine their oaths to deities. They also swore by the garlic, the leek and the onion, and Socrates is reputed to have sworn by the dog, the goose and the plane tree. Various theories have been put forward to try and explain these eccentric oaths, including the idea that they were a play on words, or oblique references to certain gods, and in Socrates' case, because he did not believe in the gods. It is now generally accepted, however, that the main motive for these choices was fun. The Ionians swore 'By the cabbage!', probably because they believed that it was an effective antidote against hangovers. This habit of swearing by vegetables is still found in Italy, where people occasionally resort to pretend swear-words, like *Pasta-Fazula*, meaning macaroni-and-beans.

The Romans also swore by the gods, usually with men invoking male gods and women appealing to goddesses. Hercules, however, was used by men, and not by women, although children were permitted to swear by Hercules, provided they were outside the house. Ashley Montagu tells us that 'In the house one could swear *Di Doni*! or *Per dios immortales*! but never by Hercules. The prohibition, however, extended only to the four walls of the house and its curtilage; out of doors the children were free to make what use of it they liked.' The Romans also had a host of colourful curses and expletives, one of the more famous being *damnosa canicula*, which means 'damned dog', and which in France became *Sacré chien*. According to Montagu, this swear-word originated in Roman times as an expression of frustration and disappointment, being used by players who had thrown a bad hand in dice – a *canicula* or *canis* referring to a particular throw that happened to be called a dog. The expression itself was not an anti-canine curse, although its foreign derivatives turned out that way.

Oaths have always invited the patronage and witness of super-natural beings, and in some cases their punishment if the oath was not fulfilled. In the Christian tradition, God, Jesus, Holy Mary, Heaven and the saints have all been invoked; so have 'God's wounds', 'God's blood' and 'The Holy Cross'. All of these oaths involve profanity, and they are therefore very different from blasphemous oaths and curses, where an attempt is usually being made to vilify the supernatural. Both the Church and the state have tried to put a stop to the use of profane oaths, but seldom with any great success. In England, linguistic censorship only came into effect after the reign of Elizabeth I, partly because she was a libertarian as far as language was concerned, but also because she was not averse to swearing herself. It is said that she seldom spared an oath where one was appropriate, and that 'God's wounds' was her favourite.

Ecclesiastical disapproval and censorship did not manage to do away with profane oaths, but they did succeed in fostering the use of 'minced oaths' – that is oaths which are modified in such a way as to disguise their true identity. By the early part of the seventeenth century, 'God's wounds', for example, had been contracted to 'zounds', 'God's truth' had become 'struth', or 'strewth', and 'God's nails' had become 'snails'. In time Jesus was shortened to 'Jeeze', while Christ became 'Cripes' and 'Crikey', and Jesus Christ became 'Jeepers Creepers', and even 'Jiminy Cricket'. Even invocations of the devil became disguised, with oaths like 'Deuce' and 'Dickens'. Many expressions which have enjoyed widespread use are in fact minced oaths with a profane origin. Who would imagine, for example, that 'Gosh' and 'Golly' are derived from God, that 'Dickens' was a diabolical invocation, or that 'Geewhizz' was a reference to Jesus Christ?

In addition to oaths that invoke gods and the assistance of supernatural beings, there are others where the person invites punishment if he fails to live up to his word. Oaths like 'Strike me dead' and 'Blow me down' are usually tagged on to a statement of fact, implying that the person is prepared to die if he is not telling the truth. These are therefore 'forfeit oaths' because they offer the person's life, their health or their welfare as a forfeit against the truth. These oaths are also subject to abbreviation. 'Gorblimey', for example, is a corruption of the forfeit oath 'God blind me (if I lie)!'.

Forfeit oaths are a form of 'self-cursing', because people who utter them curse themselves if it turns out that they are not telling the truth. There are, incidentally, also forfeit oaths that involve 'other-cursing', where, for example, an oath is extracted, on penalty of a curse being applied, usually by some appointed official. The ancient Egyptians had a rather unusual version of this type of oath. According to Gershon Legman, 'Egyptian legal documents of the last dynasties used to be reinforced, where today we might have a notary public's seal, with the stereotyped phrase: "As for him who shall disregard it, may he be fucked by a donkey." The hieroglyph for this curse makes the matter unmistakably clear with two little drawings of large, erect penises.'

The English reputation for swearing goes back a long way. 'Have we not been called in the vulgar dialect of foreign countries "The Swearing Nation"?,' asked Daniel Defoe in 1712. A century later, in 1821, William Hazlitt acknowledged that 'The English (it must be owned) are a rather foul-mouthed nation.' But even before that, during the sixteenth century, English soldiers were known to the French as *les Goddems*, after their liberal use of 'Goddamn!'. The word 'Damn' is very old, but the expression 'I don't give a damn' is fairly recent. The origins of the expression go back to the last century, when the Duke of Wellington is said to have coined the phrase 'I don't give a two-penny dām', where 'dām' referred to an Indian coin of that name. In time, it is said, 'dām' was changed to 'damn', and another oath entered the lexicon.

The English reputation for swearing rests on their readiness to use vulgar langauge and profanities, and the rather unusual character of some of their expletives. In his book on swearing, Geoffrey Hughes deals with some of the mistaken theories – or folk etymologies as they are called – that have been put forward to explain the origins of certain English swear-words. There is a widespread belief, for example, that all the four-letter words in English are Anglo-Saxon in origin. This, as it happens, is only true of 'shit', 'turd', 'arse' and 'fart' – 'piss' was probably brought over by the Normans, while the origins of words like 'crap', 'cunt' and 'fuck' continue to remain a mystery. There are indications that many of these words were originally used literally, and without any sense of shame. For example, in the thirteenth century Sherborne Lane in the City of London was known as Shitteborwelane, probably because it was the site of a privy. Other four-letter words also appeared in medieval English street names. Magpie Lane in Oxford was known as Gropecuntlane in about 1230, and during the same period there were lanes with similar names in London, York, Wells and Northampton – presumably because they were the location of brothels.

Another example of folk etymology is the widespread belief that 'bloody' originated from the expletive 'By Our Lady!', which was a reference to the Virgin Mary. In fact there are at least six theories about the origins of 'bloody', of which the 'By Our Lady' theory is probably the least convincing. It has been suggested, for example, that bloody derives from *bloidhe*, a Celtic word meaning 'rather'. This would explain how Dean Swift could write to a friend in London, reporting that it was 'bloody hot in Dublin'. It is more likely, however, that bloody comes from 'blood', a word that was used to describe an upper-class rowdy. The phrase 'bloody drunk', for example, was employed during the seventeenth century, and there is a reference to 'bluddily learned' as early as 1606, which suggests that the term first appeared in connection with the aristocracy, and then became a simple linguistic intensifier. In fact, 'bloody' remained a respectable word, and continued to be employed without giving offense, right up to the middle of the eighteenth century, when it was taken over by the working classes and transformed into a common swear-word. It was precisely because the word was so closely associated with the working classes that it came to be regarded as a swear-word. This did not, however, prevent other people from using 'bloody'; during the early part of this century George Bernard Shaw estimated that it was 'in common use by four-fifths of the English nation, including many highly-educated persons'.

The First World War helped to entrench 'bloody' and to increase its usage, especially among working-class people and country folk, to the point where it was liberally distributed in every sentence, and sometimes in the middle of words, being used almost as if it were a hesitation device like 'um' or 'er'. The reliance on bloody is captured by the following story, which was going around at the time: Two Yorkshiremen were standing in front of an election poster. 'What do they mean', asked one, 'by one man one vote?' 'Why!' answered his companion, 'it means "one bloody man, one bloody vote."' To which the enquirer replied, 'Then why the hell don't they bloody well say so?'

After the First World War 'bloody' started to lose its force as a swear-word, largely because it had been overworked and because it had lost its capacity to shock. This opened up the way for 'fuck'. 'Fuck' has also attracted several fanciful etymologies, one of the more bizarre being the theory that the word is an acronym for 'Fornicate Under Command of the King', a royal edict that was supposed to have been issued during the time of the great plague. In fact the word is believed to have appeared about 1500, coming either from the German '*ficken*', meaning 'to strike', or from the Old English '*firk*', meaning to get or to make. All the European languages have words for sexual intercourse, but only English has managed to press 'fuck' into service as an expletive. In fact, 'fuck' and its derivatives function as insults, intensifiers, descriptors, dismissives and verbal ejaculations. Grammatically, it can behave like an adjective, a noun, an adverb or a verb – as in the case where the frustrated motorist says of his car, 'The fucking fucker's fucking well fucked.'

The English habit of using the sexual act as the basis of swearing usually strikes other Europeans as peculiar. The Dutch psychiatrist, Renatus Hartogs, had this to say when he heard his English mechanic complain that he could not 'get this fucking wheel off!': 'I was astounded. At the time I was sufficiently new to the English langauge to take everything being said quite literally, and the idea of a wheel engaging in sexual intercourse perplexed me. In my former languages, German, French and Dutch, it is simply unthinkable to ascribe sexual activity to inanimate objects.' But why do the English use the symbolism of the sexual act as the basis for their swearing and cursing? The answer, according to Hartogs, lies in the grammatical structure of the language and the fact that while all the other European languages have gender, English does not. To compensate for this deficit, English speakers implicate inanimate objects in a never-ending series of sexual acts. Through repeated use of the word 'fuck', 'they turn grammatical lack of gender into a veritable linguistic orgy'.

The first time that 'fuck' was used on television was in 1965. The British drama critic, Kenneth Tynan, managed to smuggle the word into a discussion about whether the sexual act should be shown on the stage. 'I doubt if there are very many people in the world,' said Tynan, 'to whom the word fuck is particularly diabolical or revolting or totally forbidden.' Tynan, however, had seriously under-estimated the strength of the taboo and the number of people who found the word revolting. The next day the newspapers were full of indignation and coded references to the word that he had dared to use. The scandal was in fact very reminiscent of what had happened half a century before, when Mrs Patrick Campbell had appeared as Eliza Doolittle in the first production of Shaw's *Pygmalian* and uttered those immortal words, 'Not bloody likely. I am going in a taxi.' A large number of people had attended the first night, just to hear the word 'bloody' used in the theatre. Shaw was roundly attacked for violating the taboo, and for years afterwards 'bloody' was euphemised as 'the Shavian word' or disguised in expressions like 'Not Pygmalian likely'. Tynan's name was similarly used in expressions like 'Shut the Tynan door!'.

Linguistic taboos surrounding the use of vulgar and profane words are extremely powerful, but they do not last for ever. Even the strongest linguistic taboo cannot withstand the evolutionary pressures that are applied to language, and once a word has lost its emotional charge and its capacity to offend, it is automatically demoted to the ranks of the inoffensive words, from whence it came. 'Bloody', for example, managed to scandalise people from the middle of the century up to the end of the First World War. Nowadays, however, it is hardly noticed. 'Fuck' is going through the same cycle. It too started out as an inoffensive word, and has enjoyed long service as a swear-word. But it has undoubtedly passed its peak. During the next century it will probably go the way of 'bloody', and another word will move in to take its place.

Swear-words are very similar to euphemisms because they reflect the preoccupations and concerns of society. The issues that people cloak in the anodyne language of euphemism is always a good guide to the things that they cannot face directly, and which they therefore need to obscure with circumlocution. Swear-words are equally revealing, because they provide an inventory of taboo topics. There are many reasons why people swear. One is that swearing provides people with a form of emotional release, a way of expelling tension. Another purpose of swearing is to show that one is the kind of person who is not bound by the conventions of polite society, that one is 'one of the boys'. But there is also another motivating force behind the use of expletives, namely the discharge of anxiety about specific issues. The things that bother or oppress people often become incorporated into their oaths and invective, thereby enabling them to wage linguistic warfare against the sources of their anxiety. The things that people swear about can therefore tell us a great deal about their fears and concerns.

Historically there has been an enormous shift in swearing, away from religious subjects to more secular issues, particularly those connected with bodily functions and sex. This development has followed the gradual decline of religious beliefs. Even today there are quite noticeable differences between the practices of Protestant and Catholic countries, with the former basing their swear-words on sex and scatological topics, and Catholics concentrating more on blasphemy and profanity. This is a long-standing feature of Catholic countries. Dante, for example, is said to have indulged freely in obscenity, but he consigned blasphemers to the seventh level of hell.

Italy is a good example of a country where blasphemy and profanity are rife. The lexicon of swearwords in Italy is enormous, and constantly being enlarged with new imprecations, blasphemies and profanities. Most Italian profanities refer to God and the

Virgin Mary, with the majority referring to God – for example, *Dio Buono!* (Good God) or *Dio caro!* (Dear God). The same is true of Italian blasphemies, where God is frequently associated with some lowly animal – like *Porco Dio!* (That pig of a God), *Dio Cane!* (That dog of a God), or *Dio serpente!* (That snake of a God). Some imprecations try to disguise their blasphemous content, either by replacing *Dio* with *zio*, meaning 'uncle', or by contracting the oath and sticking something else on the end, as in the case of *Dio can-arino!* (That canary of a God). Another way is to expand the oath in the hope that the blasphemous content will somehow be lost in the midst of all the other verbiage – for example *Dio scapà da lett senza scarpi!* (God escaped from bed without shoes). The Madonna also features extensively in Italian imprecations – for example *Porca Madonna!* (That pig of a Virgin Mary), *Madonna troia!* (That sow of a Virgin Mary), or *Madonna puttana!* (That whore of a Virgin Mary). What is particularly interesting about Italian swearing is the paucity of blasphemies relating to Jesus Christ. There are a few profanities, like *Cristo!* and *Corpo di Cristo!* but almost no blasphemies to speak of, which suggests that God and the Madonna are much more important to Italians than Jesus. In fact the Italians only seem to pay attention to Jesus while he is a babe in arms; the moment he leaves his mother's arms they seem to lose interest in him altogether.

Numerous attempts have been made to try and discourage the Italians from swearing so much. The Church has been involved in these efforts, and so has the state. Ashley Montagu tells us that during the time of Mussolini the local authorities launched a campaign to try and persuade Italians to stop swearing. Notices appeared in the public buildings, and on the trains and buses, pleading with people not to use bad language – *Non bestemmiare per l'onore d'Italia* (Do not swear, for the honour of Italy). The campaign turned out to be a total flop because it didn't persuade anybody. If anything, it probably encouraged swearing as people gathered round to exchange views about the notices.

The Spaniards are also inveterate swearers. *Hostia!*, which means Holy Bread, is probably their favourite profanity, but it is very mild compared to some of the other religious imprecations that they employ, like *Me cago en Dios* (I shit on God) and *Me cago en todos los Santos* (I shit on all the saints). Swearwords like *coño* (cunt) and *cojones* (balls) have their equivalents in other European languages. However, the swearword for which the Spaniards are best known is *Caramba!*, which is not found in any other European countries. The curious thing about *Caramba!* is that it has no meaning at all, and the Spaniards appear to be quite unconcerned about their inability to explain its origins. In fact it was originally the stage name of a singer of comic opera who was popular during the eighteenth century; but how her name came to be used as an expletive still remains a mystery.

It is in the area of verbal obscenity that the Spaniards remain the unchallenged past masters. Their invective is highly emotive and provocative. In addition to the usual expressions like *Jodete!* (Go fuck yourself), they also have curses like *Cago en la leche de tu madre* (I shit in your mother's milk) which show definite signs of North African influence. Gershon Legman has concluded that 'Obscenity is outstandingly an Hispanic art. When Spanish-speaking people care to curse, swear, brag, or tall-talk, every other nation in the world must stand silent with their thumb up their ass.'

In spite of the differences in national styles of swearing, there are also some striking similarities. Most European countries have animal names in their swearing vocabularies – dogs, for example, are often implicated in parental insults like the British 'son-of-a-bitch', the French *Fils d'une chienne*, the Russian *sukin syn*, and the German *Hundesohn*. Pigs are connected with accusations about uncleanliness in every European language, and the Germans have invented several imprecations involving the word *Schwein*. They have even managed to cross-breed their insults with swearwords like *Schweinhund*.

'Shit' is another swearword that crops up everywhere. The Italians, for example, use *stronzo*! as an insult, while the English use 'shit!' both as an insult and as an expression of frustration. The most elaborate use of 'shit' is undoubtedly found in Germany, where *Scheiss* and *Dreck* form the mainstay of the nation's insults and obscenities. The French have *merde* and *chier*, which are usually translated as 'shit' and 'crap' respectively. Both words are used in expressions about being in the shit, or about people who are a pain in the neck, or who are unusually fortunate. To complicate matters further, *merde* is even used to wish someone good luck. *Merde* is known in polite circles as *les cinq lettres* – a five-letter word – but it is certainly not as offensive as its English equivalent. Nor does it contain any of the anal connotations that are present in words like 'shit' or *Scheiss*. In his discussion of *merde*, Renatus Hartogs comes to the conclusion that 'it implies nothing repressive, nothing loathsome. *Merde*, to the French, is simply a sort of one-syllable synopsis of the human condition. Depending on context, it may mean anything from a dispassionate, almost antiseptic, statement of annoyance to a sort of verbal good-luck charm. It has no place in dirty stories.'

Even when different societies do select the same theme as the basis for swearing, they often approach the same theme from very different directions. This is certainly evident in the way that 'shit' has been incorporated into the swearwords of different European nations. The same is true of an expletive like 'pig!'. For the English, 'pig!' implies a lack of attention to physical cleanliness, whereas for most other Europeans it also has very definite connotions of moral impurity. What is much more obvious, however, is the way that different societies select different topics for their curses and imprecations. These choices tell us a great deal about the basic assumptions of these societies, the kinds of things they find offensive, and the sources of their anxiety.

Face

One facial feature which has captured everybody's attention is the so-called 'stiff upper lip' of the British. Whenever the British are mentioned in conversation you can be sure that someone will use this expression – either literally, when discussing the peculiar facial habits of the British, or figuratively, when referring to their reputed qualities of determination, stoicism or emotional control. But is there any evidence to show that the British upper lip is as stiff as people say, and are there any grounds for supposing that the qualities associated with a stiff upper lip are any more prevalent among the British than among other nations?

There are several types of evidence which throw light on the issue of the British stiff upper lip. The first concerns the way that people move their mouths when they are speaking, and the second the conventions surrounding laughter and smiling. The mouth movements involved in spoken English are far less dramatic than those of other languages, like French and German. In fact it is quite easy for an English speaker to keep his lips and jaw perfectly still, and to produce a very plausible imitation of his normal speaking voice, despite these restrictions. This is a trick that speakers of other languages find much more difficult to perform.

Given this special quality of English, it is hardly surprising that the British should have developed a style of 'frozen speech', in which lip movements are kept to a minimum and jaw movements are barely discernible. This style of speech is by no means a new invention of the British. When the French traveller, Samuel Sorbière visited England in 1663, he noted how well the English were suited to their language, 'for it spares them the labour of moving their lips'. A few years earlier John Milton had made a similar observation about the paucity of English mouth movements, which he excused with reference to the weather: 'For we Englishmen being farre northerly doe not open our mouthes in the cold air, wide enough to grace a Southern tongue; but are observ'd by all other nations to speak exceeding close and inward.' The Spanish sociologist, José Ortega y Gasset, made a similar observation at the beginning of this century: 'To learn English you must begin by thrusting the jaw forward, almost clenching the teeth, and practically immobilising the lips. In this way the English produce the series of unpleasant little mews of which their language consists.'

The articulatory requirements involved in speaking English have almost certainly contributed to the image of the Briton as someone who has a stiff upper lip. Another important factor is the legacy of the British attitude to laughter and smiling. During the sixteenth century, for example, there was a definite aversion to laughter in courtly circles. Laughter was regarded as uncouth, as a sign of an unserious mind, and therefore something to be avoided wherever possible. Smiling, too, was regulated by various social restrictions, although it was generally felt that genteel smiling in moderation was acceptable.

There were other reasons for this early aversion to laughter. To begin with, the upper classes had just discovered the dubious attraction of Melancholy, and they were dragging their feet around, affecting an air of gravitas and scholarly seriousness, and generally looking miserable. Melancholy was an emotional fashion, which is probably best understood, in comtemporary terms, as a mild, self-inflicted form of depression. The 'Elizabethan maladie', enjoyed enormous popularity during the sixteenth century and although it started to lose favour during the seventeenth century, it made an impression on the facial habits of the English which lasted for a long time to come. The cultivation of a serious, sombre countenance was very fashionable. According to Grant McCracken, noblemen at the time attempted to assume two attitudes in their facial expression and posture – one was affability, the other was gravity. These attitudes were designed to inculcate affection and fear – in other words, by behaving in a friendly, yet distant manner the nobleman sought to be liked and yet respected.

The cultivation of an impassive, serious countenance continued well into the eighteenth century, and many of the foreigners who visited England during that time remarked on the sullen, sad appearance of the inhabitants. Jean Paul Grosley, a Frenchman who arrived in 1765, made several comments on the morose appearance of the English. He put the whole thing down to too much beef, beer, Protestantism and smog. His solution to the melancholic appearance of the English was more French wine.

In addition to social etiquette and melancholy, there was another factor which discouraged the British from laughing and smiling during the sixteenth century, namely bad teeth. When Paul Hentzner, a German lawyer, visited the court of Queen Elizabeth in 1598, he noticed that the Queen's teeth were quite black, a defect which he ascribed to 'too much use of sugar'. A century later this observation was echoed by the Swiss traveller Beat-Louis de Muralt. His journals reveal that he was not terribly impressed by the beauty of English women: 'They are all fair and of delicate complexion but nothing animates their pretty faces . . . The greatest fault I find with them is that they do not take care of their teeth.' By neglecting their teeth, the English found it difficult to open their mouths and still appear healthy and attractive, and this undoubtedly helped to discourage laughter and open-mouthed smiles. Who knows, maybe the repressed and tight-lipped smiles found in England today are a legacy of those times.

Up until the seventeenth century, laughter had focused on abnormality, deformity and the bizarre. People in the towns and countryside would gather to taunt and laugh at individuals who looked or behaved differently, or who had experienced some misfortune and were not in a position to defend themselves. During the seventeenth century, however, laughter started to become politicised, as it shifted its sights away from the misfortunes of criminals and cuckolds, and began to focus its attention on the misdemeanours of the clergy, the nobility and politicians. Laughter became a highly subversive weapon. It was uncontrollable, and as the establishment soon discovered, it was impossible to reply to on its own terms. The establishment reacted as best it could, by restricting the opportunities for satire, and by espousing a new style of behaviour that excluded laughter, or at least reduced it to a bare minimum. The historian Keith Thomas tell us that 'jokes against the Eucharist were forbidden by statute in 1547, while jests against the clergy were prohibited in the royal injunctions of 1509. A statute of 1606 forbad the jocular use of the names of God on the stage.' In conjunction with these measures various attempts were made to discredit laughter, either by representing it as a pastime of the uncouth, or as something that fed on the misfortunes of others.

By restricting its scope and giving laughter a bad name, polite society managed to gain control over the anarchic forces associated with laughter, and to introduce a much more serious demeanour. These developments did not affect the common people – at least, not at first – although they did influence a large number of eighteenth-century notables, like Jonathan Swift and Alexander Pope. According to Samuel Johnson, Swift 'stubbornly resisted any tendency to laughter', and 'by no merriment, either of others or his own, was Pope ever seen excited to laughter'. Other authors also showed their disapproval of the habit. William Congreve, for example, announced that 'There is nothing more unbecoming a man of quality than to laugh; 'tis such a vulgar expression of the passion!' In a letter to his son, the Earl of Chesterfield wrote 'Having mentioned laughing, I must particularly warn you against it. Frequent and loud laughter is the characteristic of folly and ill manners: it is the manner in which the mob express their silly joy at silly things; and they call it being merry. In my mind there is nothing so illiberal, and so ill-bred, as audible laughter'. Chesterfield also boasted to his son 'I am sure that since I have had the full use of my reason, nobody has ever heard me laugh.'

There were other reasons why polite society had such a strong aversion to laughter during the seventeenth and eighteenth centuries. First of all, laughter was recognised as a pastime of the common people, and therefore something to be avoided. Secondly, laughter was contagious and dangerously disrespectful; it therefore had to be restrained and discredited. Finally, laughter was rejected because its purpose in those days was very different from what it is today.

There are many reasons why people laugh, but the most common reasons are 'merriment' and 'mockery'; broadly speaking, we either laugh *with* people whose company we enjoy, or else we laugh *at* those who strike us as ridiculous. If we were to sample the occasions when people laugh nowadays, we would discover that the vast majority of instances involve merriment-laughter, while far fewer involve mockery-laughter. However, had it been possible to perform the same kind of survey during the sixteenth and seventeenth centuries, we would have found that the balance was much more in favour of mockery-laughter. Sir Francis Bacon, for example, informs us that the major source of laughter during the sixteenth century was 'deformity', while Thomas Hobbes tells us that during the seventeenth century it was 'infirmity'. Hobbes concluded that 'The passion of laughter is nothing else but sudden glory, arising from some sudden conception of some eminency in ourselves, by comparison with the infirmity of others, or with our own formerly.' From these and other accounts it would seem that one of the main reasons why people engaged in laughter during that time was to pour scorn on other people and to have fun at their expense. This being the case, it is quite understandable why men like Congreve and Chesterfield disapproved of laughter and recommended that it be avoided. It was, after all, not very charitable to laugh at people who were not responsible for their own misfortune.

The image of the cool, impassive Englishman has repeatedly appeared in the writings of foreign visitors. At the beginning of the last century Karl von Hardenburg reported that 'the Englishman has all the qualities of a poker, except its occasional warmth', while more recently the Czech author Karel Capek announced that the Englishman does enjoy himself, but only 'with the most solemn and leathery expression'. The Dutch author George Renier offered a very similar observation: 'Oh, these unmoving faces of a phlegmatic race! . . . The foreigner only sees the perennial puzzle of an Englishman's face that guards the secret of a soul like a sphinx before a temple where mysterious rites are celebrated.' The descriptions that foreigners offer of the English nowadays can still be very uncomplimentary, but they no longer refer to qualities like melancholy or solemnity. The reason for this is that English facial fashions have changed enormously over the past fifty years or so, becoming much more similar to those found on the continent. In spite of these changes, however, there are several facial habits which continue to distinguish the English from other people.

For example, the English are much more likely to employ a smile in which the corners of the mouth are pulled side-ways, rather than sideways and upwards. This gives foreigners the impression that the English are reserved and emotionally controlled. It may also contribute to the popular stereotype of the Englishman as someone who can't see the point of a joke.

Even in repose, the English face can look quite different from a European one. There is, for example, a tendency for the English middle classes to assume a 'resting face' with the eyebrows raised up, particularly when they are listening to someone and trying to appear attentive. This is in complete contrast to the Welsh, who have a habit of lowering their eyebrows in similar situations. These facial conventions explain why, to foreigners, the English come across as being permanently surprised, and why the Welsh seem to be chronically puzzled.

Another factor which may contribute to the image of the English as emotionally controlled is their habit of pursing their lips when their face is in repose. The ways in which people compose their face when they are ostensibly not using it are determined partly by the sensations associated with different facial postures, and partly by the society to which they belong. The English have, for some time now, shown a special attachment to the 'lip-purse' as a posture of repose. The origins of this attachment can be found in the sixteenth-century obsession with a small mouth as a sign of beauty. They may also be seen, very clearly, in Holbein's portraits of Henry VIII and, particularly, his wedding portrait of Jane Seymour.

The psychological significance of the lip-purse is that it creates a secure defence against the outside world. Pursing the lips is a way of battening down the hatches, hauling up the drawbridge and bringing down the portcullis, all in one. With the mouth pursed, nothing can enter the individual, either actually or symbolically, and nothing can come out either. The relationship between the individual and the outside world can therefore be kept stable and secure. But the real significance of the lip-purse is to be found in its power to regulate people's feelings, and the kinds of information they convey to others.

Our digestive systems are inextricably linked to our emotions, especially to negative emotions like fear, pain and anxiety. Because our mouths are part of this system, they also register these emotions, showing outwardly what we feel inwardly. We all know that our mouths are potential traitors, and they constantly threaten to pass on information about our emotions which we would rather conceal. That is why, in an attempt to control our feelings, and the impression we make on others, we frequently resort to postures, like the lip-purse, which prevent our mouths from giving us away. This may also help to explain why the English are reputed to have a stiff upper lip.

The most important clue to English facial expressions is the English attitude towards the display of emotions. Although the English face can be as animated as any other, it tends not to be, partly because the English believe that a dignified appearance requires that one conceals one's emotions, especially those which might suggest weakness or a lack of self-control. However, in recent years the situation has started to change, and there has been a growing acceptance that showing the full range of one's feelings doesn't necessarily mean that one has a defective character. Interestingly, changes have also come from English spectator sports like soccer and politics. When Paul Gascoigne left the football pitch during the World Cup, sobbing with disappointment, the English recognised that it was possible for a cult hero to show his feelings in public without losing a drop of his masculinity. Who knows, even the lachrymose confessions of British politicians like David Owen may be helping to persuade the English that crying isn't just for babies.

But are there any ways in which the British display a stiff upper lip, other than facially? Is it the case, in other words, that the reputed stiffness of their upper lip is also a feature of their psychological make-up. The answer seems to be yes. There are signs of widespread stoicism in British society, and an unusual degree of tolerance and patience that is not found on the continent. It is said that the British need something to moan about, which may be true, but it is also evident that they are slow to complain. One often notices this kind of thing in restaurants, where customers are clearly dissatisfied with the service, and are quite happy to moan to their companions, but where they wouldn't dream of complaining to the management. This reticence may be connected to the shyness of the British, but it probably has more to do with that cardinal rule, which says that one must not make a scene in public. This desire not to cause any trouble is a very powerful motivating force in British life – one which sometimes threatens to be more important than life itself. As Pamela Frankau remarked, 'The English find ill-health not only interesting but respectable and often experience death in the effort to avoid a fuss.' They are also painfully aware that death itself may be a cause of inconvenience to others. For example, when Charles II was on his death-bed, he apologised for taking so long to die.

Fascination

One of the oldest beliefs about the eyes is that certain people have the power to harm others, simply by looking at them. This belief in fascination, as it is called, can be found all round the world, but it is particularly prevalent in the mediterranean basin, where people have lived in continuous dread of the 'evil eye' since prehistoric times. The Etruscans, and the ancient Greeks and Romans all believed in the potential malevolence of the eyes, and they took special precautions to protect themselves with various charms, amulets, gestures and magical spells.

The Romans were particularly fearful of the evil eye, or the *oculus fascinus* as they called it, and they erected several statues to Nemesis, the goddess who protected her devotees from fascination. In the Equiline quarter of Rome there was an altar dedicated to *Mala Fortuna*, the goddess of bad luck, which was used exclusively by those who feared the evil eye. According to Pliny the Elder, the Romans placed statues of satyrs in their gardens to keep away evil spirits, especially those associated with fascination, and Bacchus was invoked every year in a spring festival, which was designed to protect the grain from the blighting eyes of men and devils. Cattle and orchards were thought to be particularly susceptible to fascination, and the *Decemvirales Tabulae* set out the penalties for destruction of crops by those who possessed the evil eye.

Contemporary theories of vision are very different from those which were around in the ancient world. We know today that the eyes work by absorbing and analysing light which is reflected into them, but scholars in ancient Greece and Rome had a completely different theory of vision. They believed that the eyes actually *emitted* rays, and that these rays darted out, struck objects, and were reflected back into the eyes. They also believed that these rays could be affected by the character or condition of the person from whose eyes they were emitted, and that the people most likely to harm others were those who were envious.

At some stage every European society has believed in the evil eye. This is evident from archaeological remains and written records, as well as from the dictionaries of the European languages. The Italians, for example, speak of *mal occhio*, and the Greeks of *baskania*. When the French speak of the evil eye they refer to *mauvais oeil*, and the Germans to *böse blick*. The Spanish refer to *mal ojo*, the Dutch to *booze blik*, the Norwegians to *skoertunge*, the Danish to *et ondt oje*, the Poles to *zte oko*, and the Hungarians to *szemveres*.

Although the evil eye belief once dominated the whole of Europe, its grip over the European imagination today has relaxed a great deal, and in some countries all that is left are a few linguistic finger-prints and the occasional tell-tale sign of what was once a very powerful superstition. For example, up until the turn of the century belief in the evil eye was widespread in certain parts of Scotland. Nowadays very few Scots believe in the evil eye or take precautions to protect themselves, although they still speak of people getting the 'blink o' an ill ee'. In other parts of Europe, especially along the mediterranean coast, in countries like Spain, Italy, Greece and Turkey, belief in the evil eye continues to flourish. To these people the evil eye is like a scud missile attack. People don't know where the attack is coming from, where it will strike, or what kind of damage it will cause. They recognise, though, that someone is likely to be hurt, and that they personally may be in danger. This increases the need for vigilance. It makes it essential to know which types of people possess the evil eye, where they are likely to attack, and how they can best be repelled.

There are various folk theories about how people come to acquire the evil eye. One is that children who have been weaned, and then allowed back to the breast, are likely to develop the evil eye – presumably because their demands have been indulged and rewarded. This explains why, in Greece, Romania and Slovakia – and until recently, even in Sweden – children are seldom allowed back to the breast after they have been weaned. In most countries it is acknowledged that although people can acquire the evil eye temporarily, the most dangerous cases involve those who

have been born with these powers. In Italy they are known as
jettatori. According to the Italians, some *jettatori* exercise their
power deliberately, others unknowingly; and while the evil eye is
sometimes used indiscriminately, on other occasions it is targeted
at particular individuals.

The Italians believe that there are three types of people who
possess the power to injure others by looking at them. Firstly
there are those who envy others, secondly there are those whose
condition enables them to harm others, and thirdly there are those
who occupy powerful positions in society. The first group includes
people who are disfigured or deprived in some way, and who are
capable of damaging those who are healthy and successful. This
group includes dwarfs, hunchbacks and ugly old men and women
– in fact, anyone who is predisposed to envy and therefore likely
to injure others; hence the Italian expression *Invidia Crepa*, or
'envy kills'.

Various physiognomic features are regarded as good indicators
of the evil eye. So are the shape and colour of the eyes. The
Germans, for example, are said to be suspicious of people with
bloodshot eyes, while the Irish are worried about people who have
a squint. The Italians, on the other hand, believe that a *jettatore*
can be recognised by his piercing eyes and heavy eyebrows.

Aside from these features, it is generally recognised that women
can acquire the evil eye temporarily, especially during menstrua-
tion, when they are impure, or during pregnancy, when they are
able to harness the mysterious forces of procreation. Finally, people
with power – kings, popes and priests – are believed to have the
evil eye. To this day there are Italians who, if they meet a priest
or a monk on leaving the house, will immediately return home and
wait there a while before venturing forth again. This precaution is
designed to cancel the bad luck that comes from meeting a cleric
early in the day.

Cardinals and popes are frequently reputed to have the evil eye.
The most famous ecclesiastical case was Pope Pius XI. Pope Pius
was very popular during the early years of his pontificate. But one
day, as he was being driven through the streets of Rome, his eyes
happened to fall on a nurse who was standing at an open window
with a child in her arms. A few minutes after he had passed, the
child fell to its death on the pavement below. Nobody suspected

for a moment that the Pope had wished the disaster, but the incident was enough to mark him as a *jettatore* for the rest of his life.

The case of King Alphonso of Spain provides a similar example. In 1923 the king embarked on a state visit of Italy to pay his respects to the new government of Mussolini. As his ship approached Genoa a terrible storm rose up and four sailors were drowned. When the ship entered the bay of Naples the old bronze cannon which fired the salute exploded, killing the crew, and soon afterwards an official who had shaken the king's hand collapsed and died. By the following day, King Alphonso was an acknowledged *jettatore*. Mussolini refused to receive him, and all their transactions had to be undertaken by reluctant intermediaries. Servants who were assigned to the king filled their pockets with keys and bits of metal to protect themselves, and everywhere he went he was greeted by averted eyes and the audible clink of metal objects. King Alphonso never outlived his reputation, and for the rest of his life people continued to avoid him. On one occasion, when he was dining with a companion in a restaurant, he became so frustrated that he rose up and shouted 'Look at me! Look at me! Do I look like a *jettatore*?' Within seconds the restaurant emptied out, leaving the king with his one companion, for it is believed that a *jettatore* only increases his powers by denying them.

The evil eye can be directed at people, livestock and crops – in fact, at any object of envy. Women and children are especially vulnerable when they are beautiful; domestic animals and crops are prone to death and disease when they are healthy; and personal possessions are likely to break or disappear when they are coveted. In evil eye cultures it is widely accepted that individuals who are envious cannot always contain their envy, and that they sometimes reveal themselves by flattering people whom they admire, or praising objects they would like to have as their own. It is also believed that innocent and well-meaning individuals can bring bad luck to others by complimenting them – either because the compliment makes the gods jealous, or because it encourages people to think too highly of themselves. Whatever the case may be, the general rule in these societies is that one should be wary of flatterers. At the same time one has to be careful when offering a compliment, because there is always a chance that people will misconstrue one's motives, or that one will inadvertently cast a spell on somebody.

These restrictions have far-reaching consequences for the ways in which people relate to each other in an evil eye society. It means that people are constantly on their guard, and that a great deal of effort is invested in avoiding contamination by those who are reputed to have the evil eye. It also means that people cannot afford to boast about their achievements, for fear of attracting the envy of others, and they dare not raise other people's suspicions when complimenting or praising them. When praise is called for, they have to resort to certain formulaic expressions which deny that they have any connection with the evil eye. In Romania, for example, a compliment is usually accompanied by *Sa nu-i fie de deochiu!*, meaning something like 'let it not be the cause for giving the evil eye'. The Italians sometimes use the expression, *Se mal occhio non ci fosse*, meaning that the praise is acceptable provided it is sincere. More commonly, however, they use *Benedica!* or *Dio Benedica!*, meaning 'God bless you!'. In addition to these verbal disclaimers, people sometimes spit three times, again to show that they intend no mischief, and that they are invoking the protection of good magic, rather than bad. Overall, the state of affairs is very different in a culture where people no longer believe in the evil eye. Although there may be linguistic remnants of the belief – like the English expression 'Bless you!' or the German *Gesundheit!* – people are not as suspicious about flattery, and they certainly show far less caution when it comes to blowing their own trumpet.

It is known that people who possess the evil eye can strike in all kinds of ways. The damage they produce ranges from headaches and minor injuries to the most ghastly afflictions and death. The Italians recognise that *jettatori* can cause loss of teeth, dandruff and impotence, as well as storms, floods and avalanches. However, most *jettatori* specialise in producing one kind of disaster. *Jettatori di cavalli*, for example, are responsible for maiming horses, whereas *jettatori di bambini* concentrate on children. On the other hand, the sole purpose of *jettatori sospensivi* is to delay and obstruct people who are hurrying to an appointment. If you meet one on your way to catch the train, he will ensnare you in a long conversation from which it is almost impossible to escape. When you do manage to get away, you will find that your car refuses to start, or that the taxis are all taken, or that the train has been cancelled. Whatever you do, you will not get to your destination on time. Meeting a *jettatore sospensivo* is said to be a very frustrating experience, but it has the advantage of offering a culturally acceptable excuse for being late – something which the Italians certainly need. In fact, if the *jettatore sospensivo* did not exist, the Italians would probably need to invent him.

Societies that believe in the evil eye have a wide range of defensive measures at their disposal. The best guarantee against injury is always prevention, and this can take the form of either avoidance or concealment. Some Italians think nothing of taking a long, roundabout route if it will mean that they can avoid an area that is frequented by a known *jettatore*. They will also go to enormous lengths to insulate their personal possessions from public scrutiny. There are farmers in Italy, for example, who hide their livestock in enclosures rather than allow them to graze in the open where they are likely to attract the attention of jealous neighbours and passers-by.

Other methods of protecting oneself against the evil eye include incantations, the use of amulets and gestures, and touching a protective substance such as wood, iron or one's own skin. It is commonly assumed that touching wood is connected with the cross. However, there are reasons to believe that the practice is not a Christian innovation, and that its origins go back to pagan times when people engaged in tree worship.

While most northern Europeans touch wood for luck, the Italians are more likely to touch a piece of iron. The belief that *toccaferro*, or touching iron, brings good luck probably goes back to times when people who knew how to smelt iron had a distinct advantage over those who did not. It is certainly reflected in the almost universal reverence with which blacksmiths are regarded, and the fact that they are often assumed to have magical powers. Another potent form of protection against the evil eye is guaranteed by the act of grasping one's own testicles, either inside, but more usually outside the trousers. Touching one's testicles, or *toccapalle*, is inevitably the preserve of Italian males. However, women do sometimes mimic the gesture by placing their hands between their legs and grabbing hold of imaginary testicles. Interestingly, this habit of touching one's testicles is not restricted to the evil eye, because when Italian men are in conversation with each other they are constantly adjusting their private parts. It has been suggested that this habit may have something to do with the warm climate, but the fact that it occurs with greatest frequency when men are being theatrical suggests that it has more than one explanation, and that its main function may be subtly to suggest that someone is so well endowed that he constantly needs to rearrange himself.

There are several manual signs which provide an insurance policy against the evil eye. One is the 'horns gesture', or *mano cornuta*, which is performed by extending the index finger and the little finger, while keeping the remaining fingers in the shape of a fist. The horns gesture is used throughout Italy, both as an insult and as a defensive gesture against the evil eye. In its defensive role it is sometimes used surreptitiously – for example people often make the sign behind their back to ward off evil when a funeral procession goes by – or else the horns are pointed at the suspected *jettatore*, or used to sweep away the ill effects of the evil eye when people feel in danger. The horns gesture is an extremely ancient sign, the origins of which continue to excite a great deal of debate in academic circles. The most likely explanation is that the gesture developed out of bull worship and that it was reinforced by the religion of Mithra, which dominated the ancient world for several centuries. There is also a possibility that the gestures owes its origins to the cult of Diana, whose symbol was the crescent moon, a shape that is not too different from that produced by the horns gestures.

Another pagan gesture is the *mano fica*, or fig sign, which is performed by making a fist, with the thumb protruding between the index finger and the second finger. Here the thumb represents the penis and the other two fingers the vulva – which is why the gesture is called the fig sign. Not only does the pink flesh of the fig represent that of the vulva, but the fig tree itself is renowned for its fertility and abundance, and fig leaves were the original clothing of Adam and Eve. The fact that the gesture symbolises the sexual act allows it to take on a number of sexual meanings, and as we look round Europe this is exactly what we find. In Germany, for example, the fig sign is used, quite literally, to refer to the sexual act, either in reference to a third party, or as a sexual invitation. It is also employed in Germany as an insult. In Portugal, on the other hand, the gesture is used exclusively as a form of protection against the evil eye. In fact, the gesture was used for this purpose throughout the ancient world, but it is now no longer recognised in Greece, and it is seldom used in Italy. There was a time, not long ago, when the fig sign was used extensively in Italy as a protective gesture. For example, when King Ferdinand of Naples and Sicily appeared in public, he would put his hand in his pocket from time to time. Those who understood his ways realised that he was making the fig sign in his pocket, in order to protect himself against anyone with the evil eye who may be looking at him. King Victor Emmanuel II is also reputed to have relied on the fig sign for protection, and it is said that he continually made the sign at the battle of Solferino to defend his army. Mainland Italians no longer depend on this gesture as they did in the past. The only places where it continues to fulfil a defensive role against the evil eye apart from Portugal are, to a much lesser extent, Sicily and Sardinia.

The problem with gestures which are designed to repel the evil eye is that their power only lasts as long as the gesture is being performed; they offer no protection to the unwary, or to young children or very old people. The solution, therefore, is to use a magical object which provides permanent protection against the evil eye, like an amulet. Some of the amulets that are used in Europe are derived from gestures. The Portugese sometimes wear amulets in the shape of a hand performing the fig sign, made from silver, gold or plastic, on chains around their neck. The Italians have a much wider range of amulets at their disposal. In addition to the basic horns gesture, which is made from coral, silver or plastic, they also use single horns, crescent moons, hunchbacks and horseshoes as the motifs for their amulets. Sometimes several of these symbols are incorporated into the same amulet.

The range of non-gestural amulets used in Europe is enormous. In the Balkans people carry wolfs' fangs, cocks' spurs or crabs' claws to protect themselves from the evil eye, while in Greece and Turkey they employ red or blue ribbons, wound round the wrist or tied in children's hair. In Greece the amulets, or *phylactos*, tend to incorporate Christian motifs such as the cross, but blue beads, which are of pagan origin, and glass eyes, set in silver or gold, are just as common. But what is it about an amulet that enables it to defeat the evil eye?

At least three folk theories have been put forward to explain how amulets work. The first is what one might call the 'lightning conductor theory', which assumes that the power of the evil eye can be dissipated by directing it toward an amulet. It works best with the fig amulet, where the idea is that the sexual symbolism of the amulet captures the attention of the evil eye and holds it long enough for the initial glance, which is always the most dangerous, to be spent looking at the amulet. The second theory is the 'sympathetic magic theory', which assumes that like cures like. In this case the idea is that eyes which pierce and destroy people can themselves be destroyed by horns or horn-shaped objects, just as they can be intimidated by eyes or objects which are shaped like eyes. Finally there is the 'patronage theory', which explains the efficacy of amulets in terms of higher or stronger powers. The principle here is that the evil eye is repelled when it confronts a symbol of something more powerful than itself – like a bull, the Virgin May or Christ. In effect, the person wearing the amulet says to the evil eye: 'Look, I know that you are powerful. But you are not as powerful as my patron!'

Numerous attempts have been made to explain why people believe in the evil eye. The belief might, for example, be based on the fact that unbroken gaze constitutes a threat signal in every human society, and among most other species. On the other hand, it could be based on the superstitious assumption that good luck cannot last for ever, and the idea that we should not tempt fate by drawing attention to our own good fortune.

One explanation for the evil eye points out that those things which people desire – like money, good looks and youth – are not evenly distributed, and that this causes those who are blessed with these things to feel guilty, and to assume that other people envy them. In time their guilt turns to hatred, but instead of admitting that they hate those who have less than them, they project their feelings, and conclude that those who are deprived hate them. In this way, envy becomes the basis for fears about being seen, and the excuse for hiding one's possessions from other people.

It is easy to see why people might fear the envious gaze of those who are less fortunate than themselves, but how can we explain the fact that they also dread the evil glances of powerful individuals? To understand this apparent paradox we need to remember that as people become more deprived they have *more*, not less, to fear from other people because they cannot endure any further loss, and they are therefore likely to be more concerned about other people's envy. But as people become more deprived, they also become more vulnerable to those who are in power, and these fears are likely to become embodied in beliefs about the malevolent glances of popes, kings and clergymen. Naples fits this case perfectly. Not only is poverty and corruption rife in the city, but the evil eye plays a major role in people's beliefs. For centuries the Neapolitans have been exploited by ruthless conquerors, corrupt officials and their local version of the mafia, the *Camorra*. Little wonder that they dread the envy of those who have less than them, and the rapacity of those who have more.

Belief in the evil eye once extended across the whole of Europe, but nowadays it is concentrated mainly in the circum-Mediterranean area, where it probably first originated. One of the remarkable things about the belief is the way it affects people's attitudes towards each other. The other interesting thing about the belief is its tenacity and its refusal to disappear. In spite of the advances of science, the notion that certain people can harm others, simply by looking at them, continues to exercise an important influence on the ways that people relate to each other.

Gesture

The Italians are credited with having invented opera, but it sometimes looks as though it might have been the other way round. Watching Italians talk to each other, it is difficult to escape the conclusion that Italy is just one enormous operatic performance, and that the main purpose of Italians is to appear on the streets every day so that they can wave their hands about and strike theatrical poses. In other countries one has to pay to see this kind of performance on a stage. But in Italy it's free. It's entirely unscripted, impromptu, and very revealing about the character of Italians and their relationships to each other. For the Italians, conversation is not simply a matter of exchanging opinions and information. Its real purpose is to enjoy oneself and to consolidate one's relationships. This, the Italians have discovered, is best achieved by turning conversation into a performing art, one in which expressive movements are piled on top of each other, and where the whole spectacle is designed to please and entertain the participants as well as any audience that might happen to be nearby.

The historical evidence shows that the Italians have always been a highly expressive people. We know, for example, that Roman writers like Cicero and Quintilian were very much concerned with the role of hand movements in oratory, and that the Romans adopted many of the gestures used by the ancient Greeks. Latin, we find, contains a large number of words which refer to expressive movements of the hands, face, eyes and mouth, which can be found in the works of authors like Pliny, Catullus and Ovid. When the Italian language evolved several centuries later, writers like Dante and Boccaccio described various gestures and facial expressions which were currently in use. From these descriptions it is clear that the Italians of that era were just as animated as those of today. This is supported by the author of *A Treatise of Daunces* who noted, in 1581, that 'The Italian in his . . . speeche . . . intermingleth and useth so many gestures, that if an Englishman should see him afar off, not hearing his words, would judge him to be out of his wit, or else playing some comedy upon a scaffold.' By contrast, he notes, a German preaching from a pulpit would look as though he was physically paralysed.

If one had to choose a city whose inhabitants gesticulate more than any other, it would have to be Naples. Neapolitans have elevated gesture to the status of an art, developing a system of signs which rivals and sometimes surpasses the eloquence of spoken language. When one strolls along the Via Chiaia or through the backstreets of Spaccanapoli, one is besieged by the sight of people chattering with their fingers. In the Galleria Umberto the spectacle is even more dramatic. Here, groups of men gather every morning to discuss business and politics, to trade gossip and – so it would seem – to exchange gestures. The conversation is always enthusiastic, the gesticulation intense. As points and arguments fly back and forth, the hands gyrate and puncture the air, throwing cryptic signs in every direction. To the outsider, the scene looks like a choreographed ballet of the hands, or a convention of musical conductors practising without their batons.

Visitors to Naples have always been struck by the extraordinary grace and eloquence of Neapolitan gesture. Among those who have left us a record of their impressions are Goethe, Cardinal Wiseman and Charles Dickens. When Dickens was in Naples, he noticed that 'everything is done in pantomime'. He was able to interpret several gestures: 'A man who is quarrelling with another yonder lays the palm of his right hand on the back of his left, and shakes the two thumbs – expressive of a donkey's ears – whereat his adversary is goaded to desperation. Two people bargaining for fish, the buyer empties an imaginary waistcoat when he is told the price and walks away without a word: having thoroughly conveyed to the seller that he considers it too dear. Two people in carriages, meeting, one touches his lips, twice or thrice, holding up five fingers of his right hand, and gives a horizontal cut to the air with the palm. The other nods briskly, and goes away. He has been invited to a friendly dinner at half past five o'clock, and will certainly come.'

The most complete description of Neapolitan gesture was published by Andrea Di Jorio in 1832. Di Jorio was a canon of the

Cathedral in Naples and he also held the post of curator of Greek vases at the Royal Bourbon Museum. As he was guiding local Neapolitan dignitaries round the museum, Di Jorio noticed that they sometimes accompanied their comments about the vases with gestures that were depicted on the vases. This persuaded him to produce a detailed catalogue of Neapolitan gestures, the vast majority of which are still used in Naples today. Di Jorio also discovered that many Neapolitan gestures could be traced to the ancient Greeks who had started trading along the Italian coast during the second millennium B.C. It is remarkable to think that gestures which were introduced by the Greeks in the time of Homer can still be seen on the streets of Naples today.

When considering cultural differences in gesture, we tend to assume that there is very little room for change – that nations which gesticulate a lot, like the Italians, have always been animated, while nations which gesticulate very little, like the Nordic peoples, have always been reserved and undemonstrative. This idea is not always supported by the historical facts. The French, for example, are widely acknowledged to be great gesticulators, but they were not during the sixteenth century. Before Catherine de Medici of Florence arrived in France to marry Henry IV, French courtiers made very little use of gestures because they regarded the habit as vulgar. By the Restoration, the use of stylised hand movements had permeated French society from top to bottom, and gesticulation had become so extensive that it seemed as if France was about to overtake Italy in the gesture stakes. Although this never happened, the French remained enthusiastic gesticulators.

There are several ways that the French differ gesturally from the Italians. First of all they simply do not possess as many discrete gestures as the Italians. This applies not only to those hand signs which can be used independently of speech, but also those which accompany and are used to emphasise speech. When an Italian uses his hands to underline what he is saying, he has access to an enormous range of emphatic hand postures, many of which the Italians appear to have developed specifically for this purpose. While the French also gesticulate extensively while talking, their repertoire of emphatic hand postures is not only much smaller but also much less stylised than that of the Italians.

People who are acquainted with these national groups can often distinguish a Frenchman from an Italian, simply by watching how they use their hands and arms in conversation. One of the clues to nationality is the way people arrange their fingers when they are gesticulating. Another is the way that the arms are moved through space. Italians, for example, tend to use their limbs liberally, moving their upper arms almost as much as their forearms, and extending their gestures some distance from their bodies. The French, by contrast, gesticulate more with their hands and forearms, making much less use of their upper arms. As a result, their gesticulation is seldom as expansive as that of the Italians, although this does not mean that it is any less expressive.

One group of people who gesticulate a great deal, but who are not expansive in their movements, are the Eastern European Jews. According to David Efron, who made a special study of the subject, in this style of gesticulation the elbows are tucked in and the arms are held much closer to the chest; the hands may be active and energetic, but their excursions are brief and never far from the body. It is not difficult to see in this gestural style the legacy of an oppressed people who want to communicate with others but who are worried about abandoning their defences. The hands reach out, trying to make contact, but the arms and elbows wait in reserve, protecting the body from attack. The physical geometry of Italian gestures is quite different from that of Eastern European Jews. In contrast to the confined, almost apologetic circumference of Jewish gesticulation, Italian gestures often make long excursions away from the body. These expansive movements are an expression of the theatrical attitude that Italians have towards social interaction; they also suggest that Italians feel unthreatened in each other's company.

It is generally accepted, even by the British themselves, that they are not a particularly expressive people. When they talk to each other they don't use their bodies very much, and they don't strike poses or go in for extravagant displays of gesticulation. In fact, when they do shift their hands around in conversation, it's usually because they don't know what to do with them. There are times when the British do gesticulate a lot, usually when they are angry or excited. But even when the British do use their hands, they never succeed in looking like Italians. This is because they position their hands and fingers very differently, and move their arms through very different trajectories. Moreover, Italian gesticulation is primarily an exercise in expressivity. Although the Italians do use their hands to help put their thoughts into words, this function of gesture appears to be less important than that of making an impression on other people. British gesticulation, on the other hand, is almost totally devoid of any expressive component; its main purpose, it appears, is to help people formulate what they are saying.

These national differences in gesturing styles are reinforced by the kinds of relationships that people have to their own hand movements. While people are generally unaware of the way they gesticulate, this is much more pronounced in the case of a nation like the British. Because they place much greater emphasis on spoken langauge than on body language, the British are rather insensitive to the effects that their movements have on other people. Unlike the Latins, they tend not to think of their bodies as part of their expressive equipment.

In 1827 Count Pecchio posed the question 'Why is it that the English gesticulate so little, and have their arms always glued to their sides?' Numerous commentators have addressed this question, and they have tried to explain the poverty of English gestures in terms of factors such as climate, social relations, fashion and etiquette. Few, however, have managed to match the originality of Count Pecchio's explanation, when he suggested that 'The rooms are so small that it is impossible to wave one's arm without breaking something, or inconveniencing somebody.' One of the problems with attempts to explain the paucity of English gesture is that they overlook the fact that the English share a lack of interest in gesture with many other nations. The other problem with these explanations is their assumption that the English have always disliked gesticulation. There were times when the English made much more use of their hands than they do today.

In *Pantagruel*, which was published in 1533, Rabelais describes a fictional duel between a Frenchman and an Englishman where the only permitted weapons are hand gestures and movements of the face and body. In the story the Frenchman wins the duel, but not before the Englishman has released an impressive barrage of manual insults, and forced everyone to acknowledge his gestural prowess. A thorough knowledge of postures and gestures was an important requirement for all Elizabethan actors, and strict guidelines were laid down as to how the hands, face and body should be used on stage. Shakespeare's plays are full of references to stylised hand movements. Some are recognisable and still in use today. Gesture continued to play an important role in English social life throughout the seventeenth and eighteenth centuries. John Bulwer's works show that hand signs were used extensively in seventeenth century England, and that in some cases these signs differed regionally. He tells us, for example, that there were different ways of shaking hands in London's markets, that the 'Fish dialect of Billingsgate', as he called it, was quite distinct from the 'Horse Rhetorique of Smithfield'.

Hogarth's drawings of scenes from English life show that gesticulation was also popular during the eighteenth century, and that its use was not restricted to any particular sector of society. There is documentary evidence to show that gesticulation had become an important part of the church sermon, and that the clergy were waving their arms around and performing all kinds of gestural arabesques in the pulpits. However, this new ecclesiastical style did not meet with universal approval, and there were soon complaints about the 'babbling hands' and 'apish gestures' of the clergy.

In the end the real home of English gesticulation, the place where it managed to flourish without any criticism, turned out to be Parliament rather than the pulpit. Westminster saw the evolution of the 'grand manner' of political oratory, with its emphasis on bold movements and extravagant use of the hands. Contemporary accounts tell us that Gladstone was often seen 'thundering in vehement declamation', using 'dramatic gestures', that Robert Peel was given to 'animated gestures', and that Lord Balfour employed 'much gesticulation'. What is so fascinating about this development is that it occurred in almost total isolation, because while the politicians in Westminster were busy flailing their arms around, polite society was doing everything in its power to keep its hands perfectly still. Polite society had discovered a more genteel and controlled style of social behaviour, one which was quite unsuited to sudden or florid movements of the hands. Gesture, it had decided, was vulgar and un-English, definitely something to be avoided. In time these attitudes became entrenched. As they filtered down through society, their effects became more pervasive, and people stopped using their hands in conversation. By the turn of the century, gesticulation had reduced considerably.

A comparison of the European nations suggests that they fall into three groups. In the first group are the Nordic peoples – the Swedes, Finns, Norwegians and Danes – who make very little use of gesticulation and who, to all intents and purposes, are gesturally illiterate. The second group contains nations like the British, Germans, Dutch, Belgians and Russians, who use gesture in moderation. People who fall into this group tend only to use their hands when they become excited, when they have to communicate over long distances, or when they need to threaten or insult each other. The third group of nations includes the Italians, Greeks, French, Spaniards, and those honorary Mediterraneans, the Portuguese. People in this group use gesture extensively. When they are talking to each other, their hands and arms are often moving, tracing pictures in the air, emphasising what is being said, and holding the attention of the other person. Even when they are silent, their hands are often busy, sending messages through the medium of manual semaphore.

One of the startling things about European gestures is how little correspondence there is between the gesture repertoires of different nations. One of the few gestures which is used everywhere in Europe is the gesture of thumbing the nose. This is used, typically by children but also by adults, as a sign of mockery. Another gesture which is found throughout Europe is the middle-finger gesture. There are several gestures which one would expect to find everywhere in Europe, but which are either confined to a part of Europe, or which take on different meanings in different countries. For example, the thumbs-up gesture, which we associate with images of gladiatorial contests and Second World War fighter pilots, does not mean the same thing to all Europeans. In most European countries it is used as a sign of approval or gratitude, or to show that one is ready – in other words, to convey a positive message. In Greece, however, it is an insult, sometimes accompanied by the expression *Katsa pano!*, which means 'Sit on this!'. For the Greeks, therefore, the thumbs-up sign is a vulgar, emasculating taunt, with a message very similar to that of the middle-finger gesture – something that might be worth remembering next time you are hitch-hiking in Greece.

The cheek-twist gesture also has more than one meaning in Europe. This gesture, which is performed by pressing the index finger against the cheek and twisting it round, is used by the Italians to indicate that something or someone is delicious. The reference is usually to pasta, but it can also be used in connection with an attractive woman. For the Germans, however, the cheek-twist means something quite different. In Germany, motorists are prohibited, under pain of prosecution, from using insulting gestures. One of the insulting gestures which is disallowed is the temple-screw gesture, which in Germany and elsewhere is used to show that someone is mad. To get round this restriction, German drivers have come up with an ingenious solution: instead of twisting their forefinger against their temple, they simply twist it against their cheek. By relocating their finger in this way, German motorists are able to insult each other without risking prosecution.

Although Germans do not gesticulate a great deal, there are gestural differences within Germany – or at least there were before the Berlin Wall came down. An observational study performed in the bars of Berlin by Gabriele Oettingen and Martin Seligman in 1985 revealed that West Berliners used significantly more illustrative and symbolic gestures than East Berliners. These were associated with other differences in behaviour. West Berliners, for example, were observed to smile and laugh much more, and to adopt a more upright posture, than their East Berlin counterparts. The authors interpreted these differences as signs of greater despondency and depression, caused by the political system in East Germany. Since this study was completed the political system has changed completely, although many inhabitants of East Berlin still have reason to be unhappy. It would very interesting to know whether the behaviours that were observed in East Berlin before the wall came down are any different from those that can be seen today.

Within Europe there are several gestures that are confined to a single country. The insulting British V-sign, where the first and middle fingers are extended from the fist, and the palm faces back towards the gesturer, is a prime example. Another country-specific gesture is the French *La Barbe*, meaning bored or boring. This is performed by scratching the back of the fingers down the side of the face, to mimic the act of shaving or stroking the beard. It is sometimes accompanied by the expression *être de*

Birmingham – to be from Birmingham – meaning to be bored to death. Birmingham is mentioned not because it is thought to be boring there, but because it was once famous for its razors, and *rasoir* in French means both a razor and a bore. The underlying connection between boredom and beards is probably related to the inherent boredom of shaving, and to the fact that boring people talk so much that it is possible to grow a beard while listening to them.

In addition to country-specific gestures, there are also gestures that extend across several countries. Drinking gestures are a good example of signals that mimic behaviour and cross boundaries easily. In Europe there are basically three drinking gestures – one where the fingers and thumb curl round an imaginary beer-glass, another where the hand is shaped like a wine bottle, with the thumb extended from a closed fist, pointing back at the gesturer, and a third gesture which mimics the shape of a vodka glass. This gesture is performed with the index finger resting on top, and the thumb supporting an imaginary vodka glass. The interesting thing about these gestures is that they all mimic drinking containers. The beer-glass gesture is found in Britain, Germany, Holland and Belgium – in other words, all those countries where the main drink is beer, whereas the wine-bottle gesture is found in Italy, France and Spain – the countries where wine takes precedence over other drinks. Not surprisingly, the vodka gesture is used in Russia, Ukraine and Poland – all those countries where vodka reigns supreme.

In addition to country-specific gestures, and those that cross national boundaries, there is also a category of gestures that take on different meanings within the same country. The ring sign is a good case in point. This gesture is performed by bringing the tips of the thumb and index finger together so that they form a circle. For most Europeans the gesture is a sign of approval, signifying that something is 'OK' or that everything is in order. This is the meaning attached to the gesture by most people who live in the north of France, and by some who live in the south. For the remainder of the population, the gesture contains a negative message, meaning either 'zero' or 'worthless'. The case of the ring sign would be quite straightforward if everyone in France knew that the gesture had two meanings. But this is not the case. Instead we find that some people use it as a gesture of approval, while others use it to signify zero or worthless, *and* that a large number of people deny that the gesture has a meaning other than the one they use.

How is it possible for a gesture to have such contradictory meanings within the same community, and for people not to notice what is happening? There appear to be at least two explanations for this peculiar state of affairs. First of all, when the French show their approval, they are more likely to use the thumbs-up gesture than the ring sign. Because the ring sign occupies a position of secondary importance, its ambiguity is much less obvious. Secondly, unlike most other gestures, the ring sign looks exactly like a hand posture that people make in order to emphasise what they are saying. The fact that it is used so often in conjunction with speech means that it can easily be mistaken as a means of emphasising what is being said, rather than as a gesture with a meaning all of its own.

It is because the ring sign contains both a circle and a precision contact between the thumb and forefinger, that it can take on a variety of meanings. The precise contact allows the gesture to be used for precise messages like 'good' and 'OK', while the circle makes it suitable for messages like 'zero' or 'worthless'. The circle produced by the fingers also makes the ring sign the obvious candidate for anything to do with holes or orifices. In the Middle East and Africa, as well as Greece and Turkey, it is used for this purpose. When a Greek or a Turk makes the ring sign, he is not saying that he approves of something or that it is worthless. He is referring to either the anus or the vagina, and making either an invitation or a comment, to or about a male or a female. The exact meaning of the gesture, and its serious or comic aspect, is determined by the context in which it is used and the relationship between the people concerned. As a rule, however, it tends to be used as a homosexual invitation or to refer to someone's homosexuality.

Several years ago, Olympic Airlines ran an ad in the British press showing travellers in a variety of national costumes doing the ring sign. This was intended as a reference to the 'O' of Olympic Airlines, as well as an international stamp of approval, but the ad backfired because, in several cases, the people pictured in the ad were from countries were the ring sign conveys a homosexual message rather than one of approval. Somebody must have pointed this out to the advertising agency, because the campaign was brought to an abrupt halt very soon after it had been launched. In advertising as well as foreign travel, it pays to know what one's own gestures mean to other people.

Humour

It is said that although people laugh in the same way, they don't necessarily laugh at the same things. If this is true of a single community, it is even more true of people who live in different societies, because the topics that people find amusing, and the occasions that are regarded as appropriate for joking, can vary enormously from one society to the next. Some styles of humour, like slap-stick comedy, are guaranteed to raise a laugh everywhere. But because of their reliance on shared assumptions, most jokes travel very badly. This is particularly noticeable in the case of jokes that involve a play on words. Puns and spoonerisms, for example, are notoriously difficult, and in some cases virtually impossible to translate into other languages. Add to this the fact that jokes frequently deal with local and topical issues, and it soon becomes clear why people's attempts to tell jokes to foreigners so often meet with deafening silence.

The feeling of easy familiarity that people enjoy with members of their own culture has a lot to do with the fact that they share a sense of humour, and therefore a common view of the world. In a recent Gallup poll, members of the British public were asked whether they thought certain nations have a sense of humour. The results revealed a typical ethnocentric bias, with two-thirds of the sample claiming that the British have a sense of humour, and just over half of the sample saying the same thing about the Irish. Countries like France and Russia, however, were viewed quite differently. Only 13% of the sample credited the French with a sense of humour, and only 8% were prepared to extend this description to the Russians.

What people regard as a sense of humour is very much bound up with what they personally find amusing, and if foreigners don't find the same things amusing they are assumed to have no sense of humour at all. Many nations have been tempted into the belief that their sense of humour is the only real sense of humour, but none has succumbed to this temptation with more enthusiasm than the English. Up until the seventeenth century the word 'humour' referred to the four supposed constituents of the body – blood, phlegm, choler and bile. Towards the end of the century the word also acquired the jocular meaning that we associate with it today. As far as we know Sir William Temple was the first person to write about jocular humour, which he declared to be peculiar to the English: 'Yet I am deceived, if our *English*, has not in some kind excelled both the modern and the ancient, which has been by force of a vein Natural perhaps to our Countrey, and which with us, is called Humour, a word peculiar to our Language too, and hard to be Expressed in any other.' According to Temple, humour was characterised by a natural ease, and people who had it took pride in it. It was something that proceeded 'from the Native Plenty of Our Soyl, the unequalness of our Clymat, as well as the ease of our Government, and the liberty of Professing Opinions and Factions, which our Neighbours may have about them, but are forced to Disguise.'

Since the seventeenth century there have been numerous attempts to claim humour, not only as being English in origin, but also as the exclusive preserve of the English. William Hazlitt, for example, writing in 1825, proposed that the English capacity for humour could be traced to their intellectual mediocrity: 'Now it appears to me that the English are (or were) just at that mean point between intelligence and obtuseness, which must produce the most abundant and happiest crop of humour. Absurdity and singularity glide over the French mind without jarring or jostling with it; or they evaporate with levity; – with the Italians they are lost in indolence and pleasure.' Louis Cazamian, writing in 1952, put the case for English humour even stronger. According to Cazamian, only the English have humour. We should recognise that the Frenchman 'has wit, drollery, satire, and all the brilliant manners of raising a laugh, but that all the tricks of his cleverness are conspicuous, just as they may be successful; they make him admirable and admired, but as humour they would fail because the Frenchman's fun is explicit and obviously self-conscious; you read upon his face the coming climax of the story, the point that is just going to be made; and when a man gives away the effect he is about to produce, what on earth could he have to do with humour.'

Over the years numerous authors have echoed the claim that humour is a uniquely English accomplishment, or that while other nations have 'wit', only the English possess humour. There can be no denying that the English sense of humour is very different from that of most other peoples. But to suggest that humour is the exclusive preserve of the English is pushing things a little far.

Everyday humour is expressed in various ways, the most common forms being puns, wisecracks and narrative jokes. The attraction of the pun lies in its clever manipulation of language, something which has endeared it to the English, and to the French, who know it as *jeu de mot*. However, puns are not popular in Spain, largely because the Spanish language does not encourage this kind of wordplay. Over the past few years the pun has lost a lot of its attraction, partly because it now seems a rather antique form of humour, but also because it is a bit too cerebral for some people's liking. That is why puns are sometimes greeted with grudging groans of approval, but seldom with uproarious laughter.

When the English are judging other people they tend to place more emphasis on character than on brains. In fact intellectual prowess is frequently regarded as a disadvantage, something to be hidden rather than put on display where it might show up other people. After all, it was the English who produced expressions like 'too clever by half' and 'too clever for his own good', which carry the clear message that intelligence isn't necessarily a good thing. One of the main constituents of character admired by the English is sense of humour. In fact in England one can often get further in life with a sense of humour than with qualifications or talent, and that is why people are so sensitive about their ability to amuse others. Heathcote Garrod recognised this several decades ago, when he remarked that 'the surest way, of course, to affront any Englishman is to suggest to him that he has no sense of humour. He would as soon have it said that he did not like dogs.'

But what is it about the English sense of humour that makes it so special? Is it something to do with the 'cool-headed taciturnity' of the English, as Louis Cazamian has suggested, or is it connected to the national characteristics that Harold Nicolson enumerates, like 'a love of games', 'diffidence and shyness' and 'mental laziness'?

No doubt some of these factors play a role, but what is more important are the features of English humour itself.

There are five factors that appear to characterise the English sense of humour. The first, and probably the most distinguishing feature of English humour, is its 'bitter-sweetness', a sardonic quality that emerges from a unique combination of mirth and seriousness. This conjunction of moods in English humour was noticed as early as the fourteenth century, when the French historian Jean Froissart is reputed to have commented that the English 'amused themselves sadly after the fashion of their country'. This idea was echoed in *Henry V*, when Falstaff referred to 'a jest with a sad brow', and it appeared again several centuries later, when William Hazlitt remarked that the English 'have a way of their own. Their mirth is a relaxation from gravity, a challenge to dull care to be gone, and one that is not always clear at first, whether the appeal be successful. The cloud may still hang on the brow; the ice may not thaw at once.'

The idea that English humour is some sort of amalgam, an alchemical compound of levity and melancholy, is also mentioned by the French observer Hippolyte Taine, who referred to English humour as 'the irruption of violent joviality, buried under a heap of melancholy'. In his *Notes on England*, which he compiled between 1861 and 1871, Taine included the following passage about English humour: 'They possess a form of it for their own use, which, although far from agreeable, is certainly original, powerful, poignant, and slightly bitter to the taste, as are their national beverages. They call it "humour". Generally it is the pleasantry of a man who, while joking, maintains his gravity.' While gravity no longer plays a part in English humour, wryness certainly does. Melancholy, too, has disappeared, giving way to a rather serious, more ironic sense of humour.

Another peculiar feature of English humour is its 'dryness', which is the result of people avoiding the use of overstatement or any demonstrations of enthusiasm. English humour is seldom bubbly or effervescent. Instead, it tends to be rather flat, which is exactly what one would expect from a people who are self-conscious and shy. The whole tenor of English humour is one of inconspicuousness; the intention of the English joker is to elicit a chuckle rather than a roar of laughter.

The third quality of English humour is 'stoicism'. When things go seriously wrong in England, you can be sure of two things. First of all someone will make a cup of tea, and then the same person, or someone else, will crack a joke. The use of humour in adversity is central to the English character – some would say that it is what defines Englishness. It is used, not to deny the gravity of the situation, but to demonstrate that adversity can be overcome by laughter. In his book, *The English: Are They Human?*, which was published in 1931, George Renier had this to say about English humour: 'Let me risk a definition of humour as it strikes me. It is, I think, the capacity possessed by the overwhelming majority of Englishmen to laugh or at least smile in circumstances where normal human beings curse or cry. An illustration? The soldiers who during the late war went over the top shouting "Marmalade!" No German, no Frenchman could have done that. The Germans sang hymns, the French swore and trembled – without fighting worse for that matter. But the English could laugh at death. You may fight such a people. You may trade with them. But what an undertaking to try and live with them!'

The fourth and fifth characteristics of English humour are 'childishness' and 'nonsense'. A great deal of English humour is concerned with childish themes – like practical jokes, bodily functions and lavatorial topics. This represents the giggly side of English humour, and it is closely related to the 'Peter Pan complex', which is so prevalent among the English. This desire to remain a child cannot be realised in reality, but it can be satisfied symbolically by behaving like a child, using childish catch-phrases, and of course cracking childish jokes. By resorting to these regressive devices adults can return to a time when they had no responsibilities, and all the delights of being naughty. In the 1930s, Emile Cammaerts, a Belgian who settled in London, had this to say about the regressive impulses of the English: 'This unwillingness to grow old is an essential feature of the English folk lore of the twentieth century. When the learned scientists of the future endeavour to trace the origin of the Peter Pan myth, as no doubt they will, they will be obliged to recognise that it is peculiar to this island.'

The English infatuation with nonsensical humour goes back to at least the beginning of the last century, when William Hazlitt announced that 'We are almost the only people left who understand and relish nonsense.' Other authors have made the same point. For example, in his discussion of English humour, Harold Nicolson says that 'The Germans, it is true, possess some conception of nonsense, but for pure nonsense, nonsense for nonsense's sake, one must consult the English authors.' The most famous exponents of English nonsense humour are Edward Lear and Lewis Carroll, whose bizarre tales are adored equally by adults and children. Childishness is central to nonsense humour, because it turns everything upside down and refuses to obey the rules of grown-ups. Nicolson put this point very well when he suggested that 'Nonsense is in essence a rebellion against the authority of orderly thinking . . . it is the supreme release from the constraint of reason.'

This provides an important clue as to why nonsense plays such an important part in English humour, and why it is almost totally absent from French humour. For the English, orderly thinking is a means to an end, something to be used, and then abandoned. For the French, who are weaned on the very logical philosophy of Descartes, the idea of abandoning orderly thinking for something so childish as nonsense humour is inconceivable. The French do, however, have some things in common with the English, one being a fondness for puns. In fact the French language is superior to English when it comes to punning because it contains many more open sounds. This increases the number of phrases that have different meanings, which is essential for effective punning.

There are two main types of Gallic wit – one is cerebral, the other focuses on the body. Wit of the cerebral type tends to be satirical, aggressive and biting, often employing complicated wordplay and puns, which are directed against the government, women and foreigners. The other type of Gallic wit is concerned with bodily functions and sex, and it is therefore much more earthy and direct. French sexual humour is preoccupied either with sexual technique and its infinite variations, or with the intrigue and comedy associated with seduction and infidelity. People who know France often remark on the amiable quality of French sexual humour, and the fact that it contains none of the anxious aggression that lies hidden just beneath the surface of Anglo-Saxon jokes. The main reason for this is that the French have a much more relaxed attitude to sex, which means that there is less anxiety to discharge through humour. In addition, joking in France is much more of a social pleasantry – or as J.B. Priestley put it, 'French wit has about it a public air.' It is designed not so much to impress, but to ensure that people enjoy themselves.

The sense of humour in Germany is very different from that in France, largely because the French have absolutely no interest in anal humour, while the Germans have an enormous interest in the subject. Scatalogical themes appear in children's riddles and proverbs, as well as in swearing, cursing, insults, threats, and the jokes that people tell each other. According to Gershon Legman, the slightest hint of anality is enough to elicit laughter from a German audience: 'A clever joke-teller can bring the usual German audience to quite a high pitch of screaming entertainment, rolling out of their seats, and so forth, just by *preparing* to tell a joke of which the inevitable punch-line must include the word "shit".' Legman's explanation for the anality of German humour is psychoanalytic: 'This is doubtless a reaction to excessively strict and early toilet-training, and general rigidity and compulsiveness in the Teutonic character.' This interpretation of the German sense of humour is echoed in the writings of other observers, like the Dutch psychoanalyst, Renatus Hartogs, and the American folklorist, Alan Dundes. Several foreigners have contrasted the ponderous style of German humour with the sprightly qualities of Gallic wit, and come out in favour of the latter. Stendahl, for example, said 'I believe more witticisms are bandied about in Paris in one single evening than in all Germany in a month.' Hartogs concluded that 'The difference between German and French humour roughly corresponds to the difference between potato dumplings and crêpe Suzettes. The German joke usually makes its point with elephantine emphasis. The French joke, as likely as not, simply takes wing. These traits are shared alike by clean and dirty jokes.'

The jokes that are told in a country provide a valuable source of information about the concerns and aspirations of its inhabitants and how they relate to each other other. For example, while sexual jokes are common in France, in Belgium they are very rare. This is because the Belgians still have very conservative attitudes towards sex. Italy also provides an interesting case, because what people regard as funny depends to a very large extent on where they live.

Like cuisine, wine and accent, sense of humour in Italy is still very regional.

Various students of humour, Freud among them, have concluded that jokes are a disguised weapon – that under the pretence of jollity, their real purpose is to harm the person at whom they are directed, or the people to whom they are told. This theory doesn't work too well with certain kinds of humour, but with others it does. For example, when one group of people enjoys a position of power over another it is not uncommon for the powerful group to tell jokes about the subordinate group. There are two reasons for this. Firstly these jokes serve symbolically to control the behaviour of the subordinate group, and secondly they provide a means of legitimising the position of the powerful group. However, there are also cases where this relationship is reversed, and where the subordinate group starts to tell jokes about members of the more powerful group. In Italy, for example, the carabinieri, who are one of the three police forces, have become the butt of a large number of derogatory jokes. Before the demise of communism, people in Poland, Czechoslovakia and the Soviet Union also told jokes about the secret police, politicians and the state – in other words, all of the institutions that wielded power over individuals, and against which their only available weapon was humour. For many years jokes represented the only form of political resistance in the Soviet Union. These jokes did not change the system, but they did provide individual citizens with an illusion of power, however insignificant, and with a means of getting back at the state:

> A government commission in Russia is visiting a school to find out whether the pupils are patriotic.
> 'Ivan,' asks a member of the commission, 'who is your father?'
> 'My father is the Soviet Union,' replied Ivan.
> 'Good boy! And who is your mother?'
> 'The communist party,' replied Ivan.
> 'Well done! And what do you want to be when you grow up?'
> 'An orphan.'

Intimacy

When strangers meet they often have to decide where to sit or stand in relation to each other. This is not something that they need to discuss, nor is it something they need to consider consciously – they don't, for example, have to ask themselves whether they should try to be friendly and stand close, or be formal and keep their distance. They simply assume a distance that 'feels right' in those circumstances. What feels right to people depends to a very large extent on the culture to which they belong. When two individuals are members of the same culture the issue of how close they should stand seldom presents a problem. However, when they are from cultures with different proxemic conventions, all kinds of problems can arise.

European societies can be divided, very roughly, into three geographical zones, depending on how close people position themselves. The first is what Desmond Morris calls the 'elbow zone', where people stand so close that they can touch each other with their elbows. This zone includes countries like Spain, France, Italy, Greece and Turkey. The second zone covers most of Eastern Europe, including countries like Poland, Hungary and Romania. In this, the 'wrist zone', people position themselves so that, if they wanted to, they could touch each other with their wrists. Finally there is what Morris calls the 'fingertips zone', which includes Britain, Holland, Belgium, Germany and the Scandinavian countries. In this zone people like to keep others at arms length, and they are quite content to forfeit the opportunity to touch each other.

The most striking thing about these proxemic zones is the way they are arranged, with the 'elbow zone' located in the warmest part of Europe, the 'fingertips zone' in the coolest, and the 'wrist zone' roughly in between. There are several possible reasons for this. The first and most obvious explanation is climate. It is well known that ambient temperature affects people's metabolism, their comfort levels, and their sense of well-being. The other thing about a warm climate is that it can affect people's social habits through the opportunities that it provides for contact in the open air. All along the Mediterranean the summers are dry and warm, and even the winter days can be fairly clement. This enables people to spend much more time talking to each other out of doors. It is quite possible that these frequent contacts bond people closer together, and that this in turn encourages them to stand and sit much closer to each other.

Personality is another factor which might explain different proxemic habits in Europe. It has been pointed out, for example, that cultures which are situated along the Mediterranean tend to be 'collectivistic', whereas those located in northern, central and eastern Europe are much more 'individualistic'. The suggestion here is that individualistic cultures place less emphasis on the goals and aspirations of the group than on those of the individual, whereas the reverse is true for collectivistic societies. Because they show a greater concern with group cohesion, collectivistic societies are much more likely to encourage social practices which bring people together and give them a feeling of belonging – like standing or sitting close together. Individualistic societies, on the other hand, pay far less attention to issues like group cohesion, and they are therefore unlikely to emphasise the need for physical closeness.

While it is true that people in the Mediterranean stand closer to each other, it is also the case that they vary their proximity much more than do people from northern Europe. Equally variable is the way they orient their bodies toward each other. In fact, if you watch Italians talking in public, you will notice that they spend very little time standing still. Instead, they are constantly moving back and forth, sometimes orienting their bodies towards the other person, and at other times away. This is particularly evident when men are talking to each other.

It seems therefore that variability, rather than closeness, is what defines the Mediterranean style of social behaviour. When an Italian talks to his boss, for example, he typically adopts a direct and respectful *vis-à-vis* orientation. The Englishman, on the other hand, tends to orient his body slightly away from his boss. Compare this with what happens when these people are talking to their best friend on the side of the street. Here we find that while the Englishman continues to orient his body slightly away from his friend, the Italian either faces his friend directly or assumes a casual side-by-side position, alternating back and forth between these two extremes.

The reason why Italians show so much variation in their use of physical space is that, for them, proximity and orientation are important channels of communication. Where and how an Italian positions his body in conversation says a lot about his commitment to the encounter, his attitude to the other person and his feelings about what is happening in the immediate vicinity. In England, on the other hand, proximity and orientation are weak channels of communication, which is why these aspects of behaviour show such little variation. The only time the English think about proximity is when somebody gets too close for comfort.

Like other northern Europeans, the English are very sensitive about unwarranted invasions of their personal space, and they go to enormous lengths to ensure that it doesn't happen. There are several strategies they have developed. One is to adopt a blank facial expression which discourages people from coming too close; another is to construct a physical barrier, either by folding one's arms or by holding a handbag or parcel in front of one's chest. For other versions of this strategy one need only enter a library to see how the English barricade themselves behind piles of books so that they can enjoy a bit of privacy and keep other readers at bay. This sort of spectacle is seldom seen in southern Europe.

The English often become distressed when they cannot keep a healthy distance between themselves and other people. It is interesting to see how they behave when they are packed close together, how they withdraw into themselves in an attempt to deny the presence of others. In a crowded lift, for example, they develop a peculiar fascination with the floor, the ceiling, the illuminated display – anything that will save them from the horror and embarrassment of having to look strangers in the eye. Similar patterns of withdrawal can be seen on the London Underground, where commuters hide behind newspapers or seek refuge in the hiss of their walkman. How very different this is from the scene on the Paris Metro, where the French appear so relaxed and philosophical.

In addition to those invisible boundaries which surround our bodies, and which ensure that people don't invade our personal space, there are also invisible boundaries which we erect, so to speak, in our heads. These boundaries are designed to prevent people from getting too close to us psychologically. In most societies there are unwritten rules about the kinds of information that people can try to obtain from each other. These rules can differ very widely from one society to another. For example, in southern Europe it is not uncommon for young tourists to be asked how old they are, whether they are married, and why they do not have children. In other parts of Europe this innocent probing would be regarded as an affront, as a serious invasion of someone's privacy. Similar problems can arise when people try to discover each other's occupation. In Germany, for example, it is quite in order to ask someone what they do for a living. In fact, this line of questioning is usually perceived as a flattering sign of interest. But in Britain there are social circles where it is not advisable to enquire about someone's occupation on first meeting – not because the information is regarded as sacrosanct, but simply because the question implies a certain lack of conversational inventiveness. Asking someone what they do for a living is seen as a rather lazy, uninspired way of getting to know that person.

The cultural rules which govern intimacy and self-disclosure are very different in Scandinavia from what they are elsewhere in Europe. In Norway a great deal of emphasis is placed on the values of independence and control, and the sanctity of the home is taken very seriously. This gives rise to a style of behaviour which seems very rigid and excluding to people from other parts of Europe. The anthropologist Marianne Gullestad has made a special study of the symbolic boundaries that Norwegians erect to protect their privacy. These 'gates' and 'fences', as she calls them, take several forms, all of which are designed to ensure that people do not have unlimited access to each other.

Foreigners often comment on how difficult it is to get to know the Swedes, and this is something that the Swedes have now come to accept about themselves. One of the major reasons for this is that the Swedes are an extremely private people, and as a result they have great difficulty revealing their intimate thoughts and feelings to other people. It is not that the Swedes never reveal themselves to others; it's just that they tend to delay the process and then to overdo it. Consequently, getting to know a Swede is like trying to get ketchup out of a bottle. You shake the bottle repeatedly and nothing happens; then, just when you least expect it, you get an avalanche of ketchup all over your plate. It's the same with Swedes: you spend weeks, sometimes months, in their company without finding out what they really think. Then, just when you are about to give up, the flood-gates open and you discover everything you wanted to know about your Swedish colleagues, and a lot more besides.

In many respects the Finns are very similar. People from Britain, France and Germany, for example, often find it very difficult establishing close relationships with the Finns, who give the impression that they are holding them at arm's length, both literally and figuratively. The unusual thing about the Finns is that although they may be slow to form relationships with outsiders, when they do so it is for life. The establishment of a relationship with a Finn is often marked by the ritual of taking a sauna together. If a Finn invites you to join him in the sauna, it means that you are about to enter a life-long friendship.

The English are also known for being shy and withdrawn, although their reputation cannot compete with that of the Swedes. A major factor which unites the English and the Swedes is a desire for privacy and an intolerance of outside distractions. In both societies this has led to the development of various social and psychological defences which people use to protect themselves from incursions by others. By contrast, the Italians make very little effort to protect their psychological space or to separate themselves from others. It is hardly surprising that, although they do have a word for 'private', they don't have one for 'privacy'.

When we compare northern and southern Europeans we find that southerners prefer to sit and stand much closer, and that they are also more ready to reveal themselves to other people. This connection between proximity and self-disclosure is not an empty coincidence, because both aspects of behaviour express a desire for intimacy. Psychologists discovered some time ago that there are strong links between how close people sit, how intently they gaze into each other's eyes, and how intimate they want to be. They discovered that when people are forced to sit close together, they keep their level of intimacy constant by looking at each other less, and that when they want to increase their level of intimacy they simply move closer, or look at each other more.

The evidence from these studies shows that proximity plays a crucial role in the regulation of intimacy, and that the same is true of people's readiness to reveal things about themselves to others. The fact that northerners use less of these intimate behaviours can, however, be interpreted in one of two ways – either that northerners experience less intimate relationships, or that they experience similar levels of intimacy because weak expressions of affection mean much more to them than they do to southerners.

Whichever explanation is correct, there is little doubt that the physical sensations of living in a 'fingertips culture' are very different from those of an 'elbow culture'. When people sit or stand very close, they find it much easier to see, hear, smell and touch each other. Each person fills more of the other's visual field, each can inspect the other more closely, and each knows that they are being closely watched by the other. The realisation that one is being closely scrutinised is an essential feature of close physical proximity, and it is one which a lot of people find distressing.

Jokes

A common form of jokes are the 'ethnic jokes' – like 'How do you confuse an Irishman? ... Give him two shovels', or 'The Irish attempt to climb Mount Everest has failed ... they ran out of scaffolding.' Jokes like these contain two messages. The first is that the 'butt' of the joke, in this case the Irish, are stupid. The second message is that 'we', the joke-tellers, are therefore clever. Ethnic jokes are very widespread, and every European nation appears to be involved in them as either a 'teller' or a 'butt', or in some cases as both. For example, the English tell jokes about the Irish, the French and the Dutch tell jokes about the Belgians, and the Swedes tell jokes about the Finns and the Norwegians. Frequently the joke-tellers and the butts are from the same country. For instance, the Irish tell disparaging jokes about the Kerrymen in the south of the country, the Danes tell jokes about the Jutes from Aarhus, and in Greece the local butts are the Pontians who live near the Black Sea. In Germany the inhabitants of the north tell stories about the stupidity and laziness of the southerners, who reciprocate with similar stories about the northerners.

The main themes of ethnic jokes are stupidity, followed by stinginess, craftiness, laziness, cowardice, and an inability to speak the joke-teller's language properly. All of these undesirable qualities have been incorporated into jokes and hurled at people on the other side of the ethnic border. But ethnic jokes are much more than linguistic weapons; they also erect psychological fences around groups. Like self-important border guards, they march up and down, telling everyone that the people who live on this side of the boundary are superior to those who live on the other side.

There are several factors that motivate ethnic jokes. Christie Davies, who has made a special study of the subject, points out that the butts of ethnic jokes are frequently marginal groups who have seceded, or who threaten to separate themselves from the groups that tell jokes about them. Although the butts are disliked, Davies has discovered that they are often not the group that the joke-tellers dislike or fear the most, which suggests that butts are chosen because they are small, defenceless and cannot answer back. Ethnic jokes, it appears, are used as a means of symbolically controlling these groups. They allow joke-tellers to deny that they possess certain characteristics, and to project these characteristics on to the hapless members of other groups, under the disguise of a joke. In this way nasty imputations can conveniently be hidden behind the din of laughter.

But ethnic jokes also satisfy other requirements. One is to persuade people that they occupy a position between equally unappealing extremes – for example, that they are neither so stupid as the Irish, or as crafty as the Jews. Ethnic jokes also contain hidden excuses. They legitimise the existing arrangement between groups by representing the members of the outgroup as either too stupid or too lazy to deserve anything better. This self-serving feature of ethnic jokes is again very apparent in the jokes that the English tell about the Irish and the Scots, or the jokes that the Germans tell about Turkish *Gastarbeiter*.

The folklorist Alan Dundes has identified several types of ethnic jokes. First of all there is the type that begins with a catch-phrase like 'Have you heard the one about. . .'. These jokes present a stereotyped picture of the habits of ethnic groups in different circumstances, like being shipwrecked on a desert island, discovering that there's only one parachute in the aeroplane, or finding a dead fly in one's drink. For example, what do an Englishman, an Irishman and a Scotsman do when they find a dead fly floating around in their drink? Answer: The Englishman gets hold of a spoon, removes it from the glass, and drinks. The Irishman uses his fingers to remove the fly before drinking. The Scotsman carefully picks up the fly, wrings it out over the glass, and continues drinking.

Ethnic jokes are sometimes couched in the form of a riddle – like 'What do you get when you cross a German with a Frenchman?', or 'What's the shortest book?' They also appear in the form of proverbs, like 'Hell is a place where the French are the engineers, the British are the cooks, the Germans are the policemen, the Russians are the historians, and the Americans are the lovers.' Then

In Italian conversations the hands are used to hold the floor and to attract the attention of other people.

The French are in the first league of European kissers.
(Cartier-Bresson/Magnum)

there is the post-coital variety, which tries to characterise groups in terms of what wives might say to their husbands after sex:

American wife: Gee honey, that was great.
French wife: Mon Cherie, what a beautiful lover you are.
Jewish wife: I should have held out for a fur coat.
German wife: Ach, mein herr, what authority. How masterful.
English wife: There dear. Do you feel better now?

Ethnic jokes depend on stereotypes about other groups, and they are also responsible for perpetuating these stereotypes. Joke-tellers and their butts tend to be fairly close. They are usually neighbours, often with a common culture, and in some cases the same language. The roles of joke-teller and butt are seldom reversed, and it is the unfortunate experience of butts that they have great difficulty getting back at those people who tell jokes against them. This has certainly been the experience of the Norwegians, who find Swedish jokes about them extremely annoying, and who have retaliated by producing their own jokes about the Swedes. The Dutch tell an enormous number of jokes about the Belgians. Most of these 'Belgian jokes', or *Belgenmoppen*, are told against the Flemmings, who speak Dutch. However, the Belgians also tell jokes against the people of Holland, and to complicate matters further, the Flemmings and the Walloons of Belgium are constantly telling jokes about each other, and even jokes about the inhabitants of Brussels. The pattern of ethnic joking in Belgium is therefore quite unusual, because the two main ethnic groups are fairly evenly matched in the war of words, with both sides giving as good as they get.

As far as ethnic jokes are concerned, the standard practice is for one ethnic group to either invent or adapt an existing joke, and then to apply it to another group. However, there are cases where groups tell jokes about themselves, the most famous example being that of the Jews. Jewish jokes are very different from other jokes, first of all because they tend to be Jewish in origin, but also because they frequently attribute qualities to the Jews, like stinginess and craftiness, which they might otherwise wish to reject. The whole point of Jewish jokes about the Jews is that they are designed for internal consumption, and not for use by other people. When Jews tell jokes about themselves the atmosphere that is generated is usually one of wry self-disparagement; when outsiders become involved the mood can rapidly change, and the same jokes can come across as threatening. Gershon Legman suggests that there are two important rules that cover the telling of ethnic jokes. One is that they should only be told when members of the butt-culture are absent. The other rules is that ethnic jokes can be told when *only* members of the butt-culture are present. The first rule ensures that no offense is given; the second that outsiders are not let into the secret.

The opinions that ethnic groups have about each other are often contained in the jokes that they tell about each other. These opinions may cover issues like intelligence, trustworthiness and sexual preferences, and they even extend to the kinds of jokes that other groups find amusing, and their capacity to comprehend jokes. Alan Dundes has provided the following joke, which purports to show how the French, the English, the Germans and the Jews differ in their capacity to grasp the point of other people's jokes:

> When a Frenchman hears a joke he always laughs three times, first when he hears it, second when you explain it to him, and third when he understands it. That is because a Frenchman likes to laugh. When you tell a joke to an Englishman, he laughs twice, once when you tell it and a second time when you explain it to him. He will never understand it, he is too stuffy. When you tell a joke to a German, he only laughs once, when you tell it to him. He won't let you explain it to him because he is too arrogant. Also Germans have no sense of humour. When you tell a joke to a Jew – before you finish it, he interrupts you. First, he has heard it before; second, you are not telling it right; and third, he ends up telling you the story the way it should be told.

Kissing

Although the kiss may be found all over Europe, there are some countries where its use is dictated by the familiarity and gender of the participants, and others where it is only weakly related to familiarity, and where gender plays no role at all. In Mediterranean countries, for example, the cheek-kiss is employed as a greeting by men and women, regardless of the sex of the other person, and it is frequently used when the participants hardly know each other at all. In Britain, Germany and the Scandinavian countries, however, the gesture is used between women, and between men and women, provided that they know each other well or are related. In these countries men do not, as a rule, kiss each other on the cheek, although there are signs that this is now changing.

Up until a few years ago cheek-kissing between males was definitely taboo in Britain. Although it was regarded as permissible in artistic and theatrical circles, it was felt that men should not compromise their masculinity with such intimate displays of affection. But over the past decade there has been a noticeable shift in people's attitudes about gender and identity. This, together with the influence of continental fashions, has made the British much more tolerant, with the result that in certain circles it is no longer unusual to see men kissing each other on the cheek.

Despite these changes, the British could not, by any stretch of the imagination, be labelled a nation of kissers. For most people in Britain the issue is a social minefield in which it is never entirely clear whether they should shake hands or kiss each other on the cheek, how many times they should kiss, and whether they should begin on the left or the right. This may explain why the British give the appearance of being such amateurish osculators. But how are we to explain their fondness for 'vacuum kisses', where the lips do not actually touch the other person, and why do they so often accompany their kisses with noisy vocalisations?

It appears that the main reason for the popularity of the vacuum kiss in Britain is that it involves a minimum of physical contact, and therefore only a modicum of personal commitment; it combines the best of both worlds by allowing people to go through the motions of kissing each other without having to bring their lips into contact with the other person. The reason why the British accompany their kisses with noisy suctions and 'mwah!' sounds is that these are attempts to conceal embarrassment. These vocalisations may sound like signs of appreciation and enthusiasm, but they are really self-mocking devices which are designed to disown the kiss by turning it into a joke. In countries like Italy and France people are totally relaxed about social kissing. They know when it is expected, where to kiss and how many times. For them, kissing is not a source of embarrassment, and it is therefore not something that people would ever think of disowning.

One of the ways that the cheek-kiss varies geographically is in terms of the number of times people kiss each other on the cheek. Scandinavians, for example, tend to make do with a single kiss, whereas the French are renowned for the double-kiss – the first on the left, and the second on the right. The Dutch and Belgians, on the other hand, employ a multiple-kiss with at least three separate kisses. This does not mean, however, that they are the most enthusiastic kissers in Europe, because when it comes to sheer frequency nobody beats the French.

The French are undoubtedly the kissing champions of Europe, both in terms of the way kissing pervades their lives and the keen interest that they show in the topic. It is no coincidence that the most celebrated sculptures devoted to the subject – Rodin's *Kiss* and Brancusi's *Kiss* – were both executed in Paris. The French are also said to be the originators of deep kissing, at least according to the British, who refer to the practice as 'French kissing'. This reputation could simply be the result of international projection, in other words a case of the British attributing to the French certain habits that they wish to disown. But there are two arguments against this theory. One is that the Germans also implicate the French by referring to deep kissing as *Franzosisches Kussen*, and the second is that *Maraichinage*, the French word for deep kissing, implies that the practice arose in France. *Maraichinage* is derived from the Maraichins, or inhabitants of the district of Pays de Mont in the Vendee in Britanny. Why this community should have been singled out as the inventors of deep kissing remains a mystery. Although the practice of deep kissing is very popular among the French, it seems highly unlikely that deep kissing was invented in France. Because it plays such an important role in courtship, it is much more likely that it emerged independently in several parts of the world.

Whatever the truth of the matter, there is no doubt that the French are in the first division of European kissers, while the British are somewhere near the bottom. However, there was a time when these positions were reversed – that is, when the French were much more retiring, and the English were acknowledged to be the foremost kissers in Europe. As early as 1466, a Bohemian nobleman, Leo von Rozmital, reported that in England it was customary that 'when guests arrive at an inn, the hostess with all her family go out to meet and receive them; and the guests are required to kiss them all.' He noted that 'this among the English was the same as shaking hands among other nations.'

A similar report was filed by the Dutch scholar, Desiderius Erasmus. When he visited England in 1499, he wrote to his friend, the Italian poet Fausto Andrelini, telling him to forget about his gout and to get himself to England as soon as possible, because 'here are girls with angels' faces, so kind and obliging, that you would far prefer them to all your Muses. Besides, there is a custom here never to be sufficiently commended. Whenever you come you are received with a kiss by all; when you take your leave, you are dismissed with kisses; you return, kisses are repeated. They come to visit you, kisses again; they leave you, you kiss them all around. Should you meet anywhere, kisses in abundance; in fine, wherever you move, there is nothing but kisses'.

These descriptions suggest not only that kissing had reached epidemic proportions in England by the end of the fifteenth century, but that the habit remained virtually unknown in countries like Germany, Italy and Holland. In fact there is a great deal of documentary evidence to show that the promiscuous habit of greeting strangers with a kiss was peculiar to England. For example, when the Englishman George Cavendish visited the castle of a French nobleman in 1527, he was received by the lady of the house, who declared, 'For as much as ye be an Englishman, whose custom is in your country to kiss all ladies and gentlewomen without offence, and although it be not so here in this realm, yet will I be so bold to kiss you, and so will all my maidens.' This was certainly a bold move, because in France at the time it was unheard of for a girl to kiss or be kissed by her fiancé, let alone by a complete stranger.

Things in England, however, were very different, for it was quite acceptable for courting couples to kiss each other on the mouth. In fact the choice between kissing on the lips or the cheek was not an issue, because people regularly kissed each other on the mouth. Nicander Nucius, a Greek traveller who visited England in 1545, pointed this out in his account of the English and their kissing customs: 'They display great simplicity and absence of jealousy in their usages towards females. For not only do those who are of the same family and household kiss them on the mouth with salutations and embraces, but even those too who have never seen them.'

During the sixteenth century meetings between members of the opposite sex continued to be marked by a great deal of physical contact, some of which appears, at least to us now, to have been extremely familiar. In addition to kissing, there was also a convention which allowed men to touch a woman's breasts during the greeting, provided they were 'kissing kin' and she was young and unmarried. The fact that young women exposed more of their breasts than they do today made this practice much easier, but because relatives were usually involved, breast-touching was supposed not to be erotic. That at least was the theory, even if it was not always the practice.

Kissing actually began to decline in England during the sixteenth century, but the practice managed to survive through the reigns of James I and Charles I, and up to the Restoration, when it came under renewed attack. The habit of kissing had long been abandoned as unfashionable by the French, and when James II returned to England he introduced the French code, with its disdain for kissing, into the English court. Very soon English courtiers and gentlemen started to abandon the kiss in favour of the bow, and what one correspondent in the *Spectator* called the 'fine reserved airs' of the French.

It is strange to think that the English, who are not regarded as particularly tactile or demonstrative, once enjoyed an international reputation for their osculatory excesses. In fact the spectacle of

English men and women kissing each other on the mouth, and scandalising foreigners in the process, is almost unimaginable. Something else that is difficult to accept is the idea that the disappearance of wholesale kissing from England may have been due to the introduction of French manners, and that these might also have been partly responsible for the reserved style of behaviour which is now regarded as quintessentially English. Who would have thought that, of all people, the French were to blame?

Looking

Visitors to Mediterranean countries often complain that they are being watched. As they walk down the street they get the feeling that people's eyes are locked on to them like radars tracking a foreign missile, and when they stop to talk to the locals they find that they are being drawn, almost against their will, into an intimate visual embrace. The reasons for these feelings of discomfort are quite straightforward: it is because the conventions and taboos which govern looking vary cross-culturally.

Feelings of discomfort arising from the visual habits of people on the continent are by no means new to the British. In 1728 Lady Mary Wortley Montagu wrote to Alexander Pope from Paris, reporting that 'Every body stares here; staring is á-la-mode – there is a stare of attention and *intèrêt*, a stare of curiosity, a stare of expectation, a stare of surprise, and it would greatly amuse you to see what trifling objects excite all this staring.' Writing in 1760, Oliver Goldsmith had similar remarks to make: 'The first national peculiarity a traveller meets upon entering that kingdom is an odd sort of a staring vivacity in every age; not excepting even the children; the people, it seems, have got it into their heads that they have more wit than others, and so stare in order to look smart.'

In every society, gaze serves three important social functions. First of all it performs a 'monitoring' function by allowing people to see how others are reacting and what they are doing; secondly it performs an 'expressive' function by enabling them to convey information about their attitudes and intentions; and thirdly it fulfils a 'control' function by enabling them to control and modify the actions of other people. These three functions are universal, but the amount of emphasis that is placed on each can differ from one society to another. This is certainly the case in Europe, where two quite separate zones of looking can be identified. One is the 'High-look' zone, which covers those Mediterranean countries where people also position themselves close to each other and touch a great deal. The other is the 'Low-look' zone, which covers northern, central and eastern Europe – in other words, those regions where people position themselves further apart and touch each other less.

The fact that interpersonal distance and touching are so closely linked to gaze is no coincidence, because all these channels of behaviour carry important intimacy signals. When people want to show that they like each other, they tend to stand closer and to touch each other more; they also spend much more time looking each other in the eye. The converse is also true, for when people are not feeling particularly affectionate towards each other they tend to assume a greater interpersonal distance, to reduce their physical contact, and to avoid gazing into each other's eyes.

Similar processes operate at the cultural level. In those societies where open demonstrations of intimacy are encouraged, people look at each other more intently, not only to monitor the effect they are having on each other, but also to publicise their accessibility and to express their warmth and affection. These societies are also more immediate in their style of interaction – they place greater emphasis on nonverbal cues, and therefore rely more heavily on visual signals as a means of controlling turn-taking in conversation. But one of the most important things about a 'High-look' society is the fact that it has much more mutual gaze. The more time two people spend looking at each other, the more likely it is that they will look simultaneously. When mutual gaze does occur, it enhances the sense of shared intimacy, but it also gives rise to an increase in physiological arousal, which in turn can lead to increased liking.

This is very different from what happens in a 'Low-look' society, where less emphasis is placed on gaze as a means of monitoring and controlling others, and where the eyes play a diminished role in the communication of intimacy between strangers. Children in a 'Low-look' culture are usually taught that it is rude to stare at people, and that the best way to show one's respect for strangers is to pretend lack of interest – to engage in what Erving Goffman calls 'civil inattention' – because this does not place any demands on them. Of course, not looking at someone also reduces the risk of rejection, because when one person looks expectantly at another there is always a chance that the other person will catch his or her eye and then look away, thereby rejecting the implicit invitation. This is much more likely in a Low-look society, which is why members of these societies make much less use of the eyes when initiating conversations with strangers.

Low-look societies differ from High-look societies in other ways. First of all they tend to have more pronounced taboos against staring. In a Low-look society it is quite all right for lovers to gaze at each other, and for friends and acquaintances to do so in moderation. But it is not advisable to be caught staring at a stranger – not only because it forces the person to respond in some way, but because staring can be construed as a threat signal. The chances of this happening are very much less in a High-look society, simply because there are more people staring. That is why staring so often features as a prelude, or as a pretext for a fight in a Low-look society, but not in a High-look society.

Although Low-look societies purport to protect their members from prying eyes, what they do instead is force them to find alternative ways of monitoring other people. The British, in particular, seem to have developed a whole armoury of techniques for watching each other in ways which are not obvious. One trick is to 'sneak a peek' when the other person is looking elsewhere. Another is to make full use of peripheral vision, by pretending that one's attention is elsewhere while watching the other person out of the corner of one's eye. This use of peripheral vision in Low-look cultures may help to explain why it is so hard to catch the eye of British waiters. After a life-time of watching people surreptitiously, the British waiter has become a past master at orienting his head and eyes in one direction while looking in another. For sheer ability to deceive his customers, the British waiter beats his Spanish and Italian counterparts every time.

Not only do people gaze more in a High-look society; they also get gazed at more, and they come to expect that they will attract the attention of other people. For the average person this is not a problem, but for young, attractive women it certainly is. There is very little that, say, an attractive Italian girl can do about the uninvited stares she attracts from men. Short of objecting, the only strategy available to her is to display her detachment by not returning their glances. Italian girls develop these displays of uninterest very early in life, and continue to use them until they are no longer required. Because girls from northern Europe grow up without developing these skills, they are much more likely to return a look of interest when they visit a country like Italy. This is not always advisable.

In his book, *Being and Nothingness*, Sartre refers to looking as a form of appropriation. 'Either the other looks at me and alienates my liberty, or I assimilate and seize the liberty of the other.' People who live in a Low-look society are quick to appreciate this point. They recognise that gaze which simply monitors other people is sometimes like a form of theft – which is why they have such strong taboos against staring. People who live in a High-look society seldom make this connection, which is why they have such weak prohibitions against staring. V.S. Pritchett, for example, speaks of 'the total Spanish stare', and the fact that 'it does not occur to them to conceal their admiration or their desire'. What he neglects to mention, however, is that this predatory use of gaze by men is also a means of communication between men, and in many cases a game of visual cat-and-mouse that men endeavour to play with women. The man who turns his head in order to watch a woman walking by may satisfy his curiosity; but if there are other men around he should succeed in conveying a very clear message about his interest in the opposite sex, and his virility.

Although the most pronounced differences in ocular habits occur between the High-look zone and the Low-look zone, there are nevertheless some extremely interesting differences between individual countries within the same zone. The British psychologist, Roger Ingham, has found that there are marked differences between the gaze patterns of the English and Swedes. He found that while the total amount of time that they spend looking during conversation is roughly the same, Swedes have much longer glances, their glances are more infrequent, and they engage in more mutual gaze. By administering personality questionnaires, Ingham was able to show that while mutual gaze correlated with extroversion in the case of the English, it correlated with social anxiety in the case of the Swedes. His explanation for this was that mutual gaze reflects a desire for affiliation in England, whereas in Sweden its purpose is to gather feedback and keep an eye on the other person. This interpretation has gained further support from the finding that Swedes spend disproportionately more of their time looking while they are talking than when they are listening, which suggests that they are more concerned about how *interesting* they appear, rather than how *interested* they appear to other people.

Manual Insults

There are two ways in which someone can be insulting. One involves saying something, the other doing something. Verbal insults fall into various categories, the most serious being those that cast aspersions on someone's parentage (e.g. bastard, son-of-a-bitch) or their sexual predilections (e.g. motherfucker, wanker), or which identify them with a part of the body (e.g. cunt, arsehole). After these come insults that equate individuals with body products (e.g. shit, piss) or with animals (e.g. rat, pig), and finally those that call into question their mental abilities (e.g. moron, blockhead). Most verbal insults fall into one or other of these categories, but there are also certain 'hybrid' insults, like 'Bullshit', that fall into two or more categories.

Although specific insults may differ from one society to another, they all fall into these categories. The subject of sex is a universal constituent of insulting language, partly because it is the subject of so many taboos, but also because it is a major source of anxiety. Animal insults are also universal. According to the anthropologist, Edmund Leach, their main purpose is to label people as non-human, and therefore to deny them the rights that they normally enjoy as humans. As Leach pointed out, it is very much easier to mistreat people once one has categorised them as 'pigs' or 'vermin'.

When people use insults they seldom know where they come from. In some cases they may be unaware of their meaning, and their victims may be just as ignorant. Robert Graves, for example, claimed that he witnessed a scene where a man was thrown out of the Empire Lounge in London for having called a barmaid a *maisonette*. 'Indeed, you're wrong,' she replied indignantly, 'I'm an honest woman!' The most important thing about insults is not their literal meaning, but their capacity to provoke, belittle and injure; and even though they may not be aware of it, the expletive character of insults, and the sense of release they provide, are also crucial to the experience of insulting other people.

Most verbal insults are propositional – that is, they attempt to attribute characteristics to the person being addressed. In this respect verbal insults are very different from manual insults, most of which are not propositional at all. Those that are tend to be gestural analogues of verbal insults like calling into question someone's mental abilities. In terms of message content, there is, in other words, very little difference between tapping one's forehead to tell someone that you think they are stupid, and actually saying 'Idiot!' or 'Birdbrain!' to their face.

Every European country has at least one gesture for indicating that someone is either stupid or crazy. The Italians draw a distinction between these two defects, either by tapping the forehead with the tips of the fingers to suggest stupidity, or by screwing the index finger beside the temple to show that someone is mad. Madness can also be signalled by holding an imaginary ball beside one's head and shaking it vigorously – presumably to indicate that the person's brain is small, and loose in the cranium. These gestures can either be used as insults, or as references to one's own mental shortcomings or those of a third party. Screwing the index finger beside the temple also refers to madness in other European countries, but tapping the forehead to indicate stupidity is usually replaced by tapping the temple. To make matters worse, countries like Britain and Holland actually use the temple-tap gesture for either stupidity or intelligence. Fortunately the two meanings can usually be distinguished by what the person says or by the facial expression that accompanies the gesture.

Most manual insults in Europe are concerned with sex. Like their verbal counterparts, there are certain gestural insults that impute sexual inclinations or sexual characteristics. For example, in order to refer to someone as an homosexual, the Italians either grasp the ear-lobe between their thumb and forefinger, or else they flick the ear with their forefinger. These gestures can be used to refer to someone as a homosexual, either genuinely of playfully, or they can be used as insults. In addition to these referential gestures, there are others that are designed to emasculate their victims, or to threaten them with symbolic sexual assault, or simply to tell them to 'Get fucked!'.

The 'horns sign' also says something about the sexual circumstances of its victim – in this case that they have been cuckolded by
their spouse or lover. The horns sign, or *mano cornuta* as it is called
by the Italians, is performed by extending the index and little fingers
from a closed fist – thereby producing a gesture that looks like the
horned head of an animal. The horns sign is unusual because it is
used to convey two very different messages. The message relates
to cuckoldry – it says, in effect, you have been deceived by your
wife, husband or lover, and in the process they have metaphorically
placed a pair of horns on your head. Folklorists have given a great
deal of attention to the question of whether the horns depicted in
the gesture are those of a bull, a cow, a stag, a ram or a billy goat,
or whether they relate to the spurs that are removed from the legs
of a capon and grafted on to its head. So far the debate remains
unresolved.

The gesture is not known to the British, although the link
between horns and cuckoldry was certainly known in England
as far back as the sixteenth century, when it was not unusual
for someone who had been cheated by his wife to wake up and
find that his neighbours had attached a pair of horns to the front
of his house.

Today the horns sign may be found in Spain, Portugal, Italy, and
in parts of France, Greece and the former Yugoslavia, where it is
used as an imputation of cuckoldry. In Italy, France, Greece and
what was Yugoslavia the same gesture is also used as a defensive
sign against the malevolence of others. The actual position of the
hand helps to determine its meaning. When the horns sign is being
employed defensively it is either pointed down, or directly at the
source of malevolence. For example, when a hearse goes by an
Italian might put his hands in his pockets and surreptitiously make
the horns sign to protect himself against misfortune; alternatively
he might make the sign and point it in the direction of someone
who is causing him anxiety. When the horns sign is used as an insult
it can be pointed in any direction, although there is a tendency to
direct the horns up or towards the person being insulted.

But how does the horns sign manage to exist with two very
different meanings? The answer, it seems, is connected with the
religion of Mithra, which worshipped the bull, and which was
extremely popular in Rome right up to the time when Christianity

became the favoured religion of the empire under the Emperor Constantine. Bull worship was widespread throughout the ancient world, and depictions of horns were used, sympathetically, to harness the sexual and mystical powers of the bull. The fact that the horns sign is used as a means of protection today is undoubtedly an extension of this very ancient belief about the symbolic power of horns.

This may explain the protective meaning of the horns sign, but it does not help us to understand why the gesture is also used as a reference to sexual infidelity. To do this we need to turn to what happens when one religion is supplanted by another. When this happens, the deities of the old religion are demoted and driven off to take up residence in the underworld. This is precisely what happened when Christianity was adopted as the official religion of the emperors: the displaced gods of the defeated religions were dispatched to hell, with their horns, hooves and long tails – in other words, with the physical attributes of the devil himself. At this point horns became discredited because they were the symbols of a defunct religion, and therefore available as a symbol of defeat, deceit and unfaithfulness. It is very likely, therefore, that the insulting horns sign and its protective counterpart are remnants of two phases in horn iconography – one when the gods wore horns, the other when horned gods had ignominiously been dispatched to the underworld.

In addition to manual insults that impute characteristics, there are also those that threaten their victim. The most famous gesture in this category is the 'Middle-finger' gesture, or the *digitus impudicus* as it was known to the ancient Romans. As its name suggests, this gesture is performed by extending the middle finger from a closed fist. The gesture is obviously phallic, and the expressions that sometimes accompany it show that it is basically a gesture of emasculation. It is directed at someone with the intention of showing what the gesturer will do to them if he gets the chance. This gesture is very old. It was known to the ancient Greeks and Romans, who used it both as a phallic insult and as a reference to homosexuality. We are told, for example, that when a group of strangers at a large gathering asked the Greek philosopher Diogenes where they might find the orator Demosthenes, Diogenes pointed at Demosthenes with his middle finger rather than his index finger, thereby drawing attention to his homosexuality. The Roman historian Suetonius tells us that the Emperor Caligula made a habit of insulting Cassius Charea, a tribune of the Praetorian guard who happened to be homosexual. The Emperor was constantly drawing attention to his effeminacy, and when he offered his hand to Cassius to be kissed he would provocatively extend his middle finger.

Since classical times the Middle-finger gesture has changed its meaning slightly. It is no longer used to refer to someone's sexual habits, but rather to suggest where they might insert the middle finger, or what is likely to happen to them if they are not careful. The Romans were largely responsible for transporting the Middle-finger gesture round the known world. The gesture, however, did not take root throughout the whole of Europe, because it appears to have been imported into Britain from America, rather than being a vestige of the Roman occupation of Britain. There are also several variants of the Middle-finger gesture. For example, the Russians turn the gesture round so that the palm faces towards, rather than away from the person being addressed. The person performing the gesture also holds the top of the extended middle finger with the fingers of the other hand, as if they were lifting up a cat's tail to expose its anus. The Russian version of the middle-finger gesture is not so much designed to show what will happen to the victim's anus, but rather to show what he should do to a cat's.

Another emasculatory gesture found throughout Europe is the Forearm Jerk. This is performed by jerking the clenched fist up and by slapping the other hand into the crook of the arm. Like the middle finger gesture, this is a phallic gesture, but it is of course much more pronounced than the Middle-finger gesture. Interestingly, the Forearm Jerk is not used as an insult in Britain or Ireland. Here it is executed rather slowly, and it is used as a sign of sexual appreciation, usually between men about women. In France, Belgium, Spain, Portugal, Greece and southern Germany the Forearm Jerk is used as an insult. In France it is known as the *bras d'honneur*, literally the 'arm of honour'. There and elsewhere it is accompanied by expressions like 'Take this!', meaning 'Put this up your arse'.

If the Forearm Jerk depicts the instrument of emasculation, then the 'Stretcher' gesture illustrates its consequences. The Stretcher gesture is exclusive to Italy, and it is performed by holding the hands apart, with the thumbs and forefingers extended, as if they were tilting a large plate for someone to see. The gesture is intended to depict a stretched anus – the result, in other words, of an homosexual assault. While the Forearm Jerk threatens 'This is what you'll get up your backside if you don't watch out', the Stretcher says 'This is what will happen to you if you're not careful.' The latent homosexuality of these two gestures is something that few people are aware of. When they insult someone with the Middle-finger gesture they don't realise that they are implicating themselves, if only symbolically, as the agents of emasculation.

Another anal gesture is the practice of exposing the buttocks, which was initially employed as a defence against the forces of evil, and later on as a means of disarming or insulting other people. This gesture was certainly around during the sixteenth century, because Martin Luther claimed that he managed to repulse the devil by showing him his backside. Italian and French sailors were in the habit of exposing their buttocks to unfavourable winds, again to protect themselves against misfortune, and Scandinavian soldiers are reputed to have bared their bottoms to the enemy, in the belief that the terrifying spectacle would blunt their swords. The gesture of exposing the buttocks – or 'mooning' as it is now called – continues to be used in Europe, but it has lost its power to repel evil and has become an insult instead. The gesture succeeds in being insulting because it contravenes the social norms about concealment of the body, and because it threatens, at least symbolically, to defecate on the person to whom the buttocks are exposed. But there is also something extremely infantile about the practice of baring the buttocks. Children are taught from a very early age that they should not show their backside to other people, because it is a 'rude' part of their anatomy. For adults, therefore, the attraction of mooning relies on the flaunting of parental rules, and this explains why the gesture is so often accompanied by laughter. In these instances the laughter is a form of release, a feeling of liberation that comes from defying authority, being naughty once again, and getting away with it.

Sex and scatology are not the only themes behind insulting gestures. The Greeks, for example, have a gesture called the *Moutza*, which is sometimes accompanied by the expression 'Go to Hell!'. The *Moutza* is performed by presenting the palm of the hand to one's adversary, with the thumb and fingers splayed. The insulting message can be reduced by performing a miniature version of the *Moutza* in which just the first and second fingers are splayed; this gesture looks exactly like the British victory sign. Alternatively the insulting message can be doubled by presenting the palms of both hands, with all the fingers splayed. A comic version of this gesture is sometimes performed by presenting the soles of the feet as well, but this four-fold insult is rather precarious for the gesturer.

The *Moutza* is an ancient sign, the origins of which can be found in the old Byzantine practice of parading chained criminals through the town while the local populace collected dirt and refuse from the streets and thrust it into their faces. This practice is now happily extinct, but the gesture lives on as a highly emotive insult. The peculiar shape of the *Moutza* renders it liable to misunderstanding. For most foreigners it appears to be a fairly innocuous, if not neutral sign, and the fact that it offers no clues to its distasteful origins means that it can very easily be mistaken as a gesture which has something to do with the number five. This did in fact happen a few years ago when Nottingham Forest football club played in Athens. The soccer correspondent for an English newspaper reported that young Greek fans had approached the English team and indicated what they expected the final score to be in their favour – five nil! Had the correspondent known about the *Moutza*, he would have realised that the gesture was an insult, and not some wishful prognostication.

The *Moutza* is a single-culture gesture, confined to Greece. Another single-culture gesture is the V-sign, where the first and second fingers are splayed to form a 'V', and the palm of the hand faces back, towards the person making the gesture. This is the 'Palm-back V-sign'. It is used as an insult, meaning 'Fuck off!', in Britain and Ireland.

The origins of the insulting V-sign remain something of a mystery. It has been suggested that the gesture represents the inviting legs of a woman, the 'V' of the female pubic triangle, a supernormal version of the Middle-finger gesture, and even a double penis. The most fanciful theory is one that suggests that the gesture originated during the Hundred Years War. It is said that before the Battle of Agincourt in 1415 the French had threatened that they would chop off the index and middle finger of every English archer they captured. It is reported that the English archers replied by raising their two fingers whenever they managed to shoot a French soldier – defiantly showing that they were still intact. The problem with this theory is that it fails to explain the obscene component of the gesture. It explains how the gesture might have come to be used as a taunt, but not how it came to have sexual overtones.

The task of discovering the origins of the insulting V-sign is made all the more difficult by the fact that there aren't any explicit descriptions or images of the gesture being used as an insult before the turn of the century, and many of the photographs from the last war that depict the gesture give the impression that it is being used to signal 'Victory'. In his book, *The Streets of London*, which was published in 1940, Thomas Burke provides a neat historical catalogue of English insults. 'Crude gestures,' he informs us, 'have always been a part of the London scene. In Tudor times the invitation to quarrel or combat was given by a biting of the thumb; in the middle eighteenth century, by cocking the hat; later, by a jerk of the thumb over the left shoulder, implying illegitimate birth; in the early nineteenth century, by the thumb to the nose, and within living memory by two fingers jerked upwards.' There can be no doubt that this reference to two fingers being jerked upwards is the insulting palm-back V-sign of today, which means that, at the very latest, the gesture was being used in England before the war, and possibly as far back as the turn of the century. But can we date it earlier than that?

One of the earliest references to a gesture that might have been the palm-back V-sign appears in Rabelais' *Pantagruel*, published in 1533. Rabelais describes a gestural duel between a Frenchman and an Englishman, where the Frenchman 'stretched he out the forefinger, and middle or medical of his right hand, holding them asunder as much as he could and thrusting them towards' the Englishman. Another possible reference to the palm-back V-sign may be found in Tobias Smollett's *The Expedition of Humphry Clinker*, published in 1771, where he describes a tea-party in Bath that gets out of control: 'Some cried, some swore, and the tropes and figures of Billingsgate were used without reserve in all their native zest and flavour; nor were those flowers of rhetoric unattended with significant gesticulations. Some snapped their fingers, some forked them out, some clapped their hands, and some their backside.'

The problem with these descriptions is that we cannot tell whether they are referring to a V-sign where the palm faces back, or in some other direction. It is quite likely, for example, that the Frenchman's gesture is a V-sign directed at the eyes, in which case it would have been a threat rather than an insult. Similarly, the V-sign described by Smollett could just have easily been a V-sign with the palm facing forward, rather than back. If this were the case, it would suggest that the early version of the insulting British V-sign was borrowed from the continent. For a long time the Italians have used a V-sign with the palm facing forward as an imputation of cuckoldry – usually placing it playfully behind someone's head to show that they are 'wearing horns'. This gesture can also be found in Britain, although it is quite rare now, and it appears to have lost all its associations with cuckoldry. It is quite likely that the British borrowed the cuckold V-sign from the Italians, turned it round so that it faced back rather than forward, and then changed its meaning slightly.

Scholars have also had problems trying to untangle the origins of that other famous English gesture – the thumb-biting gesture mentioned in *Romeo and Juliet*. In the scene, Sampson and Gregory, who are servants of the Capulets, are strolling through the city when they spy two servants of the Montagues coming towards them. Sampson says to Gregory, 'I will bite my thumb at them; which is a disgrace to them, if they bear it.' It is clear from this remark that Sampson intends a provocation, and this interpretation is borne out by the response he gets. Abram, at whom the gesture was directed, asks, 'Do you bite your thumb at us, sir?'. Sampson replies with deliberate ambiguity, 'I do bite my thumb, sir', so Abram is forced to pose the question again, and this time Sampson says 'No sir, I do not bite my thumb at you, sir; but I bite my thumb, sir.' Reading this exchange it is very evident what is happening, but it is not entirely clear what the act of 'biting the thumb' involves, or why it should be provocative.

Several gestures have been offered as candidates for the thumb-biting gesture. One is the act of sucking the thumb, either as a phallic gesture or as a way of suggesting that someone is childish. Another is the gesture of biting the knuckle of the thumb to show that one is containing one's rage, and the third is the gesture of flicking one's thumbnail from behind the front teeth, to suggest that someone or something is worthless. The problem with all of these gestures is that they are not actually thumb-biting gestures, or else they are not insulting, which means that one has to look elsewhere to try and discover how the act of biting the thumb might have been provocative in Shakespeare's time.

The clue to the puzzle is that during the latter half of the sixteenth century men were in the habit of wearing gloves, and these were usually removed prior to any confrontation – not unlike the present-day Irish habit of taking off one's jacket to show that one is prepared for a fight. In fact the practice of removing and throwing down one's glove had become ritualised as a challenge long before Shakespeare's time. In medieval times knights used this device to invite each other into battle, and gloves were also used in legal disputes. A defendant in court, for example, might throw down his glove, offering it as security that he would defend his case in arms; if his accuser picked it up he accepted the challenge – hence the expression 'To throw down the gauntlet'. It seems that the medieval convention of using the glove as a challenge was still around during Shakespeare's time, but that it had been abbreviated to the point where an intention movement of removing the gloves with one's teeth – that, is by biting the tip of the thumb – would have sufficed as a challenge. We see therefore that the question about Sampson biting his thumb was really an issue about whether he was challenging Abram to a fight; that is why the gesture was potentially so provocative.

Names

When we talk about other people we can either refer to them by their real name or by their nickname, if they have one. The same applies in the case of nations and ethnic groups. Instead of referring to 'the French', we might talk about 'the Frogs'. For 'the Germans' we could substitute 'Krauts', and for the Italians 'Dagos'. Giving someone in our own society a nickname does several things. First of all, it ignores their real name, and imposes a name that is not of their choosing, nor necessarily to their liking. By drawing attention to certain observable or reputed characteristics, the nickname creates the impression that the person is very different from everybody else, and it might even suggest how they should be treated. Collective nicknames are motivated by the same principles. They also ascribe names that members of the outgroup have not chosen, and in many cases names that they would totally reject. By imputing negative characteristics to the outgroup, and exaggerating ethnic differences, collective nicknames provide a ready-made excuse for treating members of the outgroup as inferiors.

Ethnic nicknames come in various guises. Some are based on names that are assumed to be common in the country in question. The English, for example, refer to the Welsh as 'Taffy', to the Scots as 'Jock' or 'Mac', to the Irish as 'Mick' or 'Paddy', and to the Germans as 'Hans', 'Fritz' or 'Gerry'. Most of these nicknames pretend to be inoffensive, but they are frequently regarded as objectionable by the people at whom they are directed, not least because they imply a uniformity of naming practices that does not exist in the community concerned. The situation is of course even worse in the case of nicknames like Taffy and Gerry. Taffy is an anglicised version of Daffydd, and not a Welsh name at all. Gerry is not common as a German name either, and its origins are uncertain. It could derive from the first syllable of 'Germany', from the English slang for a chamber pot, or even from the word 'jerry', a word which refers to a badly constructed building, and which was in use as long ago as the 1880s.

The nickname 'Dago' is regarded as offensive by Italians, even though it was originally quite innocuous. The nickname comes from the Spanish 'Diego', meaning James. During the early part of the nineteenth century it was used to refer to the Spaniards and the Portuguese, but half way through the century it was transferred to the Italians. The prize for the most offensive nickname in this category has to be 'John Crapose', which the English once used to refer to the French. The nickname originated from the French *crapaud*, meaning a toad, which the English heard the French using as a swear-word, and which had the added attraction of sounding like 'crap'. In fact this attraction was so great that the English soon shortened John Crapose to 'Crappo', and used that instead.

Another category of nicknames is that based on the foods that different nations eat – like 'Limey' for the English, 'Potato eater' for the Irish, or 'Mushroom picker' for the Czechs. The idea behind these nicknames is that the character of a people determines the kind of food they eat – an inversion, as it were, of Brillat-Savarin's famous dictum, *Dis-moi ce que tu manges, et je te dirai ce que tu es* – 'Tell me what you eat, and I will tell you what you are.' European name-calling provides a veritable banquet of culinary epithets. The French, for example, used to call the English *Rosbif*, and the English returned the compliment by calling the French 'Frogs' – the only difference being that while the French were happy to sample the delights of roast beef, the English found the whole idea of eating frogs legs quite disgusting. It is widely assumed that this is how the English came to call the French frogs, but there is an alternative explanation which suggests that the name originated with the French themselves. According to this theory, the coat of arms of the early Frankish kings consisted of three leaping frogs, or 'frogs saltant' in heraldic terminology. These were later replaced by fleur-de-lis. Much later, when the French court was established at Versailles, the courtiers tried to conjure up the glory of the old Frankish kingdom by referring to themselves as toads, and to the inhabitants of Paris as frogs – *les Grenouilles*. This, it is said, is how the French came to be known as frogs – not through any foreign reference to their eating habits.

The Dutch, Germans and Italians have also attracted culinary epithets. During the seventeenth century the Dutch were known as 'Jan Kaas' – John Cheese. During the nineteenth century they were known, together with the Germans, as 'Cabbage-heads'. The nickname 'Sauerkraut' was first applied to the Germans round about 1904. During the First World War this was shortened to 'Kraut', and then extended to 'Krauthead' during the Second World War. Since the eighteenth century the Italians have been known as 'Macaroni'. Later on the pasta metaphor was expanded to include 'Spaghetti', or 'Spag' for short, and 'Meatball', 'Greaser' and 'Greaseball' were added to the menu for good measure.

Language, and the peculiar accents of foreigners, can also form the basis of ethnic nicknames. For a long time the English were known to the French as *les Goddems*, because of their habit of blaspheming. The English have also parroted the French, firstly by calling them 'Parleyvoo', and later 'Deedonks'. Parleyvoo was a straight mimic of *parlez vous* – 'Do you speak?' – which first appeared in the 1890s. The nickname Deedonks appeared during the First World War, probably from hearing the French *dis donc* – 'Hey, tell me!'. The pronouns that other people use have also been used in the construction of ethnic nicknames. The Polish, for example, used to refer to the Germans as *Derdiedasy*, a reference to *Der*, *Die* and *Das*, the German pronouns for he, she and it.

'Wop', the nickname for Italians, also appears to have originated from linguistic usage. There are three theories that account for its origins. One theory suggests that during the 1920s there was a flood of Italians trying to enter the United States illegally, many of them without the official papers required for immigration. It is said that after they had entered the country, many of these illegal immigrants were rounded up by U.S. officials, and shipped back to Italy with 'W.O.P.', an acronym for 'With Out Papers' stamped in their documents. If you ask Italian Americans about the origins of 'Wop', they will usually repeat this story, partly because it seems so plausible, but also because it casts Italians in the role of heroic underdogs. It is very unlikely, however, that this is how the nickname evolved. For one thing, there were other groups of European immigrants trying to gain entry into the United States at the time, all of which would have been treated in the same way by officials, but none of which were ever called 'Wop'.

Another theory suggests that 'Wop' is an acronym for 'Work

On Pavement' – a reference to the fact that so many of the Italian migrants to America ended up working in the construction industry. There is, as far as we know, no support for this theory either. It appears, like the 'With Out Papers' theory, to be another case of people inventing an explanation to account for the origins of an expression – in other words, a case of 'folk etymology'.

The most likely origin of 'Wop' is the word *guappo*. According to Irving Allen, who has made a special study of ethnic epithets, during the twenties Neapolitan immigrants to America used to acknowledge each other with *'Guappo!'*, a dialect term meaning 'dude', 'dandy' or 'good-looking'. Those people who heard the greeting, but who could not speak Italian, assumed that *'guappo'* must be a form of address, so they borrowed it as a way of referring to Italians. Anthony Burgess reports that Neapolitans still refer to themselves as *Guappi* – the pretty ones – which provides further support for this theory of the nickname's origins.

Nicknames offer one way of referring to members of other groups. But there are also several other linguistic devices which make up the general category of 'ethnic slurs' – or what the French call *'blason populaire'*. One device consists of using the name of the country as an adjective – as in 'Dutch courage', 'Welsh comb', 'Irish spoon' or 'Scotch organ'. Each of these expressions provides a demeaning, and intentionally amusing, description of the group in question – Dutch courage, for example, refers to cowardice rather than courage, and a Welsh comb is a reference to the thumb and four fingers. Irish spoon refers to a shovel, and Scotch organ to a cash register.

The way that country names are used in ethnic slurs provides a fascinating record of international relations. During the fifteenth century, for example, Spain was England's most hated enemy, and it was during this period that the English language acquired all of its derogatory references to the Spanish – phrases like 'Spanish practice', meaning deceit, and 'Spanish coin', which refers to florid compliments, and 'Spanish castle', meaning a daydream. By the seventeenth century the English had lost interest in the Spaniards, and it was the turn of the Dutch. The Dutch had started to build up an enormous trading empire. This threatened the interests of the English, who responded by coining a host of derogatory phrases which involved the Dutch – like 'Dutch auction', 'Dutch bargain',

'Dutch bath' and 'Dutch clock' – all of which were designed to belittle the Dutch in the eyes of the English, and to make the English feel superior. Phrases like 'Double Dutch' and 'I'll be a Dutchman' also originated during this period of international rivalry.

Phrases referring to the French were around in England as far back as the sixteenth century. But it was the conflicts and wars of the eighteenth and nineteenth centuries that spawned most of the derogatory references to the French that we hear today – phrases like 'French kiss' for deep kissing, and 'French letters', meaning condoms. References to the Germans have been very thin on the ground, partly because for a long time the English used to refer to the inhabitants of the low countries and most of Germany as 'the Dutch' – a confusion which may have arisen from the similarity between Dutch and Deutsch. It is very surprising that the number of slurs directed against the Germans has not increased during this century. After two world wars one would have expected the Germans to be the butt of numerous English epithets, as well as the originators of numerous slurs against the British. This has not happened. Instead the only slur of any note that the English are able to throw at the Germans is the rather weak 'German measles'. The only form of retaliation that the Germans have at their disposal is *'Englisches Krankheit'*, meaning rickets – hardly the kind of mudslinging that is going to hurt anybody's feelings.

Exchanges of slurs have been much more intense between the English and the French, largely because of their close proximity to each other and their long history of animosity. The English, for example, say things like 'Excuse my French' when referring to bad language, while the French retaliate with expressions like *damné comme un Anglais* – 'damned like an Englishman'. When the English talk about someone leaving suddenly they use the expression 'French leave'. The French use *filer à l'anglaise* to mean the same thing.

Descriptions of sexual activities are virtually monopolised by references to the French and English. Casanova, who was one of the first people to use condoms, called them *redingotes d'Angleterre* (English overcoats). What the French now refer to as *une capote anglais* (an English cloak), the English call a 'French letter'. Menstruating in France is known as *avoir les anglais* (to have the Englishes), while homosexuality and flagellation are referred to as *le vice anglais* (the English vice). The English have also found it necessary to pretend that peculiar sexual practices originate on the other side of the channel. They refer to oral-genital sex as 'the French way' or 'French arts.' 'French kissing' is, of course, the English term for deep kissing, 'French lessons' refers to instructions from a prostitute, and pornography is variously known as 'French postcards' or 'French prints'.

Venereal disease is another area where nations have tried to blame each other, normally by attaching the name of another country to the disease. For the English, syphilis was once the 'Spanish pox'. Then it became the 'French pox'. After the Italian physician, Giralomo Fracastor, published a poem entitled *Syphilis sive Morbus Gallicus*, in 1530, syphilis became known all over Europe as *Morbus Gallicus* or the 'French disease'. In England the term was expanded to include names like 'French compliment', 'French fever', 'French goods', 'French malady' – or just plain 'Frenchified'. Over the centuries other people, like the Spaniards, Poles and Italians, have been associated with syphilis, but most European nations have pointed the finger at France. The French, however, have found it more convenient to blame the Florentines and Neapolitans for the disease.

The history of Europe shows that people frequently abandon the 'official' names of countries in favour of nicknames, and that they are equally ready to identify nations and ethnic groups in terms of their linguistic and culinary habits, and to accuse them of peculiar sexual practices. Ethnic slurs are much more common between countries that have some kind of relationship, particularly when the relationship happens to be based on economic competition. Ethnic slurs like 'French disease' are motivated by two principles. One is denial and the need to disown responsibility for the disease; the other is projection, that is, the need to pin the blame on someone else. The Englishman who uses the term 'French Disease' finds it easier to persuade himself that his own people have nothing to do with the disease, and that the French are totally to blame. This in turn is likely to consolidate his attachment to his own group, and to increase his stereotyped view of the French.

Odour

The English have always prided themselves on being superior to other nations, and one way this has shown itself is in the area of personal hygiene and cleanliness. This was very noticeable during the eighteenth century, when hordes of English travellers took off for the continent on the 'Grand Tour', and returned with distressing tales about smelly streets and the overpowering stench of the natives. Robert Southey, writing from Lisbon in 1797, reported that 'The filth of this city is indeed astonishing; every thing is thrown into the street, and all the refuse of the kitchen, and dead animals are exposed to these scorching suns. I believe these Portugese would throw one another out, and "leave the dead to bury the dead", if it were not the interest of the priests to prevent them.' Round about the same time, Samuel Taylor Coleridge described Cologne as a place with 'seven-and-twenty smells, all well-defined and genuine stinks', and a few years later William Thackeray reported that the city was 'in aspect unpromising, & in smell odious'. But it was Mrs Francis Trollope, in 1836, who managed to distil the essence of English attitudes to foreign odours: 'I remember being much amused last year, when landing at Calais, at the answer made by an old traveller to a novice who was making his first voyage. "What a dreadful smell!" said the uninitiated stranger, enveloping his nose in his pocket handkerchief. "It is the smell of the continent, sir," replied the man of experience. And so it was.'

Why did English people at the time object so strongly to the smells of the continent? Was it because things on the other side of the channel were really as bad as they made out, or because they were not familiar with the smells they encountered, or was it simply a case of the overbearing English using the issue of smell to look down their noses at foreigners? To answer these questions we need, first of all, to remind ourselves of the crucial role that smell plays in social interaction.

The complaints that people offer about the smells of other countries represent the mere tip of the odour ice-berg, the bulk of which remains excluded from discussion, either because it is regarded as unnoteworthy or because people are not aware of the odours to which they are responding. For a long time the faculty of smell was ignored by students of human behaviour – so much so that the philosopher Immanuel Kant actually excluded it from his scheme of the senses. However, in recent years scientists have started to recognise the full importance of odours as social and sexual signals, and the impact, often unrecognised, that they have on people. One of the important discoveries is the power that odours have to evoke associations and memories. This is called the 'Marcel Proust phenomenon', after the French novelist who dipped a Madeleine biscuit into his tea and discovered that the aroma brought back a flood of memories from his childhood which he had completely forgotten. Nothing, it seems, is so evocative of memories as odour. That is because odours act directly on the nervous system. They are rapidly absorbed by the mucous membrane, and the decoded information is transferred directly to the limbic system of the brain, the site which is associated with our emotions and our memories. This explains why smells that we have encountered in the distant past are still capable of producing such clear and powerful memories.

Odour plays a crucial role, both in our perception of the world around us, and in the way it is actually constituted. There is certainly a great deal of anecdotal evidence to show that cultures can generate quite different odours through the food they eat and the way it is prepared. There is also evidence to show that cultures can have very different preferences and degrees of tolerance where smells are concerned. In a recent study, conducted in Poland, Switzerland, Sweden, France, Norway, Finland and England, people were presented with twenty-two 'scratch-and-sniff' cards containing different aromas. They were asked to scratch each card, to name the aroma, and then to rate it according to how much they liked it. The aroma of bananas turned out to have the highest recognition and appreciation scores, while the smell of gas scored bottom on both counts. Peppermint, lemon and vanilla were also widely recognised, whereas odours like garlic, smoke, and skunk were not. National differences also emerged. Grape and cinnamon, for example, were liked by all the Europeans, except the English. The smell of root-beet, on the other hand, was liked much more by the English than by any of the other groups. The smell of wintergreen also showed regional variation, being liked much more in France, Sweden, Finland and Norway than in Poland, England and Switzerland. International research of this nature suggests that there are strong relationships between the degree to which people recognise and like a particular odour and how familiar they are with it. People like the Poles, who eat a lot of pickles, are quick to recognise the aroma of pickle, and they also report liking the smell. This is quite different from the case of, say, the Swiss, who do not eat a lot of pickle, and who neither recognise nor like the smell.

In addition to differences in odour preference, there are other reasons why cultures might regard each other as unclean. One is familiarity, the fact that cultures are not acquainted with each other's odours, and therefore respond by assuming that they are bad. This explanation is indirectly supported by research which shows that communication between members of different cultures can actually be improved by familiarising people with the odours they are likely to encounter in another culture.

Another reason why societies accuse each other of being unclean is that all societies equate cleanliness with goodness, and both of these qualities with membership of the ingroup. For a group to be successful it must have some kind of identity – an image of itself which enables its members to compare themselves favourably with the members of other groups. This can only be achieved if members of the ingroup select a suitable outgroup for comparison, and if the comparison works out in their favour. Standards of hygiene always provide a good yardstick for comparison because other cultures can always be represented as dirty and smelly, simply because their habits of personal hygiene are different.

The British often accuse the French of not washing, and of using perfume to mask their personal body odour. Market research shows that the French do take fewer baths and showers than the British, but there is no reason to suppose that the French use perfume in order to mask their body odour. In fact, there is every reason to conclude that they use perfumes to accentuate their body odours. As far as the French are concerned, body odours are quite natural, they are part of our animal nature. Any process that removes them threatens part of our animal nature, and reduces our sexual desire. Caution is therefore needed when it comes to bathing. It may be advisable to remove dirt and stale sweat, but there is no need to completely remove those familiar odours that make us what we are.

In countries like Britain and Germany courting couples try to disguise their body odours by washing themselves thoroughly and by using deodorants. In France things are much more relaxed, and people often find body odours appealing and sexy. Just before he returned from his Egyptian campaign, Napoleon wrote to Josephine, *Ne te lave pas, j'arrive* – 'Don't wash, I'm coming'. This obvious enjoyment of body odour is still very much in evidence in France, as it is in some other Mediterranean countries. The Italian king, Victor Emmanuel II, for example, is said to have complained to his courtiers when they brought a peasant girl to him whom he had admired, all scrubbed and clean. More recently, when Marcello Mastroianni was asked in an interview how he liked his women, he confessed, 'I like them to smell a little.'

Historically the French have always shown much more interest in the subject of smell that the British. During the seventeenth century they investigated the relationship between human odours and all kinds of factors. Different types of smells were identified and the effects of climate, the seasons, food, temperament, occupation and even hair colour were examined. It was discovered that people from different parts of the country exuded specific odours, largely because of the food they ate. According to Jean-Joseph de Brieude, writing in 1789, 'When harvest time brings these people together in our cantons, it is easy to tell the men from the Quercy and Rouergue regions by the fetid odour of garlic and onion they give out, while the odour of the Auvergnats is like soured whey.'

The French were well aware of the relationship between personal odour and physical attraction – after all, Henry III is said to have fallen madly in love with Mary of Cleves, simply by breathing in the odour of one of her garments – but it was in medicine and the war against disease that odour became so important. Most doctors applied the principles of 'Osphresiology', the new science of diagnosis by smell. By inhaling the odours emitted from their patients, and from their breath, stool and urine, doctors were able to reach a diagnosis of the patient's ailment as well as a prognosis. By the same

German anti-nuclear protestors present their backsides to the French police.
(Éditions Gendre)

Russians queue in front of Lenin's tomb in Red Square.
(SCR Photo Library)

principles it was recognised that certain odours offered a protection against disease. Scents, it was believed, could actually clean the air. By smelling strongly oneself, or inhaling a powerful odour from a smelling box, one could also protect oneself from pestilence and disease. These prophylactic properties of odours, coupled with their role in physical attraction, fashion and sheer hedonism, gave enormous impetus to perfumery. The early perfumiers were often glove-makers, supplying perfumed gloves and other infused accessories to the nobility and the royal court.

France is still the international centre of the perfume industry, and it is also the largest consumer of perfume, both in absolute and per capita terms. Britain is the next largest consumer, followed by Germany, Austria, Italy and Denmark. Spain, Sweden and Norway are near the bottom of the perfume league table. Spain is rather unusual, because although its perfume market is still developing, the market for bulk fragrances is well established. According to Sophie Le Norcy, who trains perfume sales personnel, the type of perfume that Spanish women are buying has a lot to do with their aspirations. 'In recent years the sophisticated young Spanish woman has had a wish to break free from the traditional, heady, floral perfumes synonymous with well-behaved, discreetly elegant and pampered housewives. They have shown a preference for frankly masculine, herbal-woody fragrances, which betokened a liberation from the traditional stay-at-home female values.' She points out that sales training also needs to take account of other national idiosyncrasies. 'To give another example, in Germany it is quite impossible to use the perfumery adjective 'animal' [*tierisch*]. In this culture anything linked to animals is perceived as unclean or dirty or primitive or even a breach of ecological behaviour. So when dealing with the popular "musk" perfumes, one must be cautious. Even though it is well known that the natural musk is an animal ingredient, it is better to avoid reference to this aspect of the phenomenon when one is selling a perfume in Germany.'

It has been suggested that the sole reason why the art of perfumery developed in France was because the French needed a way to mask their own body odours, and to shield themselves from the stench of others. The trouble with this theory is that it only tells part of the story. Firstly it ignores the fact that the French actually enjoy certain body odours, and secondly it overlooks the various purposes that early perfumes were designed to serve. True, there was a time when the streets of Paris were like an open sewer, and sensitive Parisians walked around with sweet-smelling posies and scented pomanders tucked under their noses in order to reduce their discomfort and to counteract the pestilential properties of the air.

Other perfumes, however, were designed for different purposes. Some, like extracts of rose and honeysuckle, were used to lift people's spirits and to make them feel better, while musk and civet were unashamedly employed as sexual attractants. Musk and civet were widely used until the middle of the eighteenth century, when they gave way to herbal and floral extracts that were thought to be less blatant and sexually explicit. The point about these perfumes, however, is that they were never intended as a means of masking body odours, but rather as a way of emphasising them. From the very earliest days, therefore, French perfumery was not involved in a process of concealment, but one of accentuation.

In spite of the changes that have taken place over the last century, the same situation applies today. If the main purpose of perfume for the French was to mask personal body odour, then we would expect to find the French using deodorants for the same purpose. What is interesting is that although the French market for toiletries and cosmetics is the largest in Europe, the market for deodorants is small. Less than half of the households in France have a deodorant, and male use of deodorants is only about 42%. This suggests that the French use perfume, not to disguise their body odours, but rather to surround their body odours with fragrance.

Punctuality

European countries can be divided into those that emphasise the need for time-keeping, schedules and deadlines, and those that regard these regimentations of time as artificial and unnecessary. In the first category are the 'time-bound' countries like Germany, Switzerland, Britain and the Scandinavian countries, while in the second are the 'time-blind' countries like Spain, Portugal and Greece.

The pace at which people live their lives is very different in these two types of society. In a time-bound society, where time is at a premium, there are powerful incentives for people not to squander their time, and to use it profitably. Time-blind societies, on the other hand, don't see time so much in economic terms, and as a result there is less need to hurry through life, cramming everything into schedules and deadlines. This is borne out by a series of cross-cultural studies on 'pace of life', where psychologists have recorded how fast pedestrians move along the pavement. Although this research was originally set up to look at the relationship between pace of life and population size, it has also uncovered some interesting cultural differences. It shows that there is very little difference between walking speeds in large cities like Munich, Prague, Dublin, Edinburgh and Athens, but that people who live in Mediterranean towns move at a much slower pace than those who live in towns of comparable size in northern and central Europe. This is especially noticeable in Greek villages, where life seems to be conducted at a snail's pace, confirming Evelyn Waugh's observation that 'Everything in Greece takes just twice as long as it would anywhere else. In the country they just do not use time at all.'

The psychologist Robert LeVine and his colleagues have studied pace of life in various countries, including Italy and Britain. In addition to studying pedestrian speed, they have also looked at the accuracy of clocks in banks, and measured how long it takes to buy a stamp at a post office in different countries. When they compared the inhabitants of Rome and Florence with those in London and Bristol, they found that walking speed in England was only marginally faster than that in Italy, and that the clocks in English banks were slightly more accurate than those in Italian banks. However, they discovered a large difference in post offices, because while it took an average of twenty-eight seconds to buy a stamp in an English post office, it took an average of forty-seven seconds to make the same purchase in an Italian post office. It would appear that the reputation of Italian post offices is not without foundation!

Pace of life measures may not always show a consistent pattern when one compares just two countries, but when several countries are compared a pattern of relationships between the various measures does begin to emerge, showing that those countries which are 'fast' are quite different from those that are 'slow'. There is also evidence to show that pace of life is linked to quality of life and health, because people who feel rushed off their feet report less satisfaction with their lives and they are usually less healthy. Psychologists have isolated a category of individuals, called 'A-type', who are susceptible to coronary disorders. A-type individuals often have a chronic sense of urgency. They have too much to do, and not enough time to do it in, and the resulting stress that they experience often leads to coronary problems. There is some support for this in cross-cultural research on pace of life, which shows that the 'faster' a country is, the higher the number of people who die from heart disease. Pace of life appears to affect not only enjoyment of life, but also how long people actually live.

Research has also shown that people who are A-type have a very different attitude to punctuality. Not only do A-types report being more on time for appointments, but they also feel worse about being late. Punctuality in other people is very important to them, and they are not prepared to wait around for very long when someone is late for an appointment.

Like individuals, cultures differ enormously in how much value they place on punctuality. Time-blind cultures like Spain and Greece have a casual attitude to time-keeping. In countries like these time is perceived as being more cyclical, and therefore less amenable to measurement. Time is also seen as being elastic, stretching and contracting according to the demands placed on it, and this makes it much more difficult for people to time their arrivals with precision. This usually results in people being late, but it can also cause them to be early. As George Orwell observed in *Homage to Catalonia*. 'In Spain nothing from a meal to a battle ever happens at the appointed time. As a general rule things happen too late, but just occasionally – just so that you shan't be able to depend on their happening late – they happen too early.'

The whole notion of what it means to be late is very different in time-bound and time-blind cultures. In a time-bound country like Britain, people are usually regarded as late if they arrive more than fifteen minutes after the appointed time, whereas in a time-blind country like Spain the permitted margin is more likely to be half an hour, if not longer. In time-bound and time-blind societies individuals are more prompt for meetings with important people than they are for meetings with unimportant people, but the amount of energy and anxiety expended on being punctual is quite different in the two types of society. In a time-blind society people allow much more time before they decide that someone is late or that they are not coming. Also, people are less likely to offer an explanation or an apology when they arrive late, and the person who has been kept waiting is less likely to expect one. The Spaniard, when he arrives an hour late, might mumble something which resembles an explanation, whereas the Englishman who is only a few minutes late is likely to offer a profuse apology, accompanied by an elaborate explanation.

Part of the reason for this is that people draw different inferences from lateness in different societies. In a time-bound society like Britain, lateness is usually interpreted as a sign of disorganisation or rudeness, whereas in a time-blind society like Spain it is more likely to be seen as a sign of status. In countries like Spain people see those who exceed the generous definition of lateness as having high status. The reason for this is that powerful people are much more likely to try and impress others with a sense of their own importance by keeping them waiting. This also happens in time-bound cultures, but it is far less frequent, and it certainly does not meet with the kind of grudging approval that one finds in Latin countries.

As societies become more time-bound, two things happen:

they adopt a more competitive attitude towards time, and their perceptions of 'fast' individuals become more favourable. This is very evident in Britain, where people are becoming more conscious of time and the demands that it imposes on them. There is a growing tendency for people to see tasks as tests of character, with time as a major adversary, and there is increasing talk about 'getting on top of things', 'getting ahead', 'catching up', and 'not being left behind'. The metaphorical language of time is very different in time-blind societies because time is not a cause of anxiety, and it is therefore not something which people feel they need to challenge or overcome.

The other thing that happens to societies as they become more time-bound is that their temporal centre of gravity begins to shift. Behaviours which were formerly regarded as evenly paced start to be seen as slow, and those which were once seen as pathologically fast come to be regarded as quite normal. Over the past decade or so the pace of life in Britain has increased enormously, and activities which used to be performed at a leisurely pace are now being done with much more urgency. A new breed of fast-living, fast-eating workaholics, armed with mobile telephones and time managers, has appeared on the scene, dashing about at a break-neck speed, like the images on time-lapse photography. Ten years ago this high-octane style of life would have appeared extremely odd. In fact it would probably have been diagnosed as hypermanic. But as the tempo of life in general has increased, these oddities have started to look quite normal, and all kinds of frenetic and manic behaviours have become de-pathologised. In the process, high-speed living has become a cultural model; it is now something that earns respect and which people feel they need to copy.

Queues

There are some nations that favour queues and some that don't. The British definitely fall into the first category, the Italians, Spaniards and French into the second. If there is one thing a Latin hates it is having to stand in line. So next time you are in Italy waiting to catch a bus, don't bother to look for the queue. You won't find one. What you will find instead is an amorphous crowd of people scattered round the bus-stop. There's no point trying to work out who arrived there first, who is entitled to a seat, or who is even waiting for the bus. None of this will matter when the bus arrives and you are swallowed up by a wave of people surging forward.

The Latin's disdain for queues never ceases to amaze the British, to whom it seems thoroughly inconsiderate and uncivilised. However, it is worth noting that there was a time when the British behaved exactly like the Latins whose disorderliness they despise. During the nineteenth century, the French rather than the British were the renowned queuers. The English philosopher Thomas Carlyle remarked: 'That talent of spontaneously standing in queue . . . distinguishes the French nation', an observation which is supported by the fact that the English language had to borrow the word 'queue' from the French word, meaning tail.

In the nineteenth century, national roles were completely reversed, because while the French were busy queuing like today's Britons, the English of the time were doing everything in their power to avoid standing in line. When the Russian revolutionary Alexander Herzen visited England in 1852, he noticed that 'nowhere is there a crowd so numerous, so close-packed, so frightening as in London, and it never in any case knows how to form a queue; the English always behave with their national obstinacy: they go on pressing forward for two hours, and at last they press through to somewhere. I have many times marvelled at this at the entrance to a theatre; if people walked one behind the

129

other, they could certainly get in in half an hour; but since they all press forward in one mass, the majority of those in front are thrust aside to the right and left of the door.'

The British may still be as obstinate as ever, but they have definitely abandoned the reservations they once had about queuing, and they will readily wait in line, even when it is not entirely necessary. As George Mikes remarked, 'An Englishman, even if he is alone, forms an orderly queue of one.' The British are now widely recognised as one of the world's foremost queue cultures, a doubtful honour they share with people like the Russians and the Poles. But what is it that the British find so attractive about standing in line, and are their reasons for queuing the same as those which motivate the eastern Europeans?

Several explanations have been given for the practice of queuing. According to the American anthropologist Edward Hall, queues are found in societies where people are treated as equals. Although it is true that queue cultures tend to espouse egalitarian ideals, it is certainly not the case that cultures which queue are necessarily more egalitarian than those which do not. Nor is it the case that queues guarantee identical outcomes to everyone who stands in line. In Britain, for example, everyone has to join the same queue to buy a railway ticket, regardless of whether they are travelling first or second class. Queues do not therefore guarantee equality, but they do promise to equate the amount of time that people spend waiting with how quickly they are served. The fact that queues deal with the fair distribution of time provides one of the clues why some countries favour queues and others don't: nations which value time and punctuality tend to favour queues, while those that take a more cavalier attitude to time prefer to do without them.

There are several other reasons why some nations queue more than others. One is the need for orderliness. It has frequently been noticed that the British have a compulsive need for orderliness, not in terms of requiring a neat and tidy environment, but in the sense of needing to know where they stand and what to expect. They usually feel uncomfortable when the situation is fluid or where there is a general free-for-all – when goods are not priced, when they have to bargain over a purchase, and when the rules of the game, so to speak, are not clear. Predictability is essential for the

British. That is why, when they settle abroad, they tend to produce pockets of Little Britain, microcosms of familiarity and security which fuel the illusion that home is never far away. The British attachment to queues is an expression of this need for orderliness and familiarity. When they join a queue they know what to expect and they can tell where they stand in relation to everyone else. For the British, a queue is therefore a cameo of an idealised society where everyone knows their place, accepts it, and doesn't try to steal an unfair advantage over others.

It is tempting to assume that queue cultures always queue and that non-queue cultures never do. Things, however, are not that clear-cut. Although the Italians regard queues as regimented and demeaning, it does not mean they never queue. They might refuse to line up at the bus-stop, but they will grudgingly do so at the supermarket check-out or at an airport check-in. The British are quite content to form disciplined queues at ticket counters, bus-stops, check-in counters, check-out counters, the January sales or the Buckingham Palace garden party. There are situations, however, where they are quite prepared to violate the basic tenets of queuing, and others where they simply won't queue at all. For example, when several queues are operating in parallel in a supermarket, you will often find the British hopping from one queue to another in order to gain an advantage over other customers who are standing in longer or slower queues. This is called 'jockeying', and it differs from 'colonising', which occurs when someone who is standing at the back of a queue notices a new counter opening up and moves across to start his or her own queue. What's remarkable about jockeying and colonising is that they are regarded as quite legitimate, even though they contravene the basic rule about first-come-first-served.

In this respect, the British appear to be somewhat inconsistent. They insist on applying the queuing rule to people who are in the same queue, but they won't apply it to people who hop between queues or who peel off the ends of existing queues in order to create new ones. There are other situations where the British show less than total dedication to queuing. For example, they don't usually form physical queues in shops and pubs. Instead they form 'invisible queues', expecting the person behind the counter to remember who is next. However, it doesn't always work out this way, and customers who have been overlooked frequently say so. There are even occasions where people who are about to be served forgo their turn by pointing out that someone else arrived before them. This kind of self-denial is something that the Latins cannot comprehend, unless it is performed with some ulterior motive in mind. Something the Latins do understand, however, is the scene that regularly takes place in the bar of an English theatre, where the jostle of people ordering drinks during the interval has all the self-effacing politeness of a rugby scrum. Contrary to the popular image, the British are not uncompromising queuers. They only queue where queuing is the convention, where enough people adhere to the rules, and where sanctions against queue-jumpers can be applied. Otherwise they will push and shove, behaving like the Latins whose apparent lack of public spiritedness they find so irritating.

In Russia, queuing is not only a national institution; it is a way of life. People queue for everything: for buses, trains, tickets, to buy essential foodstuffs, clothing and luxury goods, to pay their rent – they even queue to join other queues! In his book, *The Russians*, Hedrick Smith points out that although queuing is worldwide, Russian queues 'have a dimension all their own, like the Egyptian pyramids. They reveal a lot about the Russian predicament and the Russian psyche. And their operation is far more intricate than first meets the eye. To the passerby they look like nearly motionless files of mortals doomed to some commercial purgatory for their humble purchases. But what the outsider misses is the hidden magnetism of lines for Russians, their inner dynamics, their special etiquette.'

The typical ordeal for a Russian housewife might run as follows: she arrives at her local *Gastronom*, or foodstore, and promptly joins the queue for, say, sausages. When she has worked her way to the front of the queue, the person at the counter tells her the price of sausages. She then goes across and joins the queue for the cashier. When she gets to the front of this queue she pays the cashier, collects her receipt and then goes back to the sausage counter where she joins another queue to collect her purchase. Having worked her way through three queues, all the housewife has managed to buy is a few sausages. She now has to repeat the process in her search for other provisions, and she has to go through the same routine day after day. To make matters worse, certain goods are periodically not available, and the range of choice is either limited or non-existent.

Shopping may be fun in a consumer society, but for the Russians it has about as much attraction as an assault course. It is also notoriously wasteful. The Russian economist Yuri Orlov calculated that the Soviet population wasted about thirty billion hours a year queuing in shops – the equivalent, he points out, of a year's work for no less than fifteen million people. Five to six times as much time is spent queuing as actually buying articles, and the average shopper needs to visit three to five shops in order to make the daily purchases.

Russian shoppers frequently infer the scarcity of an item, and therefore its value, from the number of people who are lining up to buy it. When a housewife unexpectedly comes across a queue, her immediate reaction is to join the end of the line and only then to enquire what is being sold. Even if she does not need the item, she often ends up buying it, either because she assumes that it must be valuable if so many people want it, or because she knows she can sell it to somebody else afterwards. Consequently it is not just the needs of the individual, but the actual queue itself, which defines the value of an item.

Russians are very talkative in queues, using the opportunity to meet strangers and to while away the time in small-talk. However, the most important purpose of queue conversations is to give people a chance to persuade each other that the article they are about to buy is worth waiting for. The social pressure to agree can also lead to uniformity of purchase, with the result that individuals who wish to buy something else, or more or less of an item, are persuaded to make the same standard purchase as everyone else in the queue. This pressure to conform is also present in Polish queues. A Polish sociologist, Zbigniew Czwartosz, has described them as follows: 'I experienced this personally in a butcher's shop in Warsaw recently. The queue community agreed that, in addition to the official meat-rationing allocation, each person would get two pork legs. As that product is not used in my family kitchen, I categorically refused to buy it. I was persuaded that my wife would never forgive me, that my neighbours would be thankful if I resold it to them, etc. The saleswoman held two pork legs in her hands listening to the discussion, and then made the decision for me, putting them down on the balance and saying: "Please take them and don't hinder my work." I took it. The deviationist had been converted, and the social agreement saved.'

If there is one thing that the Russians and Poles detest more than standing in line it is someone who tries to jump the queue. People who ignore the rules usually attract a lot of noisy criticism, although certain exceptions are allowed. In Russia, card-carrying war veterans are permitted to go to the front of the queue, whereas in Poland there are generally two queues – a 'privileged' queue for the handicapped, the elderly, pregnant women and women carrying infants, and a 'normal' queue for everyone else. This explains why Polish mothers make a special point of lugging their babies round the shops with them; leaving them at home in the care of someone else deprives them of the opportunity to stand in 'privileged' queues and therefore increases the amount of time they spend shopping.

There are several reasons why the Russians, Poles and the inhabitants of other eastern European countries spend so much time queuing. Firstly there simply are not enough goods to satisfy demand. Secondly the availability of certain items is sporadic. This leads to panic buying and the formation of long queues, some of which are based on rumour. When people hear that a shop has received a consignment of new goods, they will sometimes queue up the day before the items appear on the shelves. The Russians have developed a unique system for getting round the prohibition against overnight queuing: when night falls they simply draw up a list of everyone in the queue, disband the queue, and reconstitute it the next morning before the shop opens. The third reason why eastern Europeans spend so much time queuing is that the major retail outlets for certain commodities are still controlled by the state. Where the state has a monopoly on the sale of goods and services, there is usually no incentive for it to invest in ways of speeding up the flow of customers.

Surveying the European scene, one finds marked national differences in the circumstances under which people queue, as well as quite distinct reasons for queuing. At one end of the spectrum are the Italians, Spaniards and French, the least queue-conscious of the European nations. There are situations where these nations queue, but they are rather rare. This is because Latins do not accept the basic philosophy behind queuing, namely the idea that people should be served in the order in which they arrive. For them a queue is an imposition, an unwarranted form of regulation and interference, like government. It is debasing, regimented, and it prevents individuals from using their intelligence and initiative to personal advantage.

At the opposite end of the spectrum are the other western European nations, who take an entirely different attitude to queues. For them queues are a rational solution to the problem of unnecessary competition. They are also fair because they prevent strong or scheming individuals taking advantage of others. It is perhaps not surprising that, of all the western European nations, the British should have developed the deepest attachment to queues, partly because they reduce the chances of physical contact between strangers – the British hate people breathing down their neck – but also because queues reduce the chances of people becoming angry and aggressive. The British have gained a reputation for being slow to anger because they stand in disciplined lines, but the more likely explanation is that they are so easily angered that they need the protection of queues. The Italians, on the other hand, have a reputation for being hot-blooded, but they are much less likely to resort to physical violence in public, which is another reason why they do not require the ritualised protection of queues.

Superficially the eastern Europeans appear to be as attached to queues as the British. However, their reasons for standing in line are quite different. In the eastern bloc countries, queues are primarily a consequence of shortages, commodity speculation, and the absence of competition. They are also the legacy of a deliberate policy to keep the populace uselessly occupied and docile. It did not require the intelligence of a Russian grand master to realise that people who spend their lives waiting in queues are not going to have a lot of time left over to think about ways of overthrowing the system.

Although there have been enormous changes in eastern Europe over the past few years, these have not yet affected the basic economic infrastructure. However, as central planning starts to give way to more market-based economies, we should expect to see an increase in the supply of consumer goods, and therefore less reason for people to stand in long queues. If this happens it will be interesting to see whether queues disappear altogether, whether eastern Europeans simply spend less time waiting in line, or whether their attachment to queues goes much deeper than a purely economic analysis would suggest. We may discover that the habit of queuing has become so ingrained that eastern Europeans continue to form waiting lines long after the need to do so has disappeared.

Reserve

Foreigners frequently comment on the diffident, withdrawn character of the English, and the fact that it takes so much effort to coax them out of their shells. The English have also recognised this about themselves. For example, in 1766 Tobias Smollett referred to 'this sort of reserve', which he considered to be 'peculiar to the English disposition'. Smollett compared the reticence of the English with the spontaneous affection of foreigners: 'When two natives of any other country chance to meet abroad they run into each other's embrace like old friends, even though they have never heard of one another until that moment; whereas two Englishmen in the same situation maintain a mutual reserve and diffidence, and keep without the sphere of each other's attraction, like two bodies endowed with a repulsive force.'

This is exactly what happened to the English traveller, Alexander Kinglake, as he was crossing the Syrian desert in 1835, on his way to Cairo. Kinglake had been travelling through the desert by camel for several days, without seeing anybody except the servants who were accompanying him. Then one day, without any warning he encountered another Englishman, also on a camel, travelling in the opposite direction. 'As we approached each other, it became with me a question whether we should speak. I thought it likely that the stranger would accost me, and in the event of his doing so, I was quite ready to be as sociable and chatty as I could be according to my nature; but still I could not think of anything particular that I had to say to him. Of course among civilised people, the not having anything to say is no excuse at all for not speaking; but I was shy, and indolent, and I felt no great wish to stop, and talk like a morning visitor, in the midst of those broad solitudes. The traveller, perhaps, felt as I did, for, except that we lifted out hands to our caps, and waved our arms in courtesy, we passed each other quite as distantly as if we had passed in Pall Mall. Our attendants, however, were not to be cheated of the delight that they felt in speaking to new listeners, and hearing fresh voices once more. The masters, therefore, had no sooner passed each other, than their respective servants quietly stopped and entered into conversation.'

What is it about the English that enables them to pass each other with no more than a peremptory wave of the hand? What is the 'repulsive force' that keeps them apart, and is it, as Smollett proposed, something that is peculiar to the English disposition?

One of the reasons why the English are so reserved is that they have a deep-seated desire not to impose themselves on other people, and not to be imposed upon by others. This trait, however, is not unique to the English, and it can be found in various other parts of Europe, including Finland, Sweden, Norway, and the north of Germany – in fact, everywhere where people are more concerned about not being disliked, rather than being liked. The motivating force behind interpersonal relations in these countries is a desire to avoid the negative consequences of other people's disapproval. This is quite the opposite to what one finds in the south of Europe, where people are motivated by the pursuit of approval.

Avoidance of disapproval is associated with several symptoms. First of all it causes people to give a wide berth to strangers, especially those who happen to have the additional disadvantage of being foreign. When people do encounter a stranger, they frequently position themselves as far away as possible, so that they don't have to engage the other person in conversation. In many cases it is the sheer agony of not knowing what to say that gives rise to this type of avoidance. The English, for example, often have a great deal of trouble starting up a conversation, which is part of the reason why topics like the weather and other forms of impersonal trivia feature so prominently in conversations, not only between strangers, but even between people who have known each other for years.

According to the American author, Susan Sontag, the Swedes have similar problems with conversations: 'Every time a conversation starts, you can feel the physical tension mount between the speakers . . . What to talk about is a problem.' 'Conversations,' she tells us, 'are always in danger of running out of gas, both from the imperative of secretiveness and even the positive lure of silence.' According to Sontag, the favourite topics of Swedes are the weather, money, liquor and plans of action, which, she tells us, can range from telling the assembled company that one is going to the toilet to announcing a vacation. Familiar and predictable topics ritualise the encounter, so that what is being said becomes less important than the fact that something is being said. Conversation becomes what the anthropologist Bronislaw Malinowski called 'phatic communion' – that is conversation for the sake of communion rather than for the exchange of information.

This style of conversation, which focuses on form rather than content, is particularly attractive to people like the Swedes and the English, who tend to be concerned about overstepping the mark and causing offence. The other great advantage of familiar topics is that they limit the extent to which other people can pry into one's own affairs. The English, for example, are extremely wary about disclosing personal information to other people, especially if it has something to do with the emotions. In fact it is not uncommon to find people in England who have known each other for many years, without having discovered anything of importance about each other – as the French novelist, André Maurois, found out when he shared a tent with a British officer during the First World War. Maurois and his English companion were together for six months, sharing a tent, provisions and the same bath tub, but in all that time the British officer never once asked him about his personal life.

There are two reasons why the English are so slow to ask questions of a personal nature. One is that they do not wish to impose, and the other is that they prefer to avoid a situation where other people feel entitled to impose on them. Keeping people at arms length is always advisable because it lowers the emotional tone of the relationship, and keeps things under control. One of the factors that threatens to make things less controllable is differences in social class. Like people in other stratified societies, the English prefer to fraternise with members of their own social class, and if they have to mix with members of other social classes they prefer them to be above rather than below themselves. When English people meet abroad the familiar cues of social class are often missing – particularly when nobody has had a chance to say anything and reveal their accent – and this leaves open the possibility that people may commit themselves to a conversation, and even an extended association, with individuals whom they would avoid on their native soil. The simple safeguard against this sort of error is to keep one's distance and not to have anything to do with one's compatriots when one is abroad, unless of course they have been properly vetted beforehand. This may exclude one from all kinds of interesting people, but it means that one won't have to deal with people whom one would otherwise avoid.

Shyness is another important factor behind the reserve of the English. Unlike the Latins, the English are particularly prone to shyness, self-consciousness and embarrassment. In his study of the English, which he conducted in the fifties, Geoffrey Gorer came to the conclusion that shyness was central to their character. In the large survey that he conducted, he discovered that over half the people interviewed admitted to having been 'exceptionally shy' in their youth. On the basis of this finding he came to the conclusion that the inherent shyness of the English was largely responsible for their 'distant cordiality' and the impression that they sometimes give of 'isolation and loneliness'.

Psychologists have discovered that shyness comes from the feeling that one is on display, and the concern that one might be negatively evaluated by other people. Because the English place disproportionate emphasis on negative, rather than positive evaluation, they are much more likely to experience shyness than, say, the Italians, who place relatively greater emphasis on positive rather than negative evaluation. It is not the case that Italians never experience shyness or self-consciousness; but rather that they do not experience these feelings to the same degree as the English. The English do not, for example, like to draw attention to themselves and they tend to react against people whom they perceive as show-offs. Although the English are sometimes very difficult to please, they will undergo all kinds of privations and inconvenience in order to avoid 'making a fuss'. The fact that they love moaning, but hate complaining, is often evident in restaurants, where you will hear people criticising the food or the service, but hardly ever hear them complaining to the waiter or the management. In Italy, it's often the other way round; you first see the customer complaining and then hear him moaning to his friends.

A few years ago a team of European psychologists, headed by

Robert Edelmann, conducted a cross-cultural study of embarrassment in Greece, Italy, Spain, Portugal, Britain and Germany. In
each country people were asked a series of questions about the
circumstances that caused them to feel embarrassed, the sensations
associated with embarrassment, and the strategies that they used to
cover it up. When the authors examined the physical symptoms of
embarrassment, they discovered that there were some interesting
differences between the countries. Blushing, for example, was more
strongly associated with embarrassment in Britain than it was in any
of the other countries, and the same applied to aversion of gaze and
facial touching. Increases in heart rate, however, were associated
with embarrassment more strongly in Greece and Portugal. The
social symptoms of embarrassment – that is, those that are apparent
to other people – are therefore much more prominent in Britain
than in the other countries. Whether the British experience more
embarrassment than people in other countries is difficult to say.
What does appear to be clear, however, is that they have a much
keener sense of their own embarrassment, and the feeling that
their awkwardness is evident to other people. This is partly due
to the fact that they are socially more reserved, but it may also be
a contributory factor to their feelings of reticence.

Salutations

The way that people greet and take leave of each other reveals a great deal about their relationship to each other. It also tells us a lot about the kind of society they live in. When we look round the world we find that every society has greeting rituals – some of them are very brief and basic, others are extremely elaborate. But regardless of how time-consuming or complex they are, all greeting rituals serve three basic functions. First of all, they reduce the inherent uncertainty which arises when people meet; secondly, they enable the participants to show that they have friendly intentions towards each other; and thirdly, they provide a framework within which people can establish or define the nature of their relationship.

People's relationships can be defined in many ways, but there are two underlying factors which are crucial to every relationship. One is the 'power' factor – that is, how people differ in terms of status – and the other is the 'solidarity' factor – that is, how much people like each other. This distinction between power and solidarity is reflected in the two basic types of greetings that people use – one being 'greetings of respect', which emphasise differences in power, the other being 'greetings of solidarity', which emphasise equality and affection. Greetings of respect include demeaning salutations like prostration, bowing and kneeling – in fact all those one-sided displays where one person shows respect for another, without that person doing likewise. Greetings of solidarity, on the other hand, are identifiable by their symmetry. They include salutations like embracing, mutual kissing and shaking hands – in other words, all those instances where individuals emphasise their equality or demonstrate their mutual affection by greeting each other with the same actions.

The greeting practices of different societies depend to a very large extent on how power is distributed. Traditional societies which are preoccupied with power tend to be organised hierarchically, usually with lots of social divisions and with very clear criteria for identifying everyone's position in society. In these societies a great deal of ceremonial work needs to be done, simply to support the social structure and to keep everyone in their place. One of the ways this is achieved is through elaborate greetings of respect which serve to remind people of their social position every time they meet. The situation in egalitarian societies, on the other hand, is quite different because much less emphasis is placed on status distinctions, with the result that there is less need for complicated greetings of respect. In fact in some egalitarian societies the importance of status distinctions has been reduced to the point where there are no longer specific greetings of respect. Instead, the task of conveying respect is performed by greetings of solidarity, like the handshake, which are specially adapted for this purpose when the occasion demands.

The way in which a society is structured appears to be a major factor in determining how many greetings of respect it possesses, as well as how complicated, time-consuming and demeaning the greetings of respect are likely to be. However, social structure appears to have very little effect on greetings of solidarity. The reason for this is that every society requires rituals through which individuals can display their equality and their affection for each other. This is as true of hierarchical societies as it is of those which are organised on egalitarian principles.

European conventions of greeting and parting have changed enormously over the past millennium. In medieval times it was common practice for men and women to pay homage to their over-lord by kneeling on one knee. Later on the bow was introduced. This was performed by drawing back the right leg so that both knees were bent, and by leaning forward. It was customary for men to perform the bow two or three times when approaching a king, and to repeat the process when leaving his presence. Doffing the hat was also part of the greeting ritual, and this was performed either before or during the act of bowing. The corresponding salutation for women was the curtsy, which involved genuflecting both knees and lowering the body.

These medieval greetings of respect differed from contemporary greetings of solidarity, which usually involved a mutual kiss, and sometimes an embrace. Kissing was used as a demonstration of affection and goodwill, and as a means of bestowing honour between members of the same sex, as well as between both sexes. Although the handshake was around at the time, it was not used as a salutation. Instead it was employed as a pledge and as a way of sealing agreements. Only later was it enlisted as a greeting of solidarity.

The bow and the curtsy remained popular for several centuries, but during the sixteenth century these greetings started to become much more studied and elaborate. Greater emphasis was now placed on doffing the hat, especially the manner in which it was performed. Popular etiquette decreed, for example, that the hat should always be grasped with the fingers rather than the whole hand, and that when it was removed it should be turned toward rather than away from the body, so that the inside of the hat remained concealed. To the bow was added the practice of kissing one's own hand – usually the left hand, which was regarded as the heart hand – and throwing the kiss in the direction of the person one was greeting.

This practice of throwing kisses was said to have originated in the Spanish courts during the sixteenth century, and then to have been introduced into Italy, France and England. In fact it was very much older, having been used by the ancient Greeks as a gesture of worship. The ancient Greeks employed two devotional postures in their religious activities. One involved an open-arm posture, with the hands raised and the palms exposed towards the heavens. This was used when praying to the gods. The other posture, which they called *proskynesis*, involved throwing a kiss, either towards the gods or in the direction of a religious statue. We can tell from the historical records that this gesture was performed not by placing the tips of all the fingers to the mouth – as the French do when praising something or someone – but by kissing the side of the index finger, while the other fingers remained curled up against the palm. The point of interest here is that although *proskynesis* fell out of favour with the early Christians, and was superseded by the various hand-clasp postures of prayer that are used today, it did not disappear altogether. In fact there are still places where it can still be found, and where it is executed in exactly the same way as it was by the ancient Greeks.

A good place to see *proskynesis* nowadays is at the festival of San Gennaro, the patron saint of Naples, when a glass phial containing the dried blood of the saint is brought out of safe-keeping and presented to the citizens of Naples who have gathered in the cathedral. The main purpose of the service is to pray for a miracle and to see whether the blood will turn liquid. If it fails to do so the congregation continues to pray, while the more impatient members of the congregation plead with the saint, and others curse him. This event is extremely important to Neapolitans, because when the blood fails to liquify it is regarded as an bad omen, a sign that a catastrophe like an earthquake, a volcanic eruption or the election of a communist mayor may be visited upon the city. But when the blood does turn to liquid the entire congregation erupts with joy. There are tears of ecstasy and shouts of *Miracolo! Miracolo!*. As the glass phial containing the blood is paraded past the congregation, people nearby reach out to touch it, and others to kiss it, while those who are too far away kiss their index fingers and throw their kisses at it – just as the ancient Greeks did in their devotions more than three thousand years ago.

At that time the kiss was used over the whole of Europe. It is quite possible, however, that it was not known to the ancient Irish and Welsh, because there was no Celtic word for 'kiss', and the words which were incorporated into Gaelic and Welsh later on were borrowed from the Latin for 'peace'. In fact the Irish and Welsh still retain a rather cautious attitude towards kissing. Havelock Ellis reports that up until the early part of this century the Welsh only kissed on very special occasions, and that a man could put away his wife for kissing another man, however innocently. The remnants of this attitude still persist in Celtic communities. Although the sight of necking couples is fairly common, social kissing is certainly not as prevalent in Ireland and Wales as it is in England and other parts of Europe.

English has only one word for 'kiss', whereas Latin has, or had, three. *Osculum* was the kiss of friendship, placed on the face or cheeks, *basium* was the kiss of affection, made on the lips, and *sauvium* was the lovers' kiss, again made on the lips. Social kissing was very much in vogue in ancient Rome, and it was common practice for people to salute each other with kisses on the hand, cheeks and lips. People scented their mouths with herbs and spices in order to smell sweet, and there was even a law, the so-called *jus osculi*, which decreed that all a woman's relatives were allowed to kiss her. Some people made a special point of extracting kisses from as many people as possible. These 'kissers', or *basiatores* as they were called, were constantly on the look-out for new victims on whom to clap their lips, and they were apparently everywhere. Writing at the time, Martial complained that 'Rome gives, on one's return after fifteen years' absence, such a number of kisses as exceeds those given by Lesbia to Catullus. Every neighbour, every hairy-faced farmer, presses on you with a strongly-scented kiss. Here the weaver assails you, there the fuller and the cobbler, who has been kissing leather; here the owner of a filthy beard, and a one-eyed gentleman; there one with bleared eyes, and fellows whose mouths are defiled with all manner of abominations. It was hardly worth while to return.' Eventually this vogue for kissing escalated to the point where the Emperor Tiberius was forced to issue an edict regulating these daily kisses or *cotidiana oscula*, so that life in Rome could be restored to some kind of normality.

Kissing was again very prominent during medieval times. Knights, for example, would kiss each other before the tournament, just as boxers today shake hands before a fight, and court pages were expected to kiss objects which had been handed to them to carry. Kissing was also used as a sign of solidarity, and as a way of paying one's respects. It was customary for people of the opposite sex, as well as members of the same sex, to exchange a kiss of friendship when they met, and it was common for women to greet guests and strangers with a kiss of welcome. The kiss of homage, which was one-sided, was also very prominent. The vassal would kiss the lord's hand or feet, or very occasionally his thigh, and afterwards he would offer a present or *baise-main* for the privilege of being able to kiss his master. If the lord was absent, the vassal was expected to kiss the door, the lock or the bolt of the house, all of which served as the lord's substitute.

Today, the act of kissing someone's hand has virtually disappeared. Up until the last world war it was fairly common, in countries like Poland, Hungary and Czechoslovakia, for men to kiss a lady's hand on meeting or taking leave of her. In some countries there are pockets of cultural resistance where this practice can still be found, but they are dwindling very fast. There are also countries where hand-kissing disappeared a long time ago, but where greeting expressions which refer to the habit continue to be used. In Austria, for example, when a man meets a lady he might say *Küss die Hand* to her, even though he has never kissed anyone's hand, and has no intention of doing so.

There are two major categories of greetings – namely those where the greeters make physical contact with each other, and those where they do not. 'Non-contact' greetings usually occur when people don't have enough time or the inclination to stop and talk to each other, and where they exchange 'distance greetings' instead. Typically these involve a verbal exchange, but they can also take the form of a gesture, like a wave of the hand or a dip of the head, performed either in conjunction with a verbal greeting or on its own.

The 'head-dip' is used all over Europe, but there is one version of the greeting which is peculiar to Britain. This is the British 'head-cock', an action that is executed by moving the chin to one side while the top of the head is brought forward and down on the other. This has the effect of producing a head-dip with a twist in it. Foreigners who encounter this British salutation for the first time often have difficulty deciphering its meaning, and even when they do recognise it as a localised greeting, they still find it very strange.

Interestingly, there are at least four possible origins for the British head-cock. One is the extinct action of tugging the forelock, a submissive greeting which was widely used by peasants during medieval times. Another is the equally defunct practice of touching the brim of one's cap or hat, either as a substitute or as a prelude to doffing it. Both of these actions produce an asymmetric lowering of the head, not dissimilar to that of the head-cock. Winking is another possible source of the head-cock. Winking is used as a gesture of complicity, and it frequently has the involuntary effect of cocking the head to one side. In fact it is not uncommon for the head-cock greeting to be performed together with a wink, reinforcing the suggestion that the two actions are linked historically. Moreover, even when the head-cock is produced on its own, it frequently conveys the same message of complicity as the wink itself.

Finally the head-cock may simply have originated from a

combination of the two basic head movements which are associated with submission in humans. One is the 'head-dip', and
the other is the 'head-tilt'. The head-dip is performed by drop-
ping the head forward, and it has numerous parallels in the
body-lowering displays of submission that are found throughout
the animal world. The head-tilt, on the other hand, is performed by inclining the head to one side. This gesture owes
its submissive character to overall lowering of the body, but
more importantly to the fact that tilting the head towards the
shoulder is reminiscent of the movement that children make
when seeking comfort in their parents' arms. The head-cock
is therefore a cross between the head-dip and the head-tilt, a
greeting which contains the submissive elements of both of these
actions.

The second category of salutations includes those where the
greeters make physical contact with each other. These range from
the handshake, which is the least intimate, through cheek-kissing
and embracing, to kissing on the mouth, which is the most intimate
form of contact greeting. These greetings are to be found all over
Europe, but the extent of their popularity, and the conventions
governing who uses which type of greeting with whom, can vary
enormously from one country to another.

The basic message of the handshake is equality. It provides both
parties with a chance to perform the same actions, and therefore
to express their solidarity. It is this that has made the handshake
so popular, and helped it to displace greetings like the bow
and the curtsy, which serve to emphasise rather than minimise
differences between people. Although the basic message of the
handshake is equality, the salutation permits an enormous range
of enthusiasm and affection, depending on how violently the hands
are pumped, how firmly they are gripped, and a variety of other
factors connected with the participants' demeanour.

Up until the middle ages the handshake, or handclasp, was
used almost exclusively for the purpose of sealing agreements and
showing goodwill. It was only later that the act of joining hands
became a greeting, and started to spread around Europe. According
to the historian Theodore Zeldin, the handshake was exported from
England to France, where it became known as *Le Handshake*. The
vigour with which it is performed in France today suggests that it

had an enthusiastic reception, because the French always shake hands on being introduced, and on meeting and parting, and it is not uncommon for them to shake hands with the same person several times during the same day. The Russians are also keen on shaking hands several times a day, and so are the Italians and the Spaniards. The British and the Germans tend to restrict their handshakes to one on meeting and another on parting.

There are also other cultural differences in the way the handshake is executed. The French, for example, tend to employ a determined and abrupt pump of the hand, whereas the Italians are more likely to draw out the process, and to hold on to each other while they are exchanging their verbal greetings. The conventions surrounding who should shake hands with whom also differ nationally. In France handshaking is deemed to be appropriate for strangers, regardless of their sex. However, in Britain there is a tendency for the handshake to be restricted to meetings between male strangers, whereas meetings between female strangers, and men and women who do not know each other, are much more likely to involve a non-contact greeting. This may reflect the deep sense of indecision that the British experience when meeting new people. It might also have something to do with the fact that the handshake was originally a means of sealing agreements, and therefore an action which was once very much a part of the male preserve.

If one were to take a train journey which stopped at all the capital cities of Europe, one would soon notice that people greet each other and say goodbye in all kinds of ways, and that while some practices are confined to specific countries, others show no respect for national boundaries. The embrace is a good example of a greeting which can be found in several countries. In Italy, where it is known as the *abraccio*, it is used as an expression of love and affection by both sexes and by people of all ages, sometimes with one or several kisses, sometimes on its own. The embrace is also used in Greece and Yugoslavia, as well as in eastern European countries like Poland, Bulgaria and Russia.

What is so interesting about the embrace in eastern Europe is the way it has been adapted for political purposes and used as a public expression of fraternal solidarity. For several decades the embrace, or 'bear-hug', was a standard feature of Soviet domestic and foreign policy. Khruschev and Brezhnev, in particular, made a habit of wrapping visiting dignitaries and returning cosmonauts in their arms, and planting a few kisses on their cheeks for good measure. When Gorbachev came to power he also followed this practice, but he later abandoned the bear-hug in favour of the handshake. The simple reason for this is that in eastern Europe the political embrace has become a powerful symbol of the communist establishment. It is therefore something which the new breed of politicians needs to avoid if they are to distance themselves from the old order. Here, as elsewhere, the way in which individuals greet each other says a lot about the kind of people they are.

Shrugs

Although the shrug is found throughout Europe, it is more closely associated with certain cultures than others. We speak quite readily of a 'Gallic shrug', an 'Italian shrug' and a 'Jewish shrug', but we do not, for example, refer to a 'Swedish shrug' or a 'Norwegian shrug'. This is not because the Swedes and Norwegians never shrug; it is simply that they don't use the gesture as extensively as the French, the Italians or the Jews. There are several reasons why the shrug is so popular in these societies. The first is that the shrug is highly expressive and therefore perfectly suited to societies that engage in dramatic displays. The other reasons for its popularity relate to the origins of the gesture, its constituent movements and the messages that it conveys.

The shrug is an extremely fascinating gesture, not least because it forms the basis of Darwin's theory of emotional expression, but also because it is a rather complex action which can be performed in several ways. Darwin made the mistake of suggesting that the shrug can be understood in contrast to the display of indignation. This happens to be incorrect because the major constituents of the shrug are raised shoulders and lowering of the head to one side, and there is no way of producing the 'opposite' of this display. The interesting thing about the shrug – unlike, say, a dominance display – is that it doesn't have an opposite gesture. It exists, quite separately, as a signal of helplessness, inability and resignation. This constellation of messages makes the shrug extremely attractive to people who might wish, for historical or personal reasons, to deny responsibility or to show that they are not in a position to satisfy someone's request. The shrug is the gestural cop-out *par excellence*. It is hardly surprising, therefore, that it should enjoy such widespread use in societies where, because of the close-knit nature of society, people are constantly making demands on each other and at the same time trying to keep their options open.

151

An important feature of the shrug is that it can be performed in several ways. The basic components of the gesture consist of raised shoulders, raised arms, exposed palms, raised eyebrows, the head lowered to one side, and the mouth shaped like an inverted 'U'. The shrug can be performed with all of these components, with some of them, or with just one of the components – for example, by raising just the shoulders or only shrugging the mouth. Which components people incorporate into their shrugs depends on their mood and the message they are trying to convey. But the way they assemble their shrugs also has a lot to do with their nationality.

There are two reasons why the shrug conveys a message of helplessness, and each is associated with a different component of the gesture. The first component is raising the shoulders. This action forms part of the involuntary 'startle response', which occurs when people are suddenly frightened. In the case of the startle response, the raised shoulders are designed to protect the head from injury, whereas in the case of the shrug the same action is intended to convey an image of helplessness, possibly even to give the person performing the gesture a sense of comfort. The second component of the shrug is raised arms. The reason why this action conveys an image of helplessness is that children use this gesture when they want to be picked up by their parents. This is one of the earliest gestures that children learn, and it is almost inevitable, therefore, that it should end up as part of the shrug.

Although shrugs come in different shapes and sizes, there is a tendency for Italians to shrug with raised shoulders as well as raised arms, and a corresponding tendency for Eastern European Jews to raise their shoulders but not their arms. Consequently, while the Jewish shrug tends to rely on the self-protective origins of the gesture, the Italian shrug depends on its self-protective as well as its parental origins. The French, on the other hand, show no preference either way. They do, however, show a penchant for the mouth-shrug.

The mouth-shrug is produced by forming the lips into an inverted 'U', and it can be accompanied by any combination of raised shoulders and arms, closed eyes, raised brows and a cock of the head to one side. On the whole, French shrugs tend to be rather economical, with less attention being paid to the shoulders and arms than to the head and face. The classic French mouth-shrug is accompanied by the expression *Boff!*, an ejaculation

which neatly summarises the bored, disdainful tone that the French
have managed to graft on to the basic message of the gesture. In fact,
French shrugs frequently contain a dismissive tone, almost as if the
shrugger were saying something like 'I'm helpless to comment, I'm
bored and uninterested, and anyway it's irrelevant!' This contrasts
with the messages contained in other ethnic variants of the shrug.
While the Italians, for example, seem to be saying 'What's it got to
do with me? I'm innocent!', the message conveyed by the Jewish
shrug is something like 'What can I do? I'm powerless.'

The reason why the mouth-shrug is so popular with the French
is that France is basically a mouth-culture. The gustatory preoccupations of the French, their love of wine and their deep attachment
to their language have all conspired to ensure that taste is the major
sense of the French, and the mouth their most public organ. This is
also reflected in the anatomy of French gestures and the way that
French is spoken.

The mouth is involved in a large number of French gestures.
One is lip protrusion. Like the mouth-shrug, this gesture is sometimes executed with closed eyes, raised brows and a tilted head.
The messages it conveys are boredom, indecision and rejection
– explicitly, *Je m'en fous* – I don't give a damn. According
to Lawrence Wylie, the author of *Beaux Gestes*, this attitude
has become a national lifestyle in France: 'It is inevitable in
the land of *Le Jemenfoutisme* that there should be a long list
of gestures indicating a rejection of responsibility, the belittling
of one's errors, the affectation of indifference.' An even more
famous French gesture is the act of kissing one's finger-tips as
a sign of approval. 'For foreigners,' says Wylie, 'probably the
most characteristic French gesture is *Splendide!*, the holding of
the joining tips of the fingers to one's puckered lips, and, with a
facial expression of exquisite pleasure, throwing out a kiss. Since
Les plaisirs de la bouche, eating and drinking, are so essential to the
French good life, it is natural that the sensation of exquisite taste
should be associated with the mouth.'

The other reason why the mouth plays such a prominent role
in France is that spoken French is articulated very differently from
other languages. Visitors to France often remark on the unusual
way the French move their mouth and lips when speaking. This
is quite correct. The French do employ a very different dialect of

mouth movements from other Europeans, and this is due to the fact that the sounds of the language involve very different shapes of the mouth. In *The French*, Theodore Zeldin explains the situation as follows: 'Their lips have to protrude when they speak because the French language has more sounds which require the rounding of the lips than other languages. Nine out of the sixteen French vowels involve strong lip-rounding, compared with only two out of the twenty English vowels. (Germans have five lip-rounding vowels.) The degree of lip-rounding in French is moreover greater because vowels following consonants often have to be prepared before the consonant is uttered.' In French the actual shape of vowels and consonants therefore forces speakers to use their mouths and lips quite differently. This contributes to the prominence of the mouth in French culture as well as to the overall appearance of the face when French is being spoken.

An Italian shrug

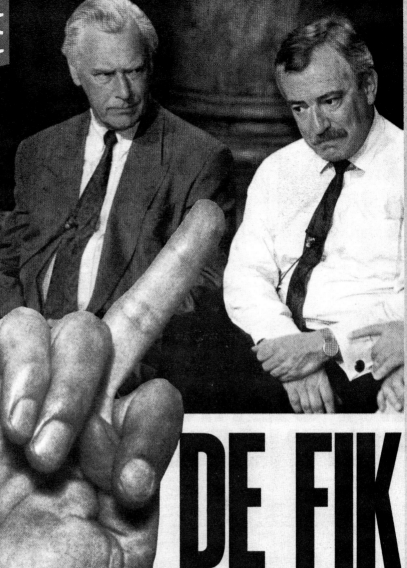

JUBEL-RUS OVER NEJ'ET

UFFE: HJÆLP MIG

ÆMPE-EPORTAGE M VALG-YSEREN

DE FIK FINGEREN

The Danish response to the European Community referendum in 1992.

Time

Time is the fundamental basis of human experience, and it is also the most mysterious. One of the reasons why we have such difficulty coming to grips with time is that it is totally intangible. It is not like physical size or distance, or like heat and cold, which we can apprehend directly through our senses. In the case of time we have to rely on changes in the outside world, or on clocks and watches, to inform us about duration. But even with the assistance of these artificial devices, it is obvious that our experience of time is not always constant because there are occasions when time appears to speed up, and others when it appears to slow down or even to stop. These sensations of the passage of time have a lot to do with the activities we perform, and how boring or enjoyable we find them. They are also intimately connected with the kind of society we live in, and the subtle ways that it prepares us to think about time and how to use it.

Historians tell us that theories about the nature of time have changed dramatically since the middle ages, and anthropologists have shown that people in other parts of the world have very different views of time from our own. Against the background of these historical and cultural variations there has been an understandable temptation to assume that Europeans have a standard set of attitudes to time – that because they are part of the same civilization, people all over Europe value and categorise time in much the same way. In fact, this is not the case.

In Europe today there is a wide range of attitudes and relationships to time. At the one extreme are those societies where people are ensnared by time, where everyone is a captive of the clock. These are the 'time-bound' societies, and they include countries like Germany, Switzerland, Sweden, Norway, Denmark and Britain. At the other extreme are the 'time-blind' societies, where people hardly notice time and where it sometimes appears to play no role in their lives at all. Spain, Portugal and Greece are the best examples of time-blind societies, followed by southern Italy and the south of France.

In a time-bound society time is seen as linear – in other words as a straight line extending from the past, through the present, to the future. In a time-blind society, on the other hand, there is a tendency for time to be seen as cyclical – that is, in terms of the natural cycles of day and night, the lunar cycle and the seasons, rather than as a progression towards an indefinite future. The linear conception of time encourages two further notions which are found in time-bound societies, but not in time-blind societies. One is the idea that time is an important yardstick of people's activities and achievements, and the other is that time is a valuable resource in its own right. In its capacity as a measure of other things, time is seen as rigid and divisible – rather like a steel tape-measure or a wooden ruler – while in its capacity as a resource, it is seen as a finite and irreplaceable form of currency. In a time-bound society, therefore, time is invariably construed in economic terms, which is why people talk about 'scarcity of time', 'investing time' and 'wasting time', and why 'time is money'.

The role of time in a time-blind society is very different. Because time is seen as cyclical, it is totally unsuitable as a measure of anything else, and it has little value in its own right. In a time-blind society time is not seen as finite and irreplaceable, but rather as something which, in the cyclical nature of things, is constantly replenishing itself. There is therefore no sense in which time could be regarded as scarce. If anything, there is a surplus of it.

The idea that time has no intrinsic value of it own is very evident in countries like Greece, particularly in the villages, where a great deal of time is devoted to idle conversation and studied inactivity. Life here is managed at an unhurried pace. There is no sense of urgency, no anxiety about deadlines, and no need to do today what can be put off till tomorrow. The economic view of time has very little attraction for the Greeks. As the anthropologist Margaret Mead has pointed out, Greeks do not try to save time or to budget it; they simply 'pass the time', experiencing things as they happen, without bothering to consider how they might fit into a schedule. Clocks seldom regulate their lives, unless they happen to live in the city. But even then, time is less important than one's relationships with other people.

In Greece – as in all time-blind societies – relationships always take precedence over time. That is why the Greeks always make a point of showing that they have time for each other, and why they are so easily offended when people fuss about time or are not prepared to donate it to the cause of friendship. In countries like Germany and Britain, clock-watching is quite acceptable, and people do not get upset when their guests have to leave slightly earlier than expected. In these countries it is generally accepted that relationships have to adapt to the requirements of time, rather than the reverse. In Greece, however, time is expected to conform to the needs of relationships. Here, an early departure can very easily cause offence, because when someone leaves his friends' home earlier than expected it is taken as a sign that he has something better to do, or that he values his time more than he values his friends.

In a time-bound society life is dominated by the clock, and by schedules, delivery dates, agendas, deadlines and all the other paraphernalia of measured time. A time-bound society operates according to what the psychologist Robert LeVine calls 'clock time'. This means that each day is carefully divided into separate time segments, and that different events are then assigned to these segments, each with a specified time for starting, and possibly a time for ending as well. In a time-blind society, however, people operate in 'event time'. This means that they pay more attention to the events themselves than to the time required to complete them. In a time-blind society an event is much more likely to be defined in terms of the people who take part in it, rather than when it is expected to start and stop. The event simply begins when a sufficient number of participants have arrived, and it ends when there is a general feeling that the event has run its course.

In a time-bound society the emphasis is often on the time at which an event occurs rather than on the event itself. Consequently the times at which events occur can more easily be changed; it doesn't matter too much when they take place, provided that everyone agrees on a time. This kind of arbitrariness is seldom found in a time-blind society, where time is seen as cyclical, and where there is therefore a much stronger sense of certain events having their proper time. In a time-blind society there may not be very much precision about when events begin and end, but there is often a very clear consensus about the approximate times when they should take place. This is certainly the case in Spain.

The Spaniards are renowned for their casual attitude to time and for their lack of punctuality. They are also famous for *mañana*, which means 'tomorrow' (or literally 'the morning'), and which has become an international byword for procrastination. Although the Spanish are very relaxed about time, there are certain events – like lunch, for example – which they are very loath to reschedule. The British and the Germans are quite prepared to abandon convention, and to take lunch much earlier or much later than usual when the need arises. But not the Spanish. For them, lunch has a 'natural' time. Consequently any attempt to shift it to another time is likely to meet with intense opposition.

There seems to be a rather interesting paradox here, because although the British and the Germans are compulsive clock-watchers, they appear to have a rather undifferentiated view of time. The Spaniards, on the other hand, pay much less attention to time, but they have fairly strong ideas about certain parts of it. It is almost as if the Spaniards possess two kinds of time – 'sacred time', which is dedicated to important activities like eating lunch, sleeping and being with one's family, and 'profane time', which is devoted to everything else. While the Spaniards are quite prepared to ignore the demands of events that occur in profane time, they steadfastly resist any attempts to rearrange those which take place in sacred time.

This is certainly borne out by Spanish business practices. For example, when a salesman calls on a client in Spain, he has to be prepared for interruptions. It is not unusual for the meeting to be repeatedly disturbed – not only by long telephone conversations, but also by interventions from the secretary and other members of staff. To the Spaniards these interruptions are quite normal. They are the way business is conducted. However, to the visitor from Britain or Germany, a Spanish business meeting looks like a three-ring circus. The constant breech in proceedings is quite unbearable because it offends the principle that time which has been put aside for a certain purpose should only be used for that purpose, until it has been agreed that it can be used for something else. The individual segments that make up business time in Britain and Germany are dedicated to specific purposes, and the boundaries of each time segment remain impermeable to intrusions by other activities. In Spain, however, this is only true of 'sacred time'. The segments which make up 'profane time', which is when most business is conducted, have highly permeable boundaries, and consequently it is very easy for activities which have nothing to do with the purpose of a meeting to intervene and to take over the proceedings.

The French also set great store by lunch, especially the so-called 'business lunch', where gustatory pleasures are combined with the needs of business. If one did not know better one might imagine that it was quite in order to talk business throughout a business lunch. But in fact the French have an unwritten rule which requires that the subject is not raised until the main course has appeared. Up to this point the conversation may cover any topic, provided it is not business. In this way the French business lunch manages to set aside sacred time for the enjoyment of food and wine, as well as profane time for the pursuit of business. It also provides people with a chance to show that they appreciate the good things in life, and that business is not the only thing that brings them together. Showing oneself to be a fully rounded person is very important in France, because a lot of business is based on liking and mutual respect. These issues also play an important role in business in other countries. But in a country like France, which has a much softer, almost feminine approach to interpersonal relations, they are absolutely crucial.

There are other ways in which time-bound and time-blind societies differ from each other. The anthropologist Edward Hall has proposed that there are two systems of time – what he calls 'monochronic time' and 'polychronic time'. Societies which operate according to monochronic time tend to do one thing at a time, whereas those which adhere to polychronic time frequently get involved in several activities at the same time. Time-bound countries like Britain, Germany and Switzerland tend to be monochronic in their outlook because they organise events in terms of schedules. Moreover, their time boundaries are usually impermeable, which makes it difficult for people to do several things at the same time, or to switch between different activities during the same time segment. Time-blind societies like Spain, Greece and France are the other way round. They are polychronic because they have a more cyclical notion of time and because their time boundaries tend, on the whole, to be more permeable. As a result, people find it easier to do several things at the same time, or in very quick succession, and they are much more tolerant of interruptions.

The French are a good example of a polychronic society because they like to get involved in parallel activities, and they don't always adhere to schedules, appointments and deadlines. But, according to Edward Hall, the French are complicated, because while they are polychronic in their behaviour, they are monochronic in their intellectual pursuits. It is certainly the case that the French like to occupy themselves with several things at the same time, while in their thinking they tend to be logical and single-minded, but there are exceptions that prove the rule. One need only think of how Balzac locked himself away for a month while he wrote *La Femme Supérieure*, without even shaving or washing, to see that the French are quite capable of behaving monochronically. Compare this with the case of Sir Richard Burton, who had eleven tables in his study, on which he prepared and wrote four different books, and one can see how the English can also behave polychronically. Clearly, individuals don't always use time in the ways that their cultures prescribe.

Another way that European cultures differ is in terms of 'time orientation' – that is, the extent to which they are oriented towards the past, the present and the future, and how far their time horizons extend, either back into the past or forward into the future. In most European countries people have a keen sense of history and a very definite orientation toward the past. In this respect they are very different from, say, the Americans, who tend to have one eye on the present and the other on the immediate future. As far as Americans are concerned, history began with the arrival of Christopher Columbus, whereas for Europeans it goes back to classical times, if not beyond. For centuries the continent has been a battleground, with armies raging back and forth, bringing death and destruction. Borders have been moved, populations displaced, and hardly a generation has passed without the map of Europe changing. It is not surprising, therefore, that Europeans have such a disturbed sense of the past, or such a cautious attitude toward the future.

There are five time periods to which cultures can orient – namely the distant past, the recent past, the present, the immediate future and the distant future. Britain, for example, is oriented very much to the distant and recent past. It is also preoccupied with the present and, to a lesser extent, with the immediate future, but it is not particularly concerned about the distant future. This may explain why such a small proportion of Britain's gross national product is devoted to basic scientific research, why British inventions are usually exploited abroad, and why business is geared to quick returns rather than to building a secure base for the future. In these respects Britain is very different from Germany, which is almost Japanese in its orientation to time. Like the Japanese, the Germans have a long view of the future, which explains why they place so much emphasis on education, training and basic research, and why investment is dictated by long-term rather than short-term considerations.

The Russian attitude to the past is very different from that of the Germans, because while the Germans prefer to concentrate on the period leading up to this century, the Russians invested an enormous amount of energy reminding themselves of their glorious achievements since the revolution. However, things in Russia have changed enormously, and much more attention is now being paid to the history of Russia under the Tsar, and to the disasters that have occurred under communism. On the whole, Russians have a very slow-moving, almost ponderous view of time. The sheer size of the country, and the slow pace of life associated with long distances and long winters, has produced a situation in which time is seen in large chunks, and patience has become an essential virtue. As the Russian expert Michael Binyon points out, 'Time for the Russians . . . comes in large units. If you drop in on friends, you stay for hours, even days. If you are ice-fishing in winter, you remain immobile beside the hole in the ice almost until you have frostbite. If you go mushrooming, you tramp through the woods from dawn till dusk. No one thinks twice about waiting three hours in a queue, travelling four days in a train or letting their grandmothers spend five hours at a Russian Orthodox Easter service.'

For a long time it was assumed that the ills of the Soviet economy, like shortages, delays and queues, were entirely the fault of communism, and that once a free-market economy was introduced, these problems would start to disappear. Although there is a lot to recommend this argument, it overlooks the fact that many of the ways in which Russians use time were established long before the introduction of communism. In some respects the Russians are like Latins, because their relationships with their family and friends are extremely important to them, and they usually take precedence over the demands of time. The official values of the state, however, were just the opposite, because they were associated with efficient production, schedules and deadlines – in other words, issues which are of secondary importance to Russians. For years a battle raged between the official ideology of the state and the indigenous values of the people, with most of the victories going to the people. The attitudes to time which the state tried to reform are very old and entrenched, and they are likely to be around long after communism has been dismantled.

Touch

The cross-cultural evidence shows that southern Europeans engage in much more physical contact in public than do other Europeans. Of the southern Europeans, the Italians are probably the most tactile. They are endlessly patting, stroking or prodding each other, or wrapping themselves in each other's arms. As D.H. Lawrence put it, they are like lemon trees, 'happiest when they are touching one another all round.'

Although (or possibly because) the Italians are so tactile, they have very strict rules about who may touch whom. It is permissible for Italian men to touch each other, provided there is no obvious status differential, in which case only the superior is permitted to touch his subordinate. In these circumstances touch is used as a power device, to keep the other person in check and subtly to remind him of his inferior position. On the other hand, when men are of roughly equal status, all kinds of social touching is allowed, and it is not unusual to see Italian men hugging each other, walking arm in arm, or even holding hands on the street. Mutual touching is also a standard feature of their conversations, where it is used to cement relationships, to regulate turn-taking, and to show that each person has access to the other's body space.

Not surprisingly, the popular image of Italians is that of a highly tactile people. But the Italians' use of touch is in fact not as extensive or as promiscuous as it might appear. With a few exceptions, men are entitled to touch each other, and so are women, but physical contact between the sexes is discouraged, particularly when people do not know each other well. Although the rules against cross-sex touch do not apply to people who are married, it is nevertheless quite remarkable how little contact occurs between husbands and wives, even in the privacy of their own homes.

In a 'contact' society like Italy, one would expect husbands and wives to hold hands in public. As it happens, this is quite unusual, much more rare in fact than it is in reputed 'non-contact' societies like Britain, Germany and Holland, where couples can often be seen linking arms or holding hands. There appear to be several reasons why Italian married couples are reluctant about touching in public. First of all, masculinity is an extremely important value in Italian society, and partly because of this the sexes tend to be separated. Holding hands, or showing one's affection for another male, is quite in order because it excludes women and respects the values of masculinity. Holding hands with one's wife, on the other hand, excludes other males and suggests that one is dependent on a woman. This is the last thing one should do in a macho society – unless, of course, the woman happens to be one's mother.

The other reason why touching is so infrequent between husband and wife is that Italian marriages rapidly become de-sexualized, if not in substance then certainly in appearance. In Italy it is very common to see young courting couples holding hands and kissing in public. But after they get married, and especially after they have had children, couples quickly abandon their public displays of affection. After marriage the Italians' ambivalent attitude towards sex comes to the fore, and all the signals which couples use to celebrate their courtship and to show that they use sex for purposes other than procreation, start to disappear.

The English have their own mixed feelings about touch, as the word and some of its derivatives demonstrate. The English expression 'keep in touch' unites the ideas of physical and social contact, giving the impression that touch plays a central role in sustaining people's relationships, which of course it doesn't. Other meanings of the word suggest that the English have a rather negative attitude to touch – as evidenced by their use of 'touched' to mean crazy, and 'touchy' meaning irritable or overly sensitive – in other words, not liking to be touched. These negative attitudes are also revealed in certain dispositions of the English, like their avoidance of close proximity and their readiness to say sorry when they accidentally bump into other people: so concerned are the English about unintended physical contact, that they will even apologise when it is not their fault.

Over the past few years the English have become much more tactile. The sight of men embracing and even kissing each other is no longer a cause for alarm, as it was a few decades ago. Although the English are changing their ways, and becoming more like the Mediterraneans, there are still certain residual signs of their deep-seated reservations about physical contact. This is evident when Englishmen hug each other, because instead of placing their head over each other's shoulders, as eastern Europeans do, they tend to turn their head away. Another revealing sign of English discomfort is the habit of patting someone on the back while hugging them. Patting is generally regarded as a sign of reassurance, a way of showing that one cares for someone. This is certainly the function of patting in some situations. However, in the case of the hug, patting serves as a 'release signal' – it pretends to be a gesture of reassurance, but its real purpose is to inform the other person that one has had enough. Englishmen who hug each other think that they are being friendly by patting each other on the back. Although they don't realise it, they are in fact bringing the hug to a close, and at the same time revealing how uncomfortable they feel about being in close physical contact with each other.

In the process of becoming more tactile, the English are slowly returning to a situation they abandoned a few centuries ago, when touch played a much more important role in people's lives. During the middle ages, it was widely believed that those who suffered from scrofula, a glandular disease, could be cured by being touched by their monarch. This belief in the 'royal touch', as it was called, lasted from the time of Edward the Confessor right up to 1714, when Queen Anne performed the last royal touch. In France, the other country where this belief was held, the last royal touch was performed in 1825, by Charles X. Some English monarchs took their responsibilities seriously, others thought the whole thing a nonsense. Elizabeth I, for example, seldom performed the ceremony, whereas Charles II is reported to have touched nearly 100,000 people between the time of his restoration and his death. It is remarkable to think that people in England believed in the power of touch for almost 700 years, and that generation after generation went to see their monarch in order to be cured. It is even more remarkable to think that there was a time when close physical contact was an integral part of English conversation.

When coffee was first imported into England during the eighteenth century, coffee-houses opened up all over London. They soon became important meeting places, full of smoke, gossip and political intrigue. Coincidentally, with the emergence of the coffee-houses, there appeared a new conversation technique 'button-holding'. This involved holding the button of someone's jacket or coat with one hand to make sure they couldn't get away, while the other hand was free to gesticulate. This method of ensnaring conversation partners soon became widespread, making it difficult for those who had been taken hostage to make their get-away. However, some people, like the author Charles Lamb, found their own solution to the problem. Lamb tells the following story:

> I was going from my house in Enfield to the India-house one morning, and was hurrying, for I was late, when I met Coleridge, on his way to pay me a visit; he was brimful of some new idea and, in spite of my assuring him that time was precious, he drew me within the door of an unoccupied garden by the road-side, and there, sheltered from observation by a hedge of evergreens, he took me by the button of my coat, and closing his eyes commenced an eloquent discourse, waving his right hand gently, as the musical words flowed in an unbroken stream from his lips. I listened entranced; but the striking of a church recalled me to a sense of duty. I saw it was of not use to attempt to break away so, taking advantage of his absorbtion in his subject, I, with my penknife, quietly severed the button from my coat and decamped.

By the end of the eighteenth century, button-holding had disappeared. Englishmen had abandoned the practice of clinging on to each other while in conversation, and they had retreated to a distance where such liberties could not be taken. By the Victorian era a more civil, detached style of behaviour had evolved, and this remained in place until very recently. It is only during the past decade or so that the English have started to become more proximate and tactile in their relations with each other – in other words, 'less English'.

Understatement

One of the things that foreigners notice about the English is their use of understatement. In his book, *The English: Are They Human?*, the Dutch author George Renier commented on the tendency of the English to downplay the significance of events, and to make everything seem less important than it really is. 'The continental, the Irishman, the American – those, in short, whom I like to call ordinary human beings – overstate. They overstate with vigour, often with art, but without the least self-consciousness, shame or wish to deceive. They are poets and advertisers. The English have their own way out: they understate.' The Hungarian George Mikes, who wrote several books on the British, arrived at a similar conclusion. 'Foreigners,' he decided, 'have souls; the English haven't . . . they have understatement instead.'

When people describe events, express their feelings or attempt to influence others, they can either do so using direct speech, or else they can resort to indirect speech. Direct speech consists of straightforward utterances that are produced without embellishments, and which are therefore relatively easy to understand. Direct speech can therefore be thought of as an 'honest' version of what the speaker thinks, feels or wants, in contrast to indirect speech, which, because it is more complicated, appears to conceal its intended messages. Indirect speech certainly requires more work on the part of the listener, and as a result it is more frequently misunderstood – a result that, in some cases, is actually intended by the speaker. The main types of indirect speech are understatement, irony, and what linguists call 'hedges'.

One of the basic skills required for language is the ability to recognise what is, and what is not, a reasonable description of an event. In the process of learning to speak we acquire various grammatical and semantic rules. We also learn that there are adequate descriptions of events, as well as descriptions that

overstate or understate their significance. As we get older we learn
that overstatement and understatement can be used as rhetorical
devices, allowing us to exercise our creative skills, and to either
accentuate or conceal what we are actually saying.

Overstatement and understatement were studied as part of traditional Greek oratory – *hyperbole* is in fact the ancient Greek word
for overstatement, and understatement was known as *litotes*. Both
of these rhetorical devices were popular during the Renaissance. In
The Courtesan, which was published in 1528, Baldesar Castiglione
recommended the use of understatement and overstatement, 'as
when to increase or diminish things be spoken that uncredibly
pass the likelihood of truth'. Castiglione also commended irony,
which he referred to as 'an honest and comely kind of jesting that
consisteth in a certain dissimulation, when a man speaketh one
thing and privily meaneth another'.

Understatement and overstatement continue to play an important role in contemporary oratory, as well as in everyday conversations where people are trying to achieve a rhetorical effect.
Although the English show a marked preference for understatement, they are happy with overstatement, provided it is not used
for boasting. However, the English generally tend to shy away
from overstatement – as Ralph Waldo Emerson observed, they
'avoid superlatives'. One of the reasons for this is that the English
do not like to appear opinionated – unless, of course, they are taking
part in a political debate, where the normal rules of self-presentation
do not apply, or in a TV chat show, where the medium demands
strong opinions, even from people who don't have them. Generally
speaking, the English do not like to parade their convictions. They
prefer to qualify their opinions, and to dissociate themselves from
all forms of extremism. This is very evident in the words that
people use to qualify their descriptions – words like 'hardly',
'almost', 'nearly' and 'rather', – all of which have the effect of
toning things down, and distancing people from what they are
saying.

When someone wants to soften the impact of a remark, they can
also use what linguists call a 'hedge'. Hedges consist of phrases
and parts of speech that mitigate the effect of utterances, usually
by allowing the speaker to show his or her concern for the listener.
When a hedge like 'I hope you don't mind me asking . . .' or 'I

don't want to impose on you . . .' precedes a request, it prepares the listener for what is to follow. It also acknowledges the effort involved in complying with the request, and the fact that the request might be rejected. Hedges are therefore designed to make requests more polite. They show that the speaker is not taking anything for granted, and that he or she is prepared to go to the trouble of producing a hedge in order to make the request more acceptable.

Hedges are used in conjunction with all kinds of utterances. In addition to requests for favours and information, they are also attached to warnings, promises, advice and criticisms. For example, one way that people dilute their criticism of others is by starting with an expression like 'I hope you don't think I'm being rude, but . . .' or 'I don't want to be critical, but . . .'. These types of hedges are basically two-faced, because while they alert the listener to what is about to follow, they also deny that it is any part of the speaker's intention to be rude or critical.

All languages appear to possess hedges, although there are enormous differences between languages, both in terms of the range of hedges that are available, and the frequency with which they are used. The English use hedges extensively, and their conversation is littered with phrases like 'Do you mind', 'Would it be possible', 'May I ask you', 'I think you ought to know', and so on.

There appear to be several reasons why the English find hedges so attractive. Firstly, because hedges show concern for the feelings of the listener, this naturally recommends them to people who value politeness. More to the point, hedges enable speakers to show that they respect the privacy of their listeners. This is particularly evident in the case of requests, where hedges manage to give the impression that the speaker does not intend to intrude upon the listener, or to impose himself in any way. In England privacy is highly valued – J.B. Priestley went so far as to suggest that England 'is a land of privacy' – and that is why forms of talk which respect privacy are so widespread.

However, the most revealing thing about hedges is their similarity to the 'appeasement displays' used by animals. Meetings in the animal world are frequently associated with complex rituals, where one individual appeases the other, usually by exposing a vulnerable part of its anatomy, in order to show that it has no aggressive intentions, and to forestall aggression from the other individual.

Hedges achieve the same end by exposing the speaker's motives, and by placing the speaker in an apologetic, and sometimes rather submissive position. Like appeasement displays, hedges also place obligations on the individual being addressed. Just as animals find it difficult to attack an individual that has subordinated itself, so too people find it difficult to dismiss someone who has used a hedge. It is much more difficult, for example, to refuse someone who says 'Would you be so good as to give me the time', than someone who simply says 'Give me the time'.

Several authors have commented on the latent aggression of the English. Geoffrey Gorer, who produced a very thorough investigation of English attitudes, went so far as to suggest that inhibition of aggression was one of the defining features of the English character. Other observers have remarked on the hypersensitivity and touchiness of the English, and the fact that they tend to shy away from confrontations, almost as if they were fearful about what might happen if they lost control and became angry. Viewed against this background of concerns, it is very clear that hedges play an important role in containing people's fears about their own aggression and that of others. Phrases like 'Do you mind' and 'Could I ask you' may sound contrived and hollow, even to the people who use them, but as long as they help to foster an illusion of security they will continue to be used.

When the English talk about their personal achievements they have difficulty avoiding understatement. The same is true of their state of health, which they are inclined to describe as being better than it really is. Understatement is now thoroughly institutionalised, with TV weathermen trying to give the impression that everything is going to be fine tomorrow, even when the charts show it's going to be raining, and with politicians attempting to persuade the public that although the economy isn't what it should be, it's never been better, and anyway it's all set to improve. When it comes to covering up the truth, politicians are the great experts, and one of the linguistic cloaks they cannot resist is understatement. A classic example of this occurred in 1958, when the whole of Harold Macmillan's Treasury team resigned. When Macmillan spoke to the press the next day he referred to the mass resignation as a 'little local difficulty'.

Irony is another device favoured by the English. Irony and

understatement are similar because they both consist of indirect statements, where the relationship between what is being said and what is meant is not entirely clear. But irony is very different from understatement because while understatement depends on subtle qualification of the message, irony consists of saying the exact opposite to what is meant. For example, someone who has just broken his leg in a skiing accident, and who is obviously in great pain, might describe his condition with an understatement like 'I don't feel brilliant', or with an ironical statement like 'I feel brilliant'. In both cases the person is letting the listener know that he feels dreadful. The understatement draws attention to his pain by understating its seriousness, the ironical statement by denying it altogether.

Because irony allows people to express themselves by saying the exact opposite of what they mean, it is ideally suited to the purposes of insulting others. It has the virtue of enabling someone to make a statement, in the hope that the person they are addressing will take it literally and not notice the intended insult – or even better, that other people who are listening will recognise the insult, while the person who is being insulted does not. Ironical insults fall into the category of sarcasm – a brand of insults which the English have virtually made their own, and which people from other countries often have difficulty understanding. Paul Gallico recognised this some years ago when he remarked that 'No one can be so calculatingly rude as the British, which amazes Americans who do not understand studied insults, and can only offer abuse as a substitute.'

To understand why understatement and irony are so popular with the English, we need to remember that with these devices there isn't a one-to-one relationship between what people say and what they mean. It is only possible to identify the intended meaning behind understatement and irony, first of all by working out which device is being used, and secondly by extracting the intended meaning. This can only be achieved if one is sensitive to the possibility of understatement or irony, and if one can recognise the subtle cues that accompany each device. Because foreigners to England tend to focus on literal meanings rather than figurative meanings, they are frequently caught out by English understatement and irony. They tend to assume that the speaker means what he says, while the speaker frequently assumes that he has conveyed sufficient signals to show that he means something very different.

One of the reasons for the enormous popularity of understatement and irony among the English is that both devices depend on shared knowledge for their success – they only work with people who think alike, who are, as it were, members of the same linguistic club. The widespread use of understatement has also been attributed to the tendency of the English to control and suppress their emotions – the theory being that understatement allows people to pretend that things are less important than they really are, which in turn enables them to deny what they really feel, both to themselves and to others. It has also been suggested that understatements which present things as being more tolerable than they really are may be motivated by what psychologists call the 'Pollyanna Principle' – that is, the tendency to look on the bright side of things, even when everything is falling apart. Remaining cheerful in the face of adversity is certainly an English trait, and one that forms the basis of a great deal of English humour. This grim side of understatement is also said to be present in Scottish humour. According to Douglas Muecke, 'Scottish humour is particularly rich in understatement and especially dry off-hand expressions of mock-commiseration that are grossly inadequate to the cruel and grim situations that call them forth.'

The other factor that motivates understatement is modesty. The English are renowned for their modesty and their reluctance to talk about their own achievements. This was not always the case, because, as far we can see, the English were rather rowdy and boastful during the sixteenth century. But by the end of the eighteenth century things had changed, and Joseph Addison was able to insist that modesty was the distinguishing feature of the English people. Since then various foreign visitors have confirmed this picture of the English. For example, in 1938 the French biographer André Maurois wrote a letter to a young man who was about to visit England, giving him the following advice: 'Be modest. If you are a world tennis-champion, say "Yes, I don't play too badly." If you have crossed the Atlantic alone in a small boat, say "I do a little sailing."' During that time the use of understatement was not confined to personal achievements;

it also extended to the achievements of other people. Nowhere was this more evident than in British institutions like the Royal Navy, where, according to Joseph Conrad 'The highest signal of commendation complimenting a ship consists exactly of those simple words *well done*, followed by the name of the ship. Not marvellously done, astonishingly done, wonderfully done – no, only just *well done, so and so*.'

The English still find it difficult to talk about their own achievements and those of other people. That is why they are so awkward when it comes to offering compliments, and so ungracious when it comes to receiving them. In fact the English show a great deal of ambivalence about success altogether. This is evident, not only in relation to things like compliments, but also in their emphasis on playing the game, rather than on winning. There is probably no other country where people identify so strongly with the underdog, or where they show more affection for heroic losers. After all, it was England that produced 'Eddie the Eagle', the Olympic ski-jumper who came last in his event, but who stole the heart of the nation in the process. It seems that a country that has lost its empire and watched its economy decline needs to find something positive to say about failure.

Verbosity

One of the things that people notice when they travel abroad is how much time, or how little time, the locals spend talking to each other. For centuries the English have regarded the French as unnecessarily verbose, to the point where they seem to spend all their time talking, simply for its own sake. 'A Frenchman,' declared Dr Johnson, 'must always be talking, whether he knows anything of the matter or not; an Englishman is content to say nothing, when he has nothing to say.' The idea that the French are more garrulous than the English is accepted by the French, but instead of seeing themselves as talkative, they naturally perceive the English as awkwardly silent. In 1938 André Maurois wrote to a young Frenchman who was about to visit England, offering him the following words of advice: 'Do not talk too much until you have found your depth. In France it is rude to let a conversation drop; in England it is rash to keep it up. No one there will blame you for silence. When you have not opened your mouth for three years they will think: "This Frenchman is a nice quiet fellow."' Other foreigners have also remarked on the taciturnity of the English. The German author Heinrich Heine defined 'silence' as 'a conversation with an Englishman', and Henry James commented that 'An Englishman is never so natural as when he is holding his tongue.' Oscar Wilde drew a wistful comparison with the Irish. 'If only one could teach the English how to talk and the Irish how to listen, society would be quite civilised.'

The Irish are widely acknowledged to be a talkative people, not only by outsiders, but by the Irish themselves. They are renowned for their colourful turns of phrase, their obvious enjoyment of conversation, and their 'Irish Blarney' – their talent for flattery. It is said that whoever kisses the Blarney Stone in Co. Cork will forever after have a flattering and cajoling tongue – something that the Irish already possess, but which outsiders need to visit Ireland in order to acquire. The reputation of the Irish for talkativeness goes back at least four hundred years. In his discussion of foreign habits, which was published in 1611, the Dutch commentator Johannes Boemus offered the following explanation for Irish verbosity: 'The hollowness of their eares is much wider than ours, and their tongues are far different, for nature ... hath indued them with this extraordinary priviledge, that their tongues are naturally so cleft and divided from the root to the tip, as they seem to have every one two tongues, by which meanes they doe not onely speake a humane and intelligible voice, but they can truely imitate the chirping and singing of divers birdes likewise, and that which is more strange, they will talke and conferre with two severall persons, of severall matters, at one and the selfe same time, the one part of the tongue speaking and giving answer unto one, and the other part to the other.'

It is often assumed that silence is the opposite of talk. In one sense it is, since two people who are together without talking, inevitably remain silent. But there is also a sense in which silence and talk are rather similar to each other, because both carry important messages. In addition, silence actually plays a crucial role in conversation, allowing the speaker to separate certain utterances, words and syllables with pauses that give special emphasis to what is being said. The other side of the story is that when people are in the listener role in a conversation, they are often anything but silent, emitting reassuring m-hms, grunts and remarks to show the speaker that they understand what is being said, and that they do not wish to take over the role of speaker. These vocal signals are often accompanied by nods and movements of the hands, which are designed to serve the same purpose. Together they are known as 'back-channel' signals – that is, signals that the listener sends to the speaker through a channel that is not the main channel of communication.

In contrast to those bits of silence that form part of conversation, there are also cases where people remain in each other's company for long spells of time without saying anything. What is regarded as silence depends to a large extent on the culture of the people concerned, and the significance that they attach to silence. Every society recognises that silence can arise from a desire to say nothing, as well as from having nothing to say, but they frequently define similar occurrences of silence in very different ways. The Italians, for example, are extremely talkative and their conversation is frequently punctuated by extravagant gesticulations and expressive movements of the body. Most people assume that this is the only way that Italians are capable of relating to each other, but there are in fact two quite distinct styles of social interaction in Italy – one being the noisy, expressive style that forms the basis of the Italian stereotype, and the other being a detached style of behaviour in which people remain largely silent.

Italians relish the theatrical aspects of conversation, as well as loud and heated exchanges. But, as the anthropologist George Saunders has pointed out, this noisy style of behaviour is reserved for issues that are unlikely to lead to serious disagreement. When there is a danger of differences of opinion over important matters, Italians tend to retreat to a silent mode of interaction, in order to ensure that they don't inflame the situation, or say something that they might later regret. In fact, both styles of behaviour can be seen as ways of avoiding having to deal with crucial issues. Two people who anticipate a serious disagreement may deflect the problem by resorting to silence, and by using an intermediary, but this is only achieved by not dealing with issues personally. The noisy, expressive style of behaviour which transforms everyday behaviour into a dramatic spectacle, can also be seen as a means of avoidance, because of its emphasis on presenting oneself in a good light. Saunders has in fact gone so far as to suggest that the theatrical character and outward display of emotion in Italian life are really a means of avoiding having to come to terms with one's own feelings, as well as an obstacle to reason.

Conversation, for an Italian, is a means of engagement, a way of showing other people that one cares, that one is committed to them, and that one enjoys their company. Talkativeness, therefore, is a sign of camaraderie, and silence an indication, either that one is not interested, or that trouble is brewing. This is very different from those European countries where silence is tolerated, and where people can sit in silence for hours, without inferring anything untoward, or even recognising that nothing has been said. The Finns, for example, have a very high tolerance for silence. This is something that they recognise and value about themselves, and which many foreign visitors to Finland find extremely difficult to handle. The premium that is placed on silence is supported by various aphorisms which extol the virtues of silence, of listening to others, and of thinking before one speaks. In fact, wisdom, for the Finns, is frequently equated with not saying anything, unless it is absolutely necessary. The Finnish penchant for silence is shared by the inhabitants of the north of Sweden, but not apparently by the inhabitants of northern Norway, who, surprisingly, have a reputation for being more garrulous and direct than Norwegians who live in the south.

After spending several months in Stockholm, the American author Susan Sontag came to the conclusion that 'Silence is the Swedish national vice.' But according to her informants, things were even worse in the north of the country. 'In Norrland, Stockholmers have told me, people hardly talk at all. Families go for months, especially during the long night of winter, without exchanging more than a few sentences with each other. The further north, everyone says here, the bigger and more unshakable the silence.' The southern Swedes tell a joke about the silence of the northerners, which could equally be applied to Finns:

> Two old men are sitting outside a log cabin near the Arctic Circle. It is early afternoon, and they are drinking together in total silence. Three hours later they are still drinking, but neither has uttered a single word. Eventually, as the sun begins to go down, one of them turns to the other and says, 'Isn't that a beautiful sunset?' The second man puts down his glass with obvious annoyance and says, 'Now look here! What do you want to do, drink or talk?'

Although the Finns have a wide variety of vocal noises that they can use as back-channel signals, they prefer to use non-verbal signals, like head nods, to reinforce the speaker and to show that they do not want the floor. The advantage of these non-verbal forms of back-channel is that they preserve the silence. Verbal back-channel, on the other hand, threatens to obscure what the speaker is saying, even if it is intended as a means of reinforcing the speaker and showing that one doesn't want to speak oneself. Two Finnish anthropologists, Jaakko Lehtonen and Kari Sajavaara, have made a special study of silence in their culture, and they have pointed out that the studied avoidance of audible back-channel by Finns often has an adverse effect on foreigners, who get the impression that the

Finns are not paying attention, that they are not interested, 'or that the Finn is indifferent, sullen or even hostile'. They also point out the Finnish tolerance for silence is correlated with an intolerance for simultaneous talk; Finns do not like to be interrupted, and generally they try to ensure that they don't interrupt others.

What is it that distinguishes the verbose style of behaviour which is so typical of the Italians, from the silent style of behaviour which is found among the Finns? The answer, it seems, has something to do with the degree to which people are seen as socially accessible, and the extent to which people are prepared to impose upon, and be imposed upon by others. The noisy, expressive style of the Italians is one of engagement, with people waving their arms around, shifting their posture, holding each other, patting and pummelling each other, and generally ensuring that their presence isn't forgotten. Here talk is recognised as a form of commitment and interest, and therefore as a means of being liked by and liking other people. In an attempt to show their affections, it is inevitable that individuals will end up talking at the same time, but because these positive motives of talk are recognised, people are usually very tolerant about being interrupted, and quite unconcerned about interrupting others.

If the Italian's aim is to use conversation as a means of displaying his affections and gaining the affections of others, the Finn's concern is to ensure that he does not impose himself upon others, and that they do not impose themselves on him. The main motive of the Finn is not to ensure that he is liked, but that he is not disliked. It is a social strategy that is designed to reduce one's losses, rather than to increase one's gains, and is largely responsible for the Finnish attitude to silence. For the Finn, silence is a way of reducing the demands that one places on others, a way of respecting their rights to privacy, and therefore a way of ensuring that nothing is done which might offend others. Requiring other people to be silent is the other side of the same coin; it too rests on the assumption that respect for others is displayed by remaining silent.

Cultural conventions associated with talk and silence are also reflected in the way that people take turns in conversation. Every society has rules about the management of conversation, as well as a repertoire of signals that individuals can use to show that they do or do not want to switch conversational roles. The reason why conversation is organised in this way is that we are incapable of understanding what someone else is saying if we happen to be talking at the same time. Of course, if we were capable of this feat, the norms governing turn-taking would not be necessary.

When someone occupies the role of speaker, he can either attempt to hold the floor so that he can continue talking, or else he can show that he is ready to give it up to the other person. Correspondingly, when someone is in the role of listener, he can signal his willingness or his reluctance to assume the role of speaker. Each of these motives is associated with a different set of conventional signals. In countries like Britain and Germany, these signals involve movements of the head and eyes, and to a much lesser extent, movements of the hands. Vocal signals are also important, and changes in pitch and volume frequently signal a change in conversational roles.

In order to hold on to the floor the speaker has to do two things. Firstly he has to signal to the listener that he intends to continue talking, and secondly he has to suppress any attempts by the listener to take the floor. One way of signalling that one intends to go on talking is by looking away intermittently. This allows the speaker to collect his thoughts; it also provides the listener with fewer opportunities to catch the speaker's eye and indicate his intention to take the floor from him. Another floor-holding technique is for the speaker to try and elicit back-channel from the listener. This is commonly done with phrases like 'Right?' and 'See what I mean?', which place demands on the listener to provide back-channel and therefore to concede any claims that he may have to the floor. In other words, getting the other person to nod his head in agreement forces him back into the role of listener, and discourages him from trying to take over the role of speaker. In addition, the speaker has to be careful not to provide the listener with opportunities to snatch the floor. Consequently, when the speaker pauses he sometimes raises one of his hands, or holds his hand in a fixed position. This has the effect of discouraging the listener from trying to take the floor, and it also suppresses back-channel because the listener obviously has less need to reassure the speaker that he does not intend to take over his role.

The speaker who wishes to relinquish the floor to the listener has a variety of signals at his disposal. These include looking at the listener to show that the turn is completed, speaking more softly, drawing out the last few words of the utterance, raising or lowering his intonation, or using a completion signal like 'You know' or 'Well, I don't know.'

Like the speaker, the listener is faced with two choices – in this case, whether to try and acquire the floor, or to indicate that he does not want it. The most effective way of indicating that one does not want the floor is by using back-channel – in other words, by nodding approvingly, smiling, looking intently, and using reassuring vocalisations like 'm-hm' and 'uh-huh'. On the other hand, when the listener wants to take the floor, he can either request a turn, or simply grab the floor from the speaker. A request for a turn, for example, can be made by an audible inhalation – which shows that one is just about to begin speaking. Usurpation of the speaker role can be achieved by jumping in while the speaker is pausing – making sure, that by looking away, the interjection does not appear to be a case of back-channel – or by interrupting with sufficient gusto to discourage the speaker from continuing.

The turn-taking signals used in Italy are very different from those employed in other parts of Europe. In Britain, for example, conversation tends to be based on the principle of cooperation, with a minimum of interruption, whereas in Italy simultaneous monologues are common, and conversations often take on the outward appearance of a contest between the participants. The other interesting difference is the way that listeners behave. In a British conversation there is tendency for the listener to look more than the speaker – partly because the speaker averts his gaze to gather his thoughts and to sustain his claim to the speaking turn, but also because listeners are, by convention, required to display their interest in what the speaker is saying. This sort of thing can also be seen in Italy, especially when the speaker has higher status than the listener, and when – as one might expect – the high-status speaker looks away while the low-status listener gazes at him intently.

But there are numerous cases where the situation is reversed, and where the listener spends much less time looking than the speaker. This pattern of looking is very much a feature of a conversation game that Italians play with each other, where the listener repeatedly denies his role by looking away, and the speaker constantly tries to reaffirm the listener's role by staring at him. In an Italian conversation it is not unusual to see the listener looking around, almost with an air of boredom, while the speaker pursues the listener, frequently by moving himself physically, so that he remains in front of the listener, but more commonly by gesticulating in front of the listener's averted face, using his hands as if they were grappling irons, to try and draw the listener's gaze back to him. The spectacle is not unlike one of those balletic sequences where the coy maiden is chased round the stage by the hero – never quite in reach, but never too far away.

Conversation turn-taking in Italy is based on what one might call a 'Conch shell model' – after the famous scene in William Golding's *Lord of the Flies*, where a group of schoolboys, who are marooned on a desert island, decide that only one person may speak at their meetings – the boy who is holding the ceremonial conch shell. Italian conversation conforms to a conch shell model – not because it has managed to eliminate simultaneous talk (anything but!), but because the person who has his hands in the air becomes the speaker.

The speaker who wants to continue talking needs only to ensure that he has his hands raised, and that they are moving around, punctuating his remarks and harnessing the attention of the other person. In other countries the speaker who wants to secure his role tries to get the listener to provide back-channel in the form of nods and vocalisations. In Italy these kinds of back-channel signals are much more rare because people are able to retain the speaker role simply by keeping their hands up, which means that there is less need for the listener to show that he accepts the speaker's claim to his role. When the listener does need to do so, he is more likely to look at the speaker than to nod his head or offer reassuring vocalisations. This explains why an Italian conversation sometimes looks like a form of courtship, with the listener repeatedly looking away, and the speaker trying to ensnare the listener's attention with his gesticulations. By getting hold of the listener's attention the speaker manages to secure his role, and by looking elsewhere the listener is able to keep his options open and deny the speaker a claim to the role.

To show that he intends to continue talking, the speaker in an

Italian conversation needs to do three things. Firstly he needs to keep his hands up and moving. Secondly he needs to ensure that the listener has no claims on the speaker role. This he can achieve by getting the listener to look at him while he is talking. Finally the speaker needs to make sure that the listener does not get his hands up so that he can grab the speaker role. This is achieved by physically restraining the listener from getting his hands in the air. If you watch an Italian conversation you will notice that there are times when the speaker gently places his hand on the forearm of the other person. Superficially this looks like a gesture of affection. Its real purpose, however, is to show the listener that the speaker is ready to counter any attempt by the listener to get his hands into the air.

When the speaker wants to relinquish his role, he simply lowers his hands, thereby indicating that he has no intention of carrying on talking. Another termination signal that is used by Italians is the shrug. When the speaker comes to the end of his turn, he sometimes shrugs his shoulders, almost as if he were displaying his helplessness. Interestingly, although the British don't use shrugs as termination signals, they do sometimes end their turns with phrases like 'Oh well, I don't know', which carry the same message of detachment and helplessness as the shrug.

The listener's role in an Italian conversation is fairly straight-forward. In order to keep his options open and deny the other person permanent occupancy of the speaker role, he needs to avert his gaze. To actually secure the speaker role, however, he needs to get the speaker's hands down, usually by grabbing them and pushing them down so that the speaker stops talking. If, on the other hand, the listener has no intention of speaking, or he wants to show his respect, then he can do so, either by looking at the speaker, or by folding his arms, or placing them behind his back. At first glance these arm postures looks like forms of relaxation; in the context of Italian conversation, however, they frequently serve as 'unintention displays', showing the speaker that the listener has positioned his hands in a way that would make it difficult for him to start speaking. The fact that these static signals are used by listeners to forgo the role of speaker, partly explains why vocal back-channel is not needed, and why it is therefore less common in Italian conversation. The other reason for the paucity of vocal back-channel is that Italians are usually so keen to occupy the role of speaker that they don't require any encouragement from the listener.

There is clearly a range of conversational styles in Europe, which extends from the boisterous style found in Italy all the way to the circumspect, more cautious style found in countries like Finland. The Greeks and Turks are more similar in their conversation style to the Italians, whereas the Swedes, the Germans, the Dutch and the British are closer in style to the Finns. The Italians enjoy talking, dislike silence, and frequently interrupt each other. They are motivated by the need to show their affections and to be liked, and that is why they adhere to a style of conversation which is more expressive in style. The Finns are more concerned with not imposing themselves on others, and not being imposed upon. Consequently their whole style of behaviour is geared towards not giving offense. That is why they are less talkative, more tolerant of silence, less happy about interruptions, and why they can afford to leave long pauses between their utterances, secure in the knowledge that others are unlikely to take advantage of the situation and steal the floor from them. For the Italians conversation is frequently a kind of contest. For the Finns it is usually an opportunity for cooperation.

Victory

The origins of most mannerisms are lost in the mists of time, but there are a few where it is possible to identify, very roughly, when they first appeared on the scene. The Churchillian gesture for 'victory', which is performed by splaying the first and second fingers, with the palm of the hand facing forward, is very unusual because its appearance can actually be narrowed down to a particular day. Although the 'victory' sign is commonly associated with Churchill, it was not Churchill who came up with the idea of using the letter 'V', or a hand gesture that depicts the letter, to signify 'victory'. There are in fact two theories about how the victory V-sign came into being.

One theory credits a Belgian lawyer, Victor de Lavelaye, with the invention of the victory V-sign. This is discussed by Desmond Morris and his colleagues in their book *Gestures*. The story goes that during the early part of the war the resistance graffito that was daubed on walls to annoy the Nazis was 'RAF' – an obvious reference to the Royal Air Force. De Lavelaye had become disenchanted with the RAF slogan because it did not translate readily into other languages, and because it wasn't particularly eye-catching. Looking around for an alternative, he suddenly came up with the idea of using 'V' for Victory, and on 14 January 1941 he broadcast his proposal on the radio. The idea of using 'V' was simple, and it was inspired because it translated into French (*victoire*), Flemish (*vrijheid*) and even into German (*Viktoria*). The BBC was persuaded by the proposal and soon afterwards it mounted a campaign, using the first four notes of Beethoven's Fifth Symphony, which also happened to correspond to the morse code for 'V' (dot-dot-dot-dash). It was after this that Churchill began to use the victory V-sign, and to make the gesture so popular.

The other theory, which has been put forward by the Oxford publisher, Bridget Hadaway, is that Sir John Hammerton was the first person to come up with the idea of using the letter 'V' to signify Victory. Hammerton was a journalist, and later on a successful compiler of popular books of reference. As he was being driven across the Sussex Downs by his chauffeur one day in November 1940, he looked up and saw an enormous 'V' that had been blazed by a Hurricane fighter plane, which he later discovered had shot down three enemy planes. On 29 November 1940, he wrote an article for *The War Illustrated*, in which he described the experience of seeing the 'vast V-shaped blaze in the sunset sky! The letter must have been a mile or more in height, and the left limb of it thinned away at the top into white vapour . . . I saw it retain its volume and density for nearly twenty minutes of my journey.' This vision inspired Hammerton to think of Victory: '. . . I would enlarge on V as the first letter of Victory, though a few miles away there is another vast V, being a plantation of trees put there to commemorate Victoria's Jubilee of 1887 or '97. But Victoria and Victory come from the same root.'

Although Hammerton's article appeared six weeks before De Lavelaye's broadcast, there is no certainty that it, rather than the broadcast, was responsible for the V-for-Victory slogan. We can be sure, however, that not long after that Churchill began to use the V-sign as a symbol of ultimate victory.

The Victory V-sign caught on very quickly. Photographs from the time show, however, that the gesture had some 'teething problems' because soldiers who were keen to use the gesture sometimes made the mistake of positioning their hand so that the palm faced back rather than forward – which meant, of course, that they were inadvertently producing the insulting V-sign instead of the victory V-sign. The records show that the insulting V-sign was definitely being used in 1940, and possibly as early as the turn of the century, and this makes it all the more difficult to understand why some people should have produced a victory V-sign the wrong way round. Desmond Morris and his colleagues point out that Churchill himself was not immune to this error because there is film footage of him making the victory V-sign with the palm of his hand facing back rather than forward. It is quite possible, of course, that people who made these errors knew of the insulting V-sign, but somehow thought that it was being taken over by the victory V-sign, so they therefore had no reason to worry. What is more likely, however, is that the insulting V-sign was a low-frequency gesture, and therefore one that was not yet widely known. This would explain why some people made the mistake. If Churchill was a part of this group, he did not remain a member for long, because by the end of the war he no longer positioned his hand so that the palm faced back. By then all his victory V-signs were being executed correctly, with the palm facing forward.

The insulting V-sign is found in Britain and Ireland, but nowhere else in Europe. The fact that it is distinguished from the Victory V-sign by the position of the palm places special demands on people in these countries to ensure that they do not produce one of these gestures in their attempt to make the other. This issue of whether to position the V-sign so that it faces either forward or back is not a problem for most Europeans because they do not have to worry about giving offense when they make the victory V-sign. That is why, if you travel through Europe, you will find people making the victory V-sign in both forms – sometimes with the palm facing forward, on other occasions with the palm facing back. The reason for this indifference is that palm position does not carry any of the message content of the gesture. The only thing that counts for them is the splayed position of the first and second fingers.

The Greeks are quite different from other continental Europeans, because they do distinguish V-signs on the basis of palm position. The major gestural insult in Greece is the *Moutza*, which is executed by splaying all the fingers of the hand and pushing the palm towards the person who is being insulted. The gesture can either be enhanced by using two hands at the same time, or its intensity can be reduced by splaying just the first and second fingers of the hand, and thrusting these, with the palm facing forward, in the direction of one's adversary. Notice that this 'Mini-Moutza' is identical to the Churchillian Victory V-sign, which means of course that when the Greeks want to signal Victory, they have to do so with the palm of the hand facing back instead of forward – that is, by producing the equivalent of the British insult.

One can immediately see the kind of problem that might arise when a Greek meets a Briton. The Greek who wants to convey a message about victory cannot use the Palm-forward V-sign because it is his insult, and he cannot use the Palm-back V-sign because it's the Briton's insult. The problem is reversed for a Briton. This

The Greeks signal 'no' by tossing their head back. This action is sometimes accompanied by raised eyebrows, closed eyes and a click of the tongue.

Winston Churchill, in 1949, with a group of Greeks who are attempting to replicate the Churchillian Victory V-sign. Because the palm-front V-sign is an insult for the Greeks, their only option is to perform the victory gesture with the palm facing back. Notice how two of the Greeks remain undecided about what to do with their hands, while one ends up making the insulting British V-sign. (Popperfoto)

dilemma did in fact arise when Churchill met a group of Greeks in Athens in 1949. They wanted to honour him by using the Churchillian gesture, but felt a little awkward about telling him to go to hell. They felt equally unhappy about using their own version of the Victory V-sign, knowing that this would be deeply insulting to most Englishmen.

Water Closets

Toilets, as we know them, are a fairly recent invention. The person responsible for the first flush toilet was Sir John Harington, a godson of Queen Elizabeth I. In fact he built two prototypes, both with cistern, pan, overflow pipe, valve, waste pipe and toilet seat. One was installed in his house at Kelstone, near Bath, the other at Richmond Palace for his godmother. Harington also wrote a book describing his invention, which contained a diatribe against the unwholesome habits of his fellow countrymen, a copy of which was apparently chained to the wall beside the water closet in Richmond. But neither this nor the patronage of his godmother succeeded in persuading the English that it was time for the flush toilet. In fact it was almost two hundred years before the first successful patent for a flush toilet was taken out. In the meantime the English and their continental cousins relied on chamber pots, which they then emptied into a cesspit or into the street below. This was often done without any warning. The inhabitants of Edinburgh, however, were reputed to be more considerate than most, because before emptying their pots over the heads of their fellow citizens they would cry out 'Gardyloo!', an expression adapted from the French, *gare l'eau* – 'Beware of the water'.

Chamber pots were widely used. But royalty and those members of polite society who were concerned with comfort and appearances tended to favour the close-stool – which consisted of an armchair with a hole in the seat, or a box with a hinged lid that closed over a padded, circular cushion. However, not everyone used these conveniences. Country folk resorted to the fields, and it was not uncommon for town folk to relieve themselves where they could. The seventeenth-century historian, Anthony à Wood, recorded how the court of Charles II spent the summer of 1665 in Oxford, avoiding the plague in London, and how they decamped, 'leaving at their departure their excrements in every corner, Chimneys, Studies, Coleholes, Cellers'. Samuel Pepys recorded in his diary how, when the maid had forgotten to put a chamber pot in his bedroom, he 'did shit twice in the Chimney fireplace'. During the eighteenth century there were men who wandered the streets, armed with a bucket and a long cloak. For a suitable fee they would wrap the cloak round their customer, concealing him while he relieved himself in the bucket. Then, of course, there were the public parks. During his stay in London, Casanova recorded how he went into St. James's Park 'to watch the Great Beauties parading, riding and driving', but he was horrified to discover 'six or seven people shitting in the bushes with their hinder parts turned towards the Publick'. He told the Earl of Pembroke that he found the spectacle disgusting. Pembroke simply shrugged his shoulders, saying that it was a common occurrence.

Most societies have a strong aversion to human faeces. This is not something that children are born with, because they continue to display a curious fascination with their own body products until they have been taught how to regulate their natural impulses, and when and where to relieve themselves. In the case of defecation, what begins for the child as a natural, often pleasurable experience ends up as a restricted cultural performance, surrounded with all kinds of taboos and conflicting attitudes. They learn, among other things, that crapping is a shameful activity, something that should be performed in private, and certainly not discussed directly.

Historically, attitudes towards privacy have varied a great deal. For example, in ancient Rome the houses did not have individual toilets. When somebody needed to relieve himself he would summon a slave to bring a chamber-pot to wherever he was, and after he had finished the slave would take it away. The Emperor Vespasian established public urinals in Rome as early as the 1st century B.C., and there were also public latrines which consisted of rows of seats suspended over a trough. Toilet paper was not yet available, so people used sponges on the end of sticks. The sponges were usually soaked in brine. After they had been used they were rinsed in running water for the next person. The fact that these sponges were not discarded, but used by one and all, reveals the extent to which defecation was regarded as a public affair.

Although private latrines came into existence during the middle ages, they continued to be a rarity, and it was more common to find rudimentary toilet seats, suspended in space, usually between two buildings – rather like the facility described in the *Decameron*, where Andreuccio, the horse-dealer, loses his balance on the planks of a latrine, and falls into the filthy ditch below. In France this public aspect of crapping even became part of royal pageantry. Louis XIV, for example, treated his close-stool as a throne, and he was not averse to granting audiences while he was perched on top of it. The English ambassador, Lord Portland, regarded it as a great honour to be received by the king under these circumstances, and it was from this vantage point that Louis announced his betrothal to Mme de Maintenon.

Sir William Wraxall offered a very similar account of the toilet habits of Ferdinand IV of Naples. Writing from Naples in 1779, he reported that 'Those arts and functions which are never mentioned in England, even by the vulgar, here are openly performed. When the king has made a hearty meal, and feels an inclination to retire, he commonly communicates that intention to the Noblemen around him in waiting, and selects the favoured individuals, who, as a mark of predilection, he chooses shall attend him. "*Sono ben pransato*," says he, laying his hand on his belly, "*Adesso bisogna una buona panchiata*." The persons thus preferred, then accompany his majesty, stand respectfully round him, and amuse him by their conversation, during the performance.'

Even today French attitudes towards bodily elimination are very different from those of other Europeans. For one thing, they do not place the same premium on privacy. This was particularly evident with the *pissoirs*, those open-air urinals that were surrounded by a half-hearted hoarding of tin which left the head and feet exposed, and allowed men inside to converse with passersby while they were busy urinating. Sadly, most of the old *pissoirs* have disappeared, giving way to vandal-proof *toilettes*. Now, instead of watching the world while he urinates, the customer pays his two francs and is enveloped in a pristine world where he doesn't even have to flush the toilet. It's all done for him as soon as he presses the button to open the door. When he steps out the *toilette* cleans itself.

Although French attitudes to elimination are concealed by the new *toilettes*, they continue to be revealed by other toilet conventions – for example, the Gallic practice of getting men and women to use a common toilet in restaurants. In British and

German restaurants there are separate toilets for men and women, which means that people have somewhere to retreat to if they want to talk about members of the opposite sex. In France, however, it is not uncommon for men and women to use the same toilet, and for the basin, the toilet and the urinal to be situated close to each other. A woman who is washing her hands in the basin may therefore find herself standing beside a strange man who is using the urinal, while he in turn may have women walking past him on their way to the toilet. A similar situation occurs in public toilets, many of which have female attendants. This arrangement can be very embarrassing for male visitors from other countries, where the facilities for men and women are kept separate, and where a strange woman would certainly not be present while men are relieving themselves and doing up their flies.

Then there is the matter of the toilet itself. In France, especially in the south and in the rural areas, the water closet often consists of a flat porcelain pan, with indentations for the feet and a hole in the middle, over which the person squats. For people who are used to this posture, nothing seems more natural. On the other hand, for foreigners who are accustomed to a sit-down toilet, the squat toilet is uncomfortable, stressful and alien. As far as they are concerned, it fails to meet the basic standards of civilization.

The French are also unique in their devotion to the bidet. It has been suggested that the appearance of the bidet, round about 1730, can be traced to the French habit of 'local washing', and to a dramatic specialisation of rooms in the great houses of France. During this period all kinds of rooms came into existence, each with their own special function – rooms like the washroom, the convenience and the privy. According to experts like Georges Vigarello, this encouraged greater attention to cleanliness, which in turn helped to make the bidet popular. The bidet was also associated with the French craze for perfumes, and the practice of applying sweet-smelling potions to the private parts. It was therefore an accessory both to hygiene and pleasure – a means of keeping the genitals clean as well as fragrant.

British and American visitors to France are frequently mystified by the bidets in their hotel rooms. Some mistake them for urinals or water closets, others used them to cool their wine or to soak their underwear. As Alexander Kira points out in his book on bathrooms, many Americans and Britons don't know that the bidet is used for cleaning oneself after defecation and urination. They think that it has something to do with sex, or that its sole purpose is 'for douching the vagina, contraceptively or otherwise, and for washing the vulva region after intercourse'. These misconceptions about the real purpose of the bidet have helped to encourage the image of the French woman as someone who is sexually active and promiscuous. Why else, the foreigner asks himself, would the French need so many bidets if it was not because their women are constantly douching themselves.

A recent study by Scott Ltd, the makers of toilet paper, shows that the British have very strong ideas about the toilets they encounter in other countries. When they were asked to compare countries, they rated France as having the worst toilets, followed by Thailand and Greece. When people were asked what they found so objectionable about foreign toilets, they mentioned dirty conditions, the absence of toilet paper, and poor washing conditions. In fact the British are rather fussy about their toilet paper. Contrary to what one might expect, the value of the market for toilet paper in Britain is almost twice that of Germany. The main reason for this is the superior quality of the paper found in Britain – reflecting the fact that the British are much more concerned about the kind of paper they use to wipe their bottoms than the Germans. If reputation is anything to go by, the French are not much better. As the American humorist Billy Wilder remarked, 'France is a place where the money falls apart in your hands but you can't tear the toilet paper.'

German toilet practices also differ in other ways. For one thing, the toilets in Germany tend to be of the flat-pan variety, which means that the faeces are deposited on a shallow ledge, which allows them to be inspected before they are flushed away. In certain circles in Germany viewing one's turds is regarded as an essential part of the toilet ritual. It is related to the ancient belief, mentioned by Pliny, that the state of a person's health can be detected by examining the colour and consistency of their faeces – a belief that is still widely held in Germany today.

With a flat-pan toilet it is almost impossible not to see one's own faeces. Instead of sinking beneath the surface of the water, they sit in the middle of the bowl, almost inviting inspection. The disadvantage of the flat-pan toilet is that it frequently requires more than one flush, and a vigorous scrub with the toilet brush, before the faeces disappear down the drain. This means that it is therefore potentially much more dirty than other types of flush toilets. In her novel, *Fear of Flying*, Erica Jong complains about the German's 'fanatical obsession with the illusion of cleanliness. Illusion, mind you, because Germans are not really clean . . . just go into any German toilet and you'll find a fixture unlike any other in the world. It has a cute little porcelain platform for the shit to fall on so you can inspect it before it whirls off into the watery abyss, and there is, in fact, no water in the toilet until you flush it. As a result German toilets have the strongest shit smell of any toilets anywhere.'

If German toilets are dirtier than most, this is certainly not reflected in the opinions that foreigners have of them. The research by Scott Ltd, for example, shows that the British rank German toilets as the fourth best in the world – after those of the United States, Britain and Switzerland. Europeans, on the other hand, rank German toilets third in the world, again after those of the United States and Switzerland. Moreover, market research shows that the per capita spending on toilet cleaners in Germany is almost double what it is in France, Italy and the United Kingdom – suggesting either that the toilets in German homes are cleaner than most, or that they require twice as much cleaning liquid to keep them clean.

Whatever interpretation is put on these findings, the fact remains that people in Germany spend a lot of money trying to keep their toilets clean. This may be related to their concern with cleanliness, but it may also have something to do with their fascination with things scatological. According to the American folklorist Alan Dundes, an obsession with shit pervades the whole of German culture. References to shit and shitting regularly appear in German jokes, riddles and proverbs, and shit-related expressions form the basis of most of their insults and obscene ejaculations. The British also have a well-developed lexicon of shitty terms – including words like crap, bullshit, and arsehole – but when it comes to using scatological obscenities they are no match for the Germans.

The most common German obscenity is *Scheiss*, meaning shit. It is used as a swear-word, an expression of frustration, and an insult – as in the case of *Scheiss drauf* (shit on it), *verdammte Scheiss* (damned shit), or *Scheissdreck* (shit-dirt). The arse itself also plays an important role in insult imagery – especially in the expression *Leck mich im Arsch*, which means 'kiss my arse', or more precisely 'lick my arse'. Like *Scheiss*, the arse-licking insult occupies a prominent position in the lexicon of German obscenities. It has attracted the attention of numerous scholars, and according to Alan Dundes 'whole books have been devoted to documenting the occurrence in literature and life of this insult. Literally dozens upon dozens of proverbs, riddles, folksongs, folktales, jokes, folk poems, etc. depend upon the articulation of *Leck mich im Arsch* . . . for their impact.'

The theme of kissing the arse is in fact extremely old, going back to the medieval belief that devil-worshippers paid homage to the devil by kissing his buttocks. The insult, however, is more recent than that. In Germany it was made famous by Goethe, but it can in fact be traced back to before the seventeenth century. It was known during the nineteenth century, because the 1811 *Dictionary of the Vulgar Tongue* refers to 'kiss mine arse', which it explains is 'an offer . . . very frequently made, but never literally accepted'. It is very likely that the insult was used all over Europe, as far back as the sixteenth century. According to James McDonald, 'The principle was familiar to Shakespeare. In *The Second Part of Henry VI* (IV.vii.31) the fawning French Dauphin is refered to as *Monsieur Basimecu*, the name being a pun on the French *baise mon cul*, literally "kiss-my-arse".'

The German image of shit is not entirely straightforward, because it has positive as well as negative components. Dundes, for example, mentions the practice of German farmers who used to stack piles of manure, human as well and animal, in front of their farm houses. Their intention was not to store the manure where it might be needed, but to put it on display for the benefit of others – in other words, to suggest to other people that one was a person of substance because one owned a large number of livestock. Obviously the larger the pile of manure, the more animals one was supposed to own. Positive references to the anus are also contained in children's stories and toys – the tale of the golden goose that lays the golden egg is a disguised example, whereas the figure of the *Dukatenscheisser*, a doll that dispenses coins from its rear – is a more explicit one. In both these cases the anus is represented not as the origin of dirty, faecal matter, but as a source of good fortune.

This equation of the anus with good luck is also found in other European countries. For example, the French sometimes use the expression *avoir du cul* when they refer to good luck, and the Italians have a hand gesture with the same meaning. Here the thumbs and forefingers are positioned so that they assume the shape of a large hole. In some cases this gesture is used as an emasculatory threat – in other words, 'Beware! I will stretch your arse to this size!' In other circumstances the gestural reference is to *un culo grande*, that is, to a large arse and good fortune. Here the person performing the gesture is saying, in effect, 'My luck was so great that it stretched my arse to this size.' The origins of this gesture are to be found in the everyday observation that people who eat a lot need to shit a lot. For the poor Italian peasant, who never knew where his next meal was coming from, a stretched arse was the natural metaphor for wealth and good fortune.

It is worth noting that although the British do not associate the arse with good fortune, they do believe that accidentally treading in a pile of shit can bring good luck. For centuries this was supported by a proverb, 'Shitten luck is good luck.' As far as we know, the proverb is no longer used, but the associated belief about treading in shit is still current.

It has been proposed that the German fascination with shit can be traced to the old practice of swaddling. Alan Dundes, for example, has suggested that the practice of wrapping up babies with long strips of material not only restricted their movements, but forced them to lie for hours in their own shit. This, he suggests, gave rise to all kinds of anxious jokes about shitting in the bed, or in one's pants, and it encouraged a personality that Freudians would label 'anal erotic' or 'anal retentive'. In fact Dundes goes so far as to suggest that Freud's observations on the anal character were based on the Austro–German society around him; without knowing it, Freud was actually describing his own society. The problem with this theory is that swaddling is no longer practised by German parents. Moreover, there are countries, like Poland and Russia, where swaddling has been practised extensively, but where there has never been any real interest in the subject of shit.

The Germans are reputed to be very concerned about their

digestive systems – the German artist Georg Grosz once referred to Germany as 'a headquarters of constipation' – but when it comes to worrying about digestion, the British take the cake. From a very early age the British are brought up to believe that a healthy constitution requires regular and frequent bowel movements. In fact a large number of people in Britain define constipation as not opening one's bowels every day – something that the average European would not even notice, let alone worry about. It is hardly surprising, therefore, that the British consumption of laxatives is the highest in Europe, or that constipation should be related to so many other symptoms. As Jonathan Miller points out in *The Body in Question*, 'The English are . . . obsessed with their bowels. When an Englishman complains about constipation, you never know whether he is talking about his regularity, his lassitude, his headaches, or his depression.'

There are several explanations for the British obsession with bowel movements. One explanation points the finger at the British diet, suggesting that an inadequate intake of fibre is the cause of constipation. Another explanation is that English public schools expose children to a daily interrogation about their bowels, asking them whether or not they 'have been'. It is said that the anxiety associated with these daily inquisitions has now permeated the whole of British society. The third explanation is a psychoanalytic one; it suggests that the British have become fixated at the anal stage of development – specifically the anal-expulsive stage, which is when children begin to enjoy defecating – and that is why the British become anxious when they fail to open their bowels. The fourth and final explanation treats the theory of auto-intoxication as the real culprit. According to Lynn Payer, who is an authority on culture and medicine, the theory of auto-intoxication was very popular during the early part of this century. It postulated that digested food that was allowed to remain in the intestine would soon begin to putrefy and poison the body. Only by opening one's bowels regularly and frequently was it possible to ensure that one did not poison oneself.

One of the things that all Europeans try to avoid is direct reference to defecating and urinating, and to the places where these activities are performed. Every society in Europe has it own euphemisms for the toilet. Even the French, who are quite content to call a *pissoir* a *pissoir*, possess a host of mealy-mouthed terms for the toilet – like *les water*, which is an abbreviation of *les W.C.*, which they borrowed from the British, and its cousin, *les lieux*, which is one of the candidates for the origins of the English 'loo'. The French are not averse to naming their conveniences after real people – a public urinal is sometimes referred to as a *Rambeteau*, after the Prefect of that name. They also use the term *Vespasienne*, which they have adapted from the Italian *Vespasiano*, which in turn derives from the Latin of the same name, after the Emperor who established the first public urinals in Rome.

Other Europeans have similar hang-ups about naming toilets. The German euphemisms include *Abort* (away place), *stilles Örtchen* (silent little place) and *Abtritt* (after 'walk away'), as well as '*D*' and '*H*' for *Damen* and *Herren*, and the English '*W.C.*'. They also refer to the toilet as *Null-Null* (after the 'OO' that sometimes appears on toilet doors) and they talk about going 'to wash the hands' or 'to make a telephone call'. The Germans also possess a few dysphemisms for the toilet, like *Donnerbalken* (thunder board) and *Plumpsklo* (plop closet). When the Russians ask for the toilet, they talk about the *ubornaya*, which literally means 'adornment place', and both the Spanish and the Italians have words that mean 'retreat'. Italian euphemisms for the toilet include *bagno*, meaning 'bath', and *servizi*, meaning 'services'. But the most popular term in Italy is *gabinetto*, which is borrowed from the French *cabinet*, meaning 'room'. The Dutch have a similar term, *bestekamer*, which means 'best room'.

The British have an enormous number of euphemisms for the toilet – a reflection, it would seem, of their fascination with toilets (Prince Charles, for example, collects toilet seats), as well as their peculiar penchant for 'lavatory humour'. Robert Burchfield, who has charted the history of English toilet names, tells us that in Chaucer's time the toilet was called a 'privy', a 'chambre foreyne', or 'foreyne' for short. 'Jakes' was used during the sixteenth century, and 'closet', 'latrine' and 'necessary house' during the seventeenth. 'Bog' and 'Bogs' appeared during the eighteenth century, together with 'water closet' and 'dunny'. 'Dunny' is no longer found in Britain, although it managed to emigrate to Australia, where it remains the principal word for toilet. The nineteenth century saw the introduction of 'bog-house', 'W.C.' and 'toilet' – the last term being adapted from the French. The present century has also witnessed a fine flush of neologisms, like 'gents', 'ladies', 'John' and 'lavatory'.

Today the most popular name for a toilet is 'loo', which appears to have entered the English language during the nineteenth century. It is generally agreed that 'loo' is French in origin, although it is not known whether it comes from *l'eau*, meaning water, or from *lieu d'aisance*, meaning 'the place of ease', or its abbreviation *lieu*. Although there is no way of finding out for certain where 'loo' came from, it is informative that the English did talk about 'easing themselves' during the eighteenth century. For example, in a letter from the continent in 1764, David Garrick reported that 'in Italy the people do *their Needs*, in Germany they *disEmbogue themselves*, but in England (& in England only) they *Ease* themselves'. This suggests that 'loo' comes from the French word for 'place', an interpretation that is supported by the fact that during the eighteenth century the French frequently referred to toilets as *cabinets d'aisance à l'anglaise* – in other words, English rooms of easement. When Blondel, the architect of Louis XV, asked his English friends about these toilets, they disclaimed any knowledge of their existence, which is not surprising, because they were extremely rare in England at the time.

It has in fact been suggested that 'loo' has nothing to do with *l'eau* or *lieu*, and that it comes from *bourdalou*, a slipper-shaped chamber-pot that French ladies used to take on their travels during the eighteenth century. According to Keith Allan and Kate Burridge, the device was named after a famous French Jesuit preacher, Louis Bourdaloue, whose sermons at Versailles were so popular that the congregation assembled hours in advance. People were not prepared to give up their places, so they relieved themselves in portable chamber-pots instead. Later on these were named after the preacher.

Yes and No

A lot of people think that the natural way to signal 'yes' with the head is to nod it up and down, and that the natural way to signal 'no' is to shake it from side to side. This assumption is incorrect. In Europe alone there are no less than three codes of head gestures for yes and no.

The first is the 'Nod–Shake' code, in which the head is nodded up and down for yes, and shaken from side to side for no. This is by far the most popular code in Europe. It extends from Portugal in the west to Russia in the east, and from Scandinavia in the north to Spain in the south. The second code is the 'Dip–Toss' code, in which the head is dipped sharply forward for yes and tossed back for no. This code is found in Greece, Turkey, Sicily and southern Italy.

There are several interesting differences between the Nod–Shake code and the Dip–Toss code. The first point to notice is that the head-nod and the head-shake operate in different planes, whereas the head-dip and the head-toss operate in the same plane. Because a sequence of head-nods (up-down-up-down-up-etc.) is very different from a series of head-shakes (left-right-left-right-left-etc.), people who use the nod–shake code are able to use uninterrupted repetition to make their messages more emphatic.

This type of emphatic repetition is not available to people who use the Dip–Toss code. Because the head-dip and the head-toss operate in the same plane, a repeated series of head-dips (down-up-down-up-down-etc.) looks disturbingly like a repeated series of head-tosses (up-down-up-down-up-etc.), and this is likely to lead to confusion. For this reason, the head-dip and the head-toss are restricted to a single movement – down in the case of the head-dip, up in the case of the head-toss. There are, however, three ways in which users of the Dip–Toss code can make their signals and their messages more emphatic. The first is by repeating a gesture, but making sure that each repetition is clearly separated

199

by a phase during which the head remains stationary, the second is by increasing the speed or amplitude of the head movement to make it more dramatic, and the third is by using certain conventionalised facial and vocal signals.

Next time you are on holiday in Greece, watch how the locals perform the head-toss. You will notice that they sometimes toss their head back without using any facial gestures. On other occasions you will find that they accompany the upward movement of the head by raising their eyebrows, by closing their eyes, and by clicking their tongue. When all of these features are used together, they produce a gesture that is maximally negative. Each feature can, however, be used singly or in combination with others to give subtle shades of emphasis, formality and familiarity to the basic message of negation. In fact, to signal no, a Greek does not have to move his head at all. If he is feeling tired or uninspired, he is much more likely just to raise his eyebrows.

Although the Dip–Toss code is often thought to be exclusive to Greece and Turkey, it is also found in Sicily and southern Italy, where it is used together with the Nod–Shake code. If you visit a northern Italian city like Rome, you will find that the Romans use the head-nod for yes and the head-shake for no. If you then take the autostrada and drive 200 kilometres south to Naples, you will discover that the Neapolitans use the head-nod and the head-shake as well as the head-toss. Research in the region between Rome and Naples by Desmond Morris and his colleagues has revealed that the northern boundary of the head-toss corresponds to a wavy line that runs from the Garigliano river on the west coast to the Gargano peninsula on the east, and that the highest concentrations of the gesture appear along the coast south of these two landmarks. The fascinating point about this discovery is that this is exactly where the ancient Greeks settled when they colonised southern Italy from the second millennium B.C. onwards. It is known that the ancient Greeks used the head-toss, just as their descendants do to this day. The fact that this gesture is still found in the area that the ancient Greeks colonised more than 3000 years ago is remarkable testimony to the conservativism of gesture.

Because the Nod–Shake code and the Dip–Toss code coincide in southern Italy, the local inhabitants have a choice of gestures at their disposal. Analysis of film material gathered in this area shows that when southerners signal no with their head, they use either the head-shake or the head-toss, but that when they signal yes they use the head-nod rather than the head-dip. But this is not the whole story, because further analysis reveals that there is a marked difference between the head-nods used by northern and southern Italians: while southerners begin their nods with a downward movement, northerners initiate theirs with either an upward or a downward movement. This is more than an idle anthropological curiosity; it shows that northern and southern Italians can be distinguished from each other, purely on the basis of how they nod their heads! If you are in Italy, and you feel inclined to play the part of Professor Higgins, watch how people answer in the affirmative. It they start their head-nod with a downward movement, they could be either northerners or southerners. If they begin with an upward movement, they are almost certainly from the north.

The third code of head gestures for yes and no is the 'Roll–Toss' code. To signal 'yes' the head is wobbled from shoulder to shoulder, rather like the Western European gesture for indecision. To signal no it is tossed back. The Roll–Toss code is unique to Bulgaria. Although the code itself is not used anywhere else in the world, the individual gestures that comprise the code can be found elsewhere. To find the head-toss, one only needs to cross the border into neighbouring Greece or Turkey. But in order to find the head-roll, one needs to venture as far as Pakistan and India.

The isolated appearance of the head-roll in Europe is a real mystery. Why do the Bulgarians share this gesture with the inhabitants of the Indian sub-continent? After all, the Bulgarians are a Slavic people. Racially, linguistically and culturally they have nothing in common with Indians, and there is nothing to suggest that they ever enjoyed the kind of contact that would have encouraged them to borrow the Indian gesture for affirmation. It is possible that the presence of the head-roll in both Bulgaria and India is merely a coincidence, but given the unusual character of the gesture, this seems highly unlikely. A more feasible explanation is to be found in the history of what is now Bulgaria. Very little is actually known about the ancient history of this region or the Proto-Bulgarians who inhabited the region before the arrival of the Slavs. It is possible, therefore, that the Proto-Bulgarians came originally from the Indian sub-continent to Europe, bringing the head-roll gesture with them. When the Slav ancestors of the present-day Bulgarians invaded the region later on, they could have assimilated the local population and borrowed their gesture for affirmation.

If the Bulgarians did borrow the head-roll from another people, this would help to explain why their gestures for yes and no sometimes seem so confused. Careful study of Bulgarian head gestures reveals that they do not form a neat, logical system. Although Bulgarians usually employ the head-roll for yes, they sometimes use the head-shake to convey the same message. Given that a head-roll is not all that different from a head-shake, this kind of substitution is quite understandable. What is not understandable, however, is the habit that some Bulgarians have of using the head-roll and the head-shake to signal either yes or no! Fortunately this tends not to happen when Bulgarians are relying on head gestures alone; only when they are using head gestures as an accompaniment to speech. Under these circumstances, it is not uncommon for someone to roll their head while saying 'yes', and a few moments later to execute the identical movement while saying 'no'. This shows that Bulgarian head gestures play a subservient role to speech. They can easily lose their significance as independent signals, and become a means of simply emphasising what is being said.

Because the messages conveyed by Bulgarian head gestures are not entirely consistent, there is always the threat of misunderstanding between individual Bulgarians. But this potential for misunderstanding and confusion is even greater when Bulgarians meet foreigners. For example, when an Englishman deals with Bulgarians he is liable to misconstrue their affirmative head-roll as a head-shake, and to interpret both of these gestures as signals of negation. This occurred with rather dramatic consequences during the last century when the Russians were helping the Bulgarians to defeat the Turks. The Russians, who used the Nod–Shake code, could not understand why their Bulgarian comrades were shaking their heads in reply to questions that normally elicited an affirmative answer. Having an ally who spoke another language was bad enough; fighting alongside people who signalled 'no' when they meant 'yes' only confused matters further.

Misunderstandings can also occur between people who use the Nod–Shake code and the Dip–Toss code. An Englishman in Greece, for example, is liable to mistake the Greek head-toss for a curt nod of affirmation. Imagine a situation where an Englishman who is visiting Athens parks his rented car in a restricted zone. He spots a traffic policeman and, using pantomime, inquires whether it is alright for him to leave the car there for a few minutes. The policeman responds by tossing his head back to signal 'no'. The Englishman interprets the gesture as a sign of approval because it looks to him like an upward nod, so he thanks the policeman and begins to walk away. To the policeman this looks like a case of provocation, so he chases after the Englishman, grabs him by the arm, and a violent argument ensues.

Scenes like this can easily occur when people attach different meanings to the same signal. But even when the Greeks don't use the head-toss, there is ample opportunity for misunderstanding. For example, when they raise their eyebrows to signal negation, they sometimes accompany the movement with a widening of the eyes. To us this gesture looks like a faintly surprised form of approval, but to the average Greek it definitely means no.

Because the head-shake plays no part in the Greek code, the gesture of shaking the head is available for messages other than yes and no. The Greeks have exploited this opportunity by enlisting the head-shake as a gesture of incomprehension. If you are talking to a Greek and you say something he doesn't understand, he is likely to shake his head rapidly from side to side. This gesture is more of a head-shuttle than a head-shake, but because it looks to us like a head-shake we automatically take it to mean that the person doesn't agree with us or that something is being denied. In fact, nothing of the sort is intended; the gesture is simply a request for clarification.

Knowing which head and face gestures other nations use for yes and no usually helps to ease communication. But beware! It is never a guarantee against misunderstanding. If you visit Bulgaria, for example, there is always the possibility that your Bulgarian host will decide to use your system of head gestures rather than his own. If this happens, he may be shaking his head to mean no, while you are blissfully assuming he means yes.

Bibliography

ALLAN, K. and BURRIDGE, K. (1991). *Euphemism and Dysphemism*. Oxford: Oxford University Press.

ALLEN, I.L. (1983). *The Language of Ethnic Conflict*. New York: University of Columbia Press.

ALLEN, I.L. (1983). You are what you eat: dietary stereotypes and ethnic epithets. *Maledicta*, 7, 21–30.

ANON (1581). *A Treatise of Daunces*. London.

ARDAGH, J. (1991). *Germany and the Germans*. London: Penguin.

ARMOUR, R.W. and HOWES, R.H. (1940). *Coleridge the Talker*. New York: Cornell University Press.

AUSTIN, P.B. (1968). *On Being Swedish*. London: Secker & Warburg.

AVERNA, G. (1982). Italian blasphemies. *Maledicta*, 6, 63–70.

BARZINI, L. (1983). *The Europeans*. Harmondsworth: Penguin.

BEATTIE, G. (1983). *Talk: An Analysis of Speech and Non-verbal Behaviour in Conversation*. Milton Keynes: Open University Press.

BECK, S.W. (1883). *Gloves: Their Annals and Associations*. London.

BERGER, M. (1964). *Madame de Staël on Politics, Literature and National Character*. London: Sidgwick & Jackson.

BERNSTEIN, R. (1991). *Fragile Glory: A Portrait of France and the French*. London: Bodley Head.

BINYON, M. (1983). *Life in Russia*. London: H. Hamilton.

BLOCH, M. (1973). *The Royal Touch: Sacred Monarchy and Scrofula in England and France* (trans. J.E. Anderson). London: Routledge & Kegan Paul.

BOEMUS, J. (1611). *The Manners, Lawes, and Customes of All Nations*. London.

BORNSTEIN, M.H. and BORNSTEIN, H.G. (1976). The pace of life. *Nature*, 259, 557–559.

BOURKE, J.G. (1891). *Scatological Rites of All Nations*. Washington, DC: W.H. Lowdermilk.

BREMMER, J. and ROODENBURG, H. (eds.) (1992). *A Cultural History of Gesture*. Oxford: Polity.

BRIEUDE, J-J. de (1789). Mémoire sur les odeurs que nous exhalons, considérées comme signe de la santé et des maladies. *Histoire et Mémoires de la Société Royale de Médecine, 10*.

BROWN, R. and GILMAN, A. (1960). The pronouns of power and solidarity. In T.A. Sebeok (ed.), *Style in Language*. Cambridge, Mass: MIT Press.

BULWER, J. (1644). *Chirologia; or the Natural Language of the Hand. Whereunto is added Chironomia: or, the Art of Manual Rhetoricke*. London.

BURCHFIELD, R. (1985). An outline history of euphemisms in English. In D.J. Enright (ed.), *Fair of Speech*. Oxford: Oxford University Press.

BURKE, T. (1940). *The Streets of London*. London: Batsford.

CALBRIS, G. (1990). *The Semiotics of French Gestures*. Bloomington: Indiana University Press.

CAMMAERTS, E. (1930). *Discoveries in England*. London.

CAPEK, K. (1925). *Letters From England* (trans. P. Selver). London.

CARLYLE, T. (1837). *The French Revolution*. London.

CAZAMIAN, L. (1952). *The Development of English Humour*. Durham: Duke University Press.

CHIARO, D. (1992). *The Language of Jokes*. London: Routledge.

CIARDI, J. (1980). *A Browser's Dictionary*. New York: Harper.

COCKBURN, P. (1989). *Getting Russia Wrong*. London: Verso.

COLLETT, P. (1982). Meetings and misunderstandings. In S. Bochner (ed.), *Cultures in Contact*. Oxford: Pergamon.

COLLETT, P. (1985). History and the study of expressive action. In K. Gergen and M. Gergen (eds.), *Historical Social Psychology*. New York: Erlbaum.

COLLETT, P. and CONTARELLO, A. (1987). Gesti di assenso e di dissenso. In P. Ricci Bitti (ed.), *Communicazione e Gestualità*. Milan: Franco Angeli.

CONRAD, J. (1921). *Notes on Life and Letters*. London: J.M. Dent.

CORBIN, A. (1986). *The Foul and the Fragrant*. Leamington Spa: Berg Publishers.

CRAWLEY, E. (1929). The nature and history of the kiss. In *Studies of Savages and Sex*. London: Methuen.

CZWARTOSZ, Z. (1988). On queuing. *Archives of European Sociology*, 29, 3–11.

DAHRENDORF, R. (1969). *Society and Democracy in Germany*. New York: Doubleday.

DARWIN, C. (1872). *The Expression of the Emotions in Man and Animals*. London: John Murray.

DAVIES, C. (1982). Ethnic jokes, moral values and social boundaries. *British Journal of Sociology*, 33(3), 383–403.

DAVIES, C. (1988). The Irish joke as a social phenomenon. In J. Durant and J. Miller (eds.), *Laughing Matters*. London: Longman.

DAVIES, C. (1988). Stupidity and rationality: jokes from the iron cage. In C. Powell and G. Paton (eds.), *Humour in Society: Resistance and Control*. London: Macmillan.

DEFOE, D. (1951). A tilt at profanity, *Review*, 1711, 8(61). Reprinted in W.L. Payne (ed.), *The Best of Defoe's Review*. New York: Columbia University Press.

DE STAËL-HOLSTEIN, A.L.G. (1859). *Germany* (trans. by O.W. Wright). Boston: Houghton Mifflin.

DICKENS, C. (1846). *Pictures From Italy*. London.

DI JORIO, A. (1832). *La Mimica Degli Antichi Investigata Nel Gestire Napoletano*. Naples: Fibreno.

DI STASI (1981). *Mal Occhio*. San Francisco: North Point Press.

DUNDES, A. (ed.) (1968). *Every Man His Way*. Englewood Cliffs, NJ: Prentice-Hall.

DUNDES, A. (1975). Slurs international: folk comparisons of ethnicity and national character. *Southern Folklore Quarterly*, 39, 15–38.

DUNDES, A. (1978). Wet and dry, the evil eye; an essay in semitic and Indo-European worldviews. In V. Newall (ed.), *Folklore Studies in the Twentieth Century*. Totowa, NJ: Rowman & Littlefield.

DUNDES, A. (1982). Misunderstanding humour: an American stereotype of the Englishman. *International Folklore Review*, 2, 10–15.

DUNDES, A. (1984). *Life is Like a Chicken Coop Ladder*. New York: Columbia University Press.

EDELMANN, R.J., ASENDORPF, J., CONTARELLO, A., ZAMMUNER, V., GEORGAS, J. and VILLANEUVA, C. (1987). Self-reported verbal and non-verbal strategies for coping with embarrassment in five European cultures. *Social Science Information*, 26, 869–883.

EDELMANN, R. and NETO, F. (1989). Self-reported expression and consequences of embarrassment in Portugal and the U.K. *International Journal of Psychology*, 24, 351–366.

EDELMANN, R., ASENDORPF, J., CONTARELLO, A., ZAMMUNER, V., GEORGAS, J. and VILLANEUVA, C. (1989). Self-reported expression of embarrassment in five European cultures. *Journal of Cross-Cultural Psychology*, 20(4), 357–371.

EFRON, D. (1972). *Gesture, Race and Culture*. The Hague: Mouton.

ELLIS, H. (1936). *Studies in the Psychology of Sex*, 4 vols. New York: Random House.

ELWORTHY, F. (1895). *The Evil Eye*. London: John Murray.

EMERSON, R.W. (1856). *English Traits*. London.

ENRIGHT, T. (1986). *Fair of Speech*. Oxford: Oxford University Press.

ERASMUS, D. (1540). *Opera Omnia*, 9 vols. Basle.

EUROMONITOR (1990). *The European Cosmetics and Toiletries Report 1990*. London: Euromonitor.

EYSENCK, H.J. (1944–5). National differences in 'sense of humour': three experimental and statistical studies. *Character and Personality* (now *Journal of Personality*), 13, 37–54.

FORGAS, J. (1976). An unobtrusive study of reactions to national stereotypes in four European countries. *Journal of Social Psychology*, 99, 37–42.

FRIEDRICH, P. (1972). Social context and semantic features: the Russian pronominal usage. In J.J. Gumperz and D. Hymes (eds.), *Directions in Sociolinguistics*. New York: Holt, Rinehart & Winston.

FRYER, P. (1963). *Mrs Grundy: Studies in English Prudery*. London: Dennis Hobson.

FRYKMAN, J. and LÖFGREN, O. (1987). *Culture Builders: A Historical Anthropology of Middle-Class Life*. New Brunswick: Rutgers University Press.

GARROD, H.W. (1947). Humour. In E. Barker (ed.), *The Character of England*. Oxford: Clarendon Press.

GEIJER, E.G. (1932). *Impressions of England 1809–1810* (trans. E. Sprigge and C. Napier). London.

GIFFORD, E.S. (1958). *The Evil Eye: Studies in the Folklore of Vision*. New York: Macmillan.

GLASSER, R. (1972). *Time in French Life and Thought* (trans. C.G. Pearson). Manchester: Manchester University Press.

GOFFMAN, E. (1971). *Relations in Public*. Harmondsworth: Penguin.

GOLDSMITH, O. (1760). A comparative view of races and nations. In A.

Friedman (ed.), *Collected Works of Oliver Goldsmith*. Oxford: Oxford University Press.

GOLDSMITH, O. (1762). *Citizen of the World*. London.

GORER, G. and RICKMAN, J. (1949). *The People of Great Russia: A Psychological Study*. London: The Cresset Press.

GORER, G. (1955). *Exploring English Character*. London: The Cresset Press.

GRABER, R.B. and RICHTER, G.C. (1987). The capon theory of the cuckold's horns: confirmation or conjecture? *Journal of American Folklore*, 100, 58–63.

GRAVES, R. (1927). *Lars Porsena or The Future of Swearing and Improper Language*. London: Kegan Paul.

GROSE, F.H. (1785). *A Classical Dictionary of the Vulgar Tongue*. London.

GROSLEY, M. (1772). *A Tour to London* (trans. Th. Nugent). London.

GROTJAHN, M. (1957). *Beyond Laughter*. New York: McGraw-Hill.

GULLESTAD, M. (1986). Symbolic 'Fences' in Urban Norwegian Neighbourhoods. *Ethnos*, 51, 52–70.

HALL, E.T. (1959). *The Silent Language*. New York: Doubleday.

HALL, E.T. (1964). *The Hidden Dimension*. New York: Doubleday.

HAMMERTON, J.A. (1944). *Books and Myself*. London: Macdonald.

HARTOGS, R. (1968). *Four-letter Word Games: The Psychology of Obscenity*. New York: Dell.

HAZLITT, W. (1825). Merry England. *New Monthly Magazine*, 14(2), 557–565.

HEALD, G. and WYBROW, R.J. (1986). *The Gallup Survey of Britain*. London: Croom Helm.

HELMAN, C. (1987). Heart disease and the cultural construction of time: the Type A behaviour pattern as a western culture-bound syndrome. *Social Science and Medicine*, 25, 969–979.

HERZEN, A. (1968). *My Past and Thoughts* (trans. C. Garnett). London: Chatto & Windus.

HÜBLER, A. (1983). *Understatements and Hedges in English*. Amsterdam: John Benjamins.

HUGHES, G. (1991). *Swearing*. Oxford: Blackwell.

HUME, D. (1882). Of national characters (1748). In T.H. Greene and T.H. Grose, *The Philosophical Works of David Hume*. London.

INGHAM, R. (1971). The Swedish condition. *New Society*, 446, 624–626.

INGHAM, R. (1972). Cross-cultural Differences in Social Behaviour. D.Phil thesis, Oxford University.

INKELES, A. (1972). National character and modern political systems in F.L.K. Hsu (ed.), *Psychological Anthropology*. Cambridge, Mass: Schenkman.

JAKOB, S.I. (1992). Pronominal address in the east and west of the Federal Republic of Germany. Unpublished.

JAKOBSON, R. (1972). Motor Signs for 'yes' and 'no'. *Language in Society*, 1, 91–96.

KINGLAKE, A. (1844). *Eothen*. London: Ollivier.

KIRA, A. (1966). *The Bath Room*. New York: Bantam Books.

LAMBERT, W.L. and TUCKER, G.R. (1976). *Tu, Vous, Usted: A Social-Psychological Study of Address Patterns*. Rowley, Mass.: Newbury House.

LAWRENCE, D.H. (1923). *Sea and Sardinia*. London.

LEACH, E. (1964). Anthropological aspects of language: animal categories and verbal abuse. In E.H. Lenneberg (ed.), *New Directions in the Study of Language*. Cambridge, Mass.: MIT Press.

LEACH, E. (1979). The official Irish jokesters. *New Society*, December 20.

LEACOCK, S. (1935). *Humour*. London: Bodley Head.

LEE, A.M. (1966). *Applied Queuing Theory*. London: Macmillan.

LEECH, G. (1983). *Principles of Pragmatics*. London: Longman.

LEEDS, C. (1992). Bilingual Anglo-French humour. *Humor* 1992, 5 (1/2), 129–148.

LEGMAN, G. (1968). *Rationale of the Dirty Joke*, Vols 1 and 2. London: Jonathan Cape.

LEGMAN, G. (1977). A word for it! *Maledicta, 1*, 9–18.

LEHTONEN, J. and SAJAVAARA, K. (1985). The silent Finn. In D. Tannen and M. Saville-Troike (eds.), *Perspectives on Silence*. Norwood, NJ: Ablex.

LE NORCY, S. (1988). Selling perfume: a technique or an art? In S. Van Toller and G.H. Dodd (eds.), *Perfumery: the Psychology and Biology of Fragrance*. London: Chapman & Hall.

LEVINE, R.V. (1988). The pace of life across cultures. In J.E. McGrath (ed.), *The Social Psychology of Time: New Perspectives*. London: Sage.

LEVINE, R. (1989). The pace of life. *Psychology Today*, October, 42–46.

LEVINE, R.V. and BARTLETT, K. (1984), Pace of life, punctuality, and coronary heart disease in six countries. *Journal of Cross-cultural Psychology, 15*, 233–255.

LEVINE, R. and WOLFF, E. (1985). Social time: the heartbeat of culture. *Psychology Today*, March, 28–35.

LIBERMAN, E.G. (1968). The queue: anamnesis, diagnosis, therapy. *Soviet Review*, March 20, 12–16.

McCRACKEN, G. (1982). Politics and ritual sotto voce: the use of demeanour as an instrument of politics in Elizabethan England. *Canadian Journal of Anthropology, 3*(1), 85–100.

McDONALD, J. (1988). *A Dictionary of Obscenity, Taboo and Euphemism*. London: Sphere Books.

McGRATH, J.E. and KELLY, J.R. (1985). *Time and Human Interaction: Toward a Social Psychology of Time*. New York: Guilford Press.

MALONEY, C. (ed.) (1976). *The Evil Eye*. New York: Columbia University Press.

MARSH, P. and COLLETT, P. (1986). *Driving Passion: The Psychology of the Car*. London: Cape.

MAUROIS, A. (1938). *Three Letters on the English*. London.

MAUROIS, A. (1965). *Les Silences du Colonel Bramble* (orig. 1950). Paris: Grasset.

MEAD, M. (1953). *Cultural Patterns and Technical Change*. Paris: UNESCO.

MIKES, G. (1946). *How To Be An Alien*. Harmondsworth: Penguin.

MIKES, G. (1983). *English Humour for Beginners*. London: Unwin.

MIKES, G. (1984). *How To Be A Brit*. Harmondsworth: Penguin.

MILLER, J. (1978). *The Body in Question*. London: Cape.

MILTON, J. (1644). *Of Education*. London.

MONTAGU, A. (1967). *The Anatomy of Swearing*. London: Rapp & Whiting.

MONTAGU, A. (1986). *Touching: The Human Significance of the Skin*. New York: Harper & Row.

MONTESQUIEU, C. (1990). *The Spirit of the Laws* (orig. 1747). Cambridge: Cambridge University Press.

MORRIS, D. (1977). *Manwatching: A Field-guide to Human Behaviour.* London: Cape.

MORRIS, D., COLLETT, P., MARSH, P. and O'SHAUGHNESSY, M. (1979). *Gestures: Their Origins and Distribution.* London: Jonathan Cape.

MUECKE, D. (1980). *The Compass of Irony.* London: Methuen.

MÜHLHÄUSLER, P. and HARRÉ, R. (1990). *Pronouns and People.* Oxford: Blackwell.

MUIR, F. (1990). *The Oxford Book of Humorous Prose.* Oxford: Oxford University Press.

MURALT, B.L. DE (1726). *Letters Describing the Characters and Customs of the English and French Nations.* London.

NASH, W. (1985). *The Language of Humour.* London: Longman.

NEAMAN, J. and SILVER, C. (1991). *In Other Words: A Thesaurus of Euphemisms.* London: Angus & Robertson.

NICHOLS, J. (1598). *Progress of Queen Elizabeth: Paul Hentzner's Travels in England During the Reign of Queen Elizabeth.* London.

NICHOLS, P. (1973). *Italia, Italia.* London: Macmillan.

NICOLSON, H. (1946). *The English Sense of Humour.* London: The Dropmore Press.

NYROP, C. (1901). *The Kiss and Its History.* London.

OETTINGEN, G. and SELIGMAN, M.E.P. (1990). Pessimism and behavioural signs of depression in East versus West Berlin. *European Journal of Social Psychology, 20,* 207–220.

ORWELL, G. (1938). *Homage to Catalonia.* London: Secker & Warburg.

PANGBORN, R.M., GUINARD, J-X. and DAVIS, R.G. (1988). Regional aroma preferences. *Food Quality and Preference, 1,* 11–19.

PAPAS, W. (1972). *Instant Greek.* Athens: Papas.

PARTRIDGE, E. (1933). *Words, Words, Words.* London: Methuen.

PARTRIDGE, E. (1937). *A Covey of Partridge.* London.

PAYER, L. (1989). *Medicine and Culture.* London: Victor Gollancz.

PEABODY, D. (1985). *National Characteristics.* Cambridge: Cambridge University Press.

PECCHIO, Count (1833). *Semi-Serious Observations of an Italian Exile.* London.

POPS, M. (1982). The metamorphosis of shit. *Salmagundi, 56,* 26–61.

PRITCHETT, V.S. (1954). *The Spanish Temper.* London: Chatto & Windus.

PUDNEY, J. (1954). *The Smallest Room.* London: M. Joseph.

RABELAIS, F. (1533). *Pantegruel.* Lyons.

RAWSON, H. (1991). *A Dictionary of Invective.* London: Robert Hale.

RENIER, G.J. (1931). *The English: Are They Human?* London: Williams & Northgate.

REYNOLDS, R. (1969). *Cleanliness and Godliness.* London: Allen & Unwin.

ROBACK, A.A. (1944). *A Dictionary of International Slurs.* Cambridge, Mass.: Sci-Art Publishers.

ROUTH, J. (1966). *The Guide Porcelaine – The Loos of Paris.* London: Wolfe Publishing Co.

RYE, W.B. (1865). *England as Seen By Foreigners.* London: John Russell Smith.

SAGARIN, E. (1962). *The Anatomy of Dirty Words*. New York: Lyle Stuart.
SAUNDERS, G. (1985). Silence and noise as emotion management styles: an Italian case. In D. Tannen and M. Saville-Troike (eds.), *Perspectives on Silence*. Norwood, N.J.: Ablex.
SCHIFFMAN, S.S. and SIEBERT, J.M. (1991). New frontiers in fragrance use. *Cosmetics and Toiletries, 106*, 39–45.
SCHWARTZ, B. (1978). Queues, priorities and social process. *Social Psychology, 41*(1), 3–12.
SELIGMANN, S. (1910). *Der Böse Blick und Verwandtes*. Berlin.
SEMIN, G. and RUBINI, M. (1990). Unfolding the concept of person by verbal abuse. *European Journal of Social Psychology, 20*(6), 463–474.
SHERZER, J. (1985). Puns and jokes. *Handbook of Discourse Analysis, Vol. 3*. London: Academic Press.
SHIPLEY, J.T. (1977). The origin of our strongest taboo-word. *Maledicta, 1*, 23–29.
SMITH, H. (1978). *The Russians*. London: Sphere Books.
SMOLLETT, T. (1766). *Travels Through France and Italy*. London.
SMOLLETT, T. (1771). *The Expedition of Humphry Clinker*. London.
SONTAG, S. (1969). A letter from Sweden. *Ramparts*, July, 23–38.
SORBIÈRE, S. (1709). *A Voyage to England*. London.
STENDHAL, H.B. (1907). *Racine et Shakespeare*. Oxford: Clarendon Press.
TAINE, H. (1872). *Notes on England* (trans. W.F. Rae). London.
Taylor Nelson European Usage Panel (1992). London: Taylor Nelson.
TEMPLE, W. (1690). *Miscellanea, Vol 2*. London.
THOMAS, K. (1977). The place of laughter in Tudor and Stuart England. *Times Literary Supplement*, No. 3906, Jan. 21, 77–81.
USENIER, J.C. (1991). Business time perceptions and national cultures: a comparative survey. *Management International Review, 3*, 197–217.
VAN TOLLER, S. and DODD, G.H. (eds.) (1988). *Perfumery: The Psychology and Biology of Fragrance*. London: Chapman & Hall.
VIGARELLO, G. (1988). *Concepts of Cleanliness: Changing Attitudes in France Since the Middle Ages*. Cambridge: Cambridge University Press.
WALMSLEY, D.J. and LEWIS, G.J. (1989). The pace of pedestrian flows in cities. *Environment and Behaviour, 21*(2), 123–150.
WATSON, O.M. (1970). *Proxemics* (Advances in Semiotics, 8). The Hague: Mouton.
WHITE, D. (1975). Queues in the mind. *New Society*, January.
WILDEBLOOD, J. (1965). *The Polite World*. London: Oxford University Press.
WISEMAN, N.P.S. (1853), *Essays on Various Subjects*, Vol 3. London.
WORTLEY MONTAGU, M. (1763). *Letters*. London.
WRIGHT, L. (1980). *Clean and Decent*. London: Routledge & Kegan Paul.
WYLIE, L. (1977). *Beaux Gestes: A Guide to French Body Talk*. New York: Undergraduate Press.
ZELDIN, T. (1988). *The French*. London: Collins Harvill.
ZIV, A. (ed.) (1988). *National Styles of Humor*. New York: Greenwood Press.

Acknowledgements

I would like to express my gratitude to the Harry Frank Guggenheim Foundation in New York and to the Economic and Social Research Council in the United Kingdom for the research funds they have provided. I would also like to thank my wife, Jill, for her support and encouragement, and the following friends and colleagues for their help and suggestions: Michael Argyle, Nicholas Brealey, Anne-Pascale Bruneau, Giovanni and Christine Carnibella, Nina Castell, Alberta Contarello, Enriques Gracia, Bridget Hadaway, Allan and Lena Hjorth, Sigrid Jakob, Kåre Jacobsen, Caradoc King, Zuleika Kingdon, Roger Lamb, Kay Lattimore, Christopher Leeds, Aruna Mathur, Carol O'Brien, Marie O'Shaughnessy, Peter Marsh, Desmond Morris, Gonzalo Musitu, Sian Parkhouse, Chantal Rawlence, Peter Rosman, Anja Spindler, Paddy Summerfield and Andy Swapp.

Index